THE
GREEN
START-UP

Juliet Davenport OBE founded Good Energy, one of the UK's first 100% renewable electricity suppliers, in 1999 at the age of 31, making her the first female CEO of a UK energy supplier. Stepping away as CEO in May 2021, Juliet sits on the boards of a string of companies that are helping tackle the climate crisis. She is chair of solar innovator Atrato Onsite Energy, whose flotation in November made it the first company with an all-female board to list on the London Stock Exchange. She is also the host of the successful podcast *Great Green Questions* and a regular speaker on climate action and sustainable business.

THE GREEN START-UP

Juliet Davenport OBE

Heligo
Books

First published in the UK by Heligo Books
An imprint of Bonnier Books UK
4th Floor, Victoria House,
Bloomsbury Square,
London, WC1B 4DA

Owned by Bonnier Books
Sveavägen 56, Stockholm, Sweden

twitter.com/heligobooks

Trade Paperback – 978-1-788707-50-3
Ebook – 978-1-788707-51-0
Audio – 978-1-788707-52-7

A CIP catalogue of this book is available from the British Library.

Typeset by IDSUK (Data Connection) Ltd
Printed and bound in Great Britain by Clays Ltd, Elcograf S.p.A.

1 3 5 7 9 10 8 6 4 2

Heligo Books is an imprint of Bonnier Books UK
www.bonnierbooks.co.uk

To my very own futureholders – Moji and Bella,

this book is for you and for your future

Contents

Introduction

Imagine standing on a cliff edge and peering over. You can't judge how far the drop is, or how deep the water is below. You know there are currents swirling underneath, but you can't see them. There's no one to guide you, or rescue you if the dive goes wrong. But you feel this strange sensation. You have to jump, but you don't know why. Suddenly you're falling. The rush is overwhelming, and you can barely breathe, yet all the time you have this unshakeable faith – a determined voice in your head telling you that everything is going to be okay.

For an entrepreneur, this is what your first days and months at work can feel like. There's no welcome at the door, no meet-and-greet around the office, no induction, no laptop waiting for you on your desk. The chances are you may not even have a desk! In short, there's no corporate support system to catch you. There's just you, an idea, and the compulsion to drive that idea forward, regardless of what lies ahead. That's certainly how I felt when I started my company, Good Energy, 20 years ago.

Back in 1999, Good Energy was one of the first companies to offer 100% renewable electricity to UK householders. But when I started it, renewable energy was hardly the buzzword on everyone's lips. In fact, it was consigned to the margins while the fossil fuel industry burned brightly.

The Green Start-Up

It's hard for me to imagine it now, but back then, there was no Greta Thunberg or activists like Extinction Rebellion. David Attenborough's *Blue Planet,* which so devastatingly exposed plastic pollution in our oceans, would not air on TV until 2001. There was no government talk of a carbon neutral future. Instead, there were a terrifying number of people either denying climate change outright or burying their heads in the sand, hoping something would sort itself out somehow without life radically changing – an inconvenient can to kick down the road.

I was viewed as an upstart – worse still, a female upstart – and I faced a steep learning curve. Yet two decades later, not only is the scientific evidence for climate change incontrovertible, but saving the planet has become the defining element of mainstream debate. Limiting global warming to 1.5° C – the temperature the world needs to reach to avoid the worst impacts of climate change – has now been enshrined in the historic Paris Agreement of 2015. In 2020 renewable energy generated almost half of Britain's electricity. There's still a long way to go, but the pace of progress is accelerating fast.

Of course, green energy is just one piece of a vast climate change jigsaw, and it happens to be the business that I've dedicated my life to. But thorny, intractable questions like: how can we save our planet? will require a myriad of people from all kinds of backgrounds coming up with a myriad of solutions. For entrepreneurs, whose natural instinct is to innovate, it's an exciting time – I would go as far as to say it's a 'golden age'.

Because climate change is endemic in everything we do – from getting on a plane at the drop of a hat, to buying supermarket food flown in from around the world – it is such an uncomfortable problem that there's now a pressing need to rethink every part of our lifestyle.

Introduction

The Covid-19 pandemic has only magnified this: it's shown us how interconnected we are and how vulnerable humans are to a rapidly changing environment. Through countless numbers of unnecessary deaths, it's thrown global inequality into sharp focus and shown what seismic shocks can do to economies, countries, communities and families. And it has exposed our systemic frailty in dealing with multiple crises – health, economic, financial and climate.

All this has presented a major threat to both consumers worldwide and established corporations, but if positives are to be found, it has also shown the world an opportunity. Successive lockdowns have given us a glimpse of what permanent recovery of our global ecosystem might look like, and the potential of collective action in responding to an emergency.

In my view, business is also part of this collective action. It has a responsibility to drive change and a role to play in challenging the status quo. It's what I set out to do when I started Good Energy. It's what still gets me out of bed every morning, and it's why I wanted to write this book.

The idea for *The Green Start-Up* was born out of a podcast I had been hosting called *Great Green Questions*. When I launched it in March 2021, the idea was to ask some *really big* questions around climate change. These are the sorts of questions I ask every day: Must I stop flying? Is becoming vegan the only way to save the planet? Can I be an environmentalist and still love cars? By exploring these topics I wanted to highlight how imperfect the road to saving the planet is, and how we don't get it right all of the time.

While *Great Green Questions* focused around what we as citizens and consumers can do and think about in our daily lives, it struck me that entrepreneurs ask exactly the same kinds of questions when building a 'green' business – some have built a business directly around solving some of these problems, while others are incorporating green practices into their business. Whatever the goal, the process is just as imperfect.

Throughout my business career I've learned, often through painful trial and error, how fraught with complexity it can be when values collide with realities; how ethical conundrums you didn't even know existed keep you awake at night; how overwhelming it can feel to navigate through a sea of false or conflicting information; and how progress is haphazard, to say the least.

The Green Start-Up is my attempt to unpick some of those conundrums and to help others starting out. From choosing the right physical space to house a business in, to deciding on your core mission, right through to how to ethically finance your business, I wanted to shine a light on the issues that eco-entrepreneurs and founders wrestle with every single day. Some may seem like small actions, like installing solar panels or switching to an ethical bank account, but incrementally and collectively these decisions have real impact. So as well as exploring some very practical solutions, underpinning each chapter is a new way of thinking about creating change in your business and the optimum time to make those changes.

Of course, it would be impossible to cover every type of business or every type of business model. Instead, I have chosen ten broad topics and provided readers with enough actionable advice to kick-start change, peppered with some blue-sky thinking to inspire further discussions.

Context is important, and so I start with an exploration of the evolution of impactful businesses and eco-entrepreneurialism and make the case for why we need to go further to save the planet. Then, I guide you

Introduction

through how to choose and inhabit the physical business space before moving to Chapter 3 on how to power your business. In Chapter 4 I discuss how best to think about your purpose and values, and in Chapter 5 I look at your people. The link between diversity and inclusion and better decision-making around climate change is becoming more established, so getting it right is key. Finance comes under scrutiny in Chapter 6. It's probably the most difficult part of any business and thinking ethically adds another layer of complexity so I break it down into manageable steps. In Chapter 7 I cover the supply chain by looking at three examples of businesses revolutionising the manufacturing process. Trust me, they are truly inspirational! Then, I move on to how to market your business with the environment in mind. Transport takes centre stage in the penultimate chapter and finally I draw everything together and look at how eco-businesses can achieve wider impact and create transformational change.

This book doesn't have to be read cover to cover, although it can be. Each chapter stands alone, and readers can dip in and out depending on what type of business you are, what stage you are at, and what budget you are working to. It recognises that everyone is on their own journey, which is why, at the end of Chapters 2–10, I have summarised information into three sections. 'Quick wins' are actions that don't require too much planning or budget. 'Moving up a gear' is aimed at businesses wanting to move their green credentials to the next level. And lastly, 'Going for it' is aimed at more established businesses who are ready to take bolder decisions.

Writing *The Green Start-Up* has been a journey for me too. I have run one business in a unique sector, and while I've drawn on my own experience throughout, I've also sought answers from experts and entrepreneurs from a number of industries already making their mark towards a greener, cleaner future. My hope is that we can all learn from each other's successes and failures – after all, in this brave new world, there are no easy answers.

But if you're a climate-change optimist like me, you won't be burying your head in the sand. You'll have picked up this book because you're asking: how can we challenge ourselves to be a greener, fairer, more equitable business? What can we do tomorrow, or in two, three or five years' time to work towards our goal? Mostly, you'll be asking: how can we build a business that contributes towards a better world for ourselves and for many future generations to come?

Juliet Davenport OBE
October 2022

Chapter 1
Sparking Change

It was in 2003 when I received an invitation from an entrepreneur called Tony Marmont to tour around his hillside eco-farm nestled in the Leicestershire countryside. At the time, I had not long since founded Good Energy. Tony had phoned with a problem and he needed a solution: how could he feed his green energy supply into the national grid?

Tony is a multimillionaire who, when I first met him, had recently sold his family-run soft drinks company. But as far back as the 1980s, he'd become acutely aware of the negative effect humans were having on the planet. Action was needed before it was too late, so he committed to using his personal fortune to change perceptions about energy. But while Tony was busy pioneering small-scale renewable power generation in his back garden, the prevailing system dominated by the large suppliers known as the 'big six' shut out individuals like him.

Tony's then energy supplier, Powergen, was refusing to let him supply the grid with any of his home-built renewable energy supply. This meant he wasn't going to receive any credit for the power he was producing above and beyond his own usage. In Powergen's view, Tony, and others like him, couldn't produce enough power to justify metering their output; the administration to pay them for the supply just wasn't worth it. But while large companies couldn't be bothered with the Tonys of this world, he was exactly the type of customer that I, and Good Energy, wanted to grow.

I'd also begun Good Energy in 1999 trying to solve a problem: how can I help save the planet by challenging the fossil fuel status quo? My solution was to place power directly into the hands of people who could collectively make a difference. From the start, Good Energy was supplying customers with clean power sourced from a handful of small renewable generators, usually medium-sized smallholders or farmers. Visiting Tony gave me further food for thought: how could we force a mechanism whereby individuals with a power supply as small as Tony's could also feed into the national grid?

Even now my first meeting with Tony makes me smile. As I jumped off the train in Loughborough, he was waiting for me behind the wheel of an electric vehicle. But this was not a sleek '0-to-60 mph-in-four seconds' Tesla – it was more like a converted milk float. 'It's fully electric,' he boasted as we scooted off to his large bungalow set in around 50 acres of land.

The whole shebang was thrillingly James Bond. In one field he had fixed rotating diamond-shaped solar panels that would tilt with the direction of the sun and were used to power his home. In the garden, he'd fashioned two wind turbines, giant enough to look like they'd been built by Don Quixote, but makeshift enough to make you terrified of walking underneath them, given that they'd practically been stuck together with Sellotape and string. Plus they were incredibly noisy – not the best poster child for wind power!

'And I've got a hydro-plant over in the lake,' he announced enthusiastically, before showing off the micro turbine he'd constructed, now with water gushing through it. All this kit was rigged up to a battery bank from which he could heat and power his home, charge his car, and recharge from the mains, especially during the winter months when the solar panels would not generate as much power.

However, Tony's *pièce de résistance* was yet to be revealed. 'What is it?' I thought. 'A giant homemade weather balloon to harness cloud power?' He pressed a button on a large outbuilding. 'It's my toy,' he said with a childlike excitement. As the doors slowly opened, my mouth did the same. In the midst of Tony's mecca to green energy, I watched as a *massive* helicopter glided majestically from its hangar on a mechanised trolley. This fossil-fuel behemoth was powerful enough to get you to the North Pole!

Listening to him reel off its top speed, its hovering capability and its fuel efficiency particulars (eight miles to the gallon), I have to admit that I was more than a little impressed. My father was a professional rally car co-driver and I grew up with high-speed engineering around me. Despite him being a very early green adopter, I completely appreciated that the petrolhead in Tony was hard to suppress.

But therein lay another question – one that Tony had already started asking: how can I power this beast with climate-friendly, commercially viable fuel? Now, at the ripe old age of 92, Tony gave up his helicopter a couple of years ago and so never got to crack that conundrum. However, in the intervening years, he did invest in a business that creates fuel from air – by sucking CO_2 from the atmosphere and mixing it with hydrogen. It's still early days for this type of technology, but one for the future, I hope.

Back then, as I came away from our meeting, Tony became my inspiration to figure out a way to work with more individual generators. I began asking: how do we get these guys with small amounts of power and treat them as customers and not power stations?

Back then, I was at the beginning of my entrepreneurial journey, yet the seed had been sown many years before. I had been a student studying atmospheric physics at Oxford University in the 1980s when I became aware of the potential devastating impact of climate change. I describe it as my 'epiphany moment': the spark that eventually fused together my undergraduate studies and real-world events. One afternoon, when I was reading in the library I landed on an article. It was one of those long reads with stunning photography in a Sunday supplement that asked, 'Is climate change *really* happening?' It was unputdownable.

The article drew together everything that I'd been trying to learn up until that point: all the theoretical maths and that module in thermo-dynamics, when I'd spend two days stuck on one page trying to figure out what the hell entropy is, anyway. Suddenly, I'd been placed at the epicentre of a potential global disaster. What's more, I'd found a prac-tical application for science that I could focus on and act upon: a vital mission for the future which I could dedicate myself to. The question I asked myself that day remains the same: how can I help save the planet and build a better future?

I'd travelled a particular route to becoming an entrepreneur. For starters, I was a graduate. On leaving university I'd gone to work as an intern in the European Commission helping to formulate a high-carbon charter dealing with gas and oil pipelines across Eastern Europe. There, I was exposed to the entrenched nature of the fossil fuel lobby and the limitations of centralised policy making. Both left me feeling more than a little frustrated and this led me to think about how to achieve a more direct, democratic and distributive approach to energy: I imagined a company that put people at the heart of the climate crisis solution. A few years down the line, one business partner and several roller-coaster rides later, the first iteration of Good Energy was formed – a bumpy journey but I got there in the end.

I'd already learned some hard lessons, and I was about to be faced with even more. Being a start-up, I lacked the financial backing that I needed to obtain the energy licence I needed to operate. Plus, no one at that time was interested in funding a female entrepreneur looking to deliver a green energy proposal to the market. Yet I kept going. What propelled me was an unshakeable faith in my idea – an idea that had been formed over many years and, just like Tony's early eco-farm, an idea born from asking questions.

Today, I spend a lot of time talking to entrepreneurs across a range of industries. Many have come from different backgrounds and taken a different route into business than I did. Like me, some are graduates who have undertaken work experience before going it alone. Others haven't climbed any corporate or organisational ladder at all. Some haven't even gone on to further education but left school with a burning passion to execute their idea. Then, there are those who have already had an established career but, at some point, spotted a gap in the market and decided to branch out and fill it, sometimes alone or perhaps with a trusted business partner. Whoever they are, or wherever they come from, entrepreneurs have a unique talent for harnessing their passion and an unshakeable vision for what they want to create. These are not regular nine-to-five people. The entrepreneurial process is far from linear, and it's never predictable, so these are people who can ride the peaks and troughs. They have a special knack of turning failure into opportunity, and learn quickly from their mistakes through a can-do, action-oriented attitude. It takes guts to be an entrepreneur.

The Green Start-Up

Whatever the permutations of how entrepreneurial businesses come to life, what's clear is that the number of people wanting to run one is rising. This is especially so among Gen Z – the cohort born between 1997 and 2012. According to one 2018 survey, 58% of Gen Z want to own their own business and 14% are already owners of entrepreneurial start-ups. Given that I started Good Energy when I was a spritely 31, this seems a far more exciting landscape than the one I entered into.

Perhaps this phenomenon is not so surprising. Traditional employment has never felt so uncertain – a job for life is considered a thing of the past. University tuition fees seem insurmountable to many, with no real guarantee of long-term employment at the end of a three- or four-year course. Plus the technological revolution has made starting an entrepreneurial business much more accessible. Born and raised with the internet and mobile technology, it is not only easier for twenty-somethings to connect to potential marketplaces, but it has given people a degree of creative control and independence, and a greater access to information than the world has ever witnessed. Whether it's a primary venture or a side hustle, these days anyone can learn how to build a website or an app or any other kind of platform at low cost and get started. And not everyone needs a headquarters to operate from – many start-ups draw on the do-it-yourself ethos of establishing themselves in a bedroom, or a garage, or sitting at a kitchen table.

In my mind, what connects these disparate individuals is a curious mind coupled with a creative spark. In fact, without creativity, entrepreneurialism cannot thrive. It's all about people finding creative solutions to problems. It's about talking to others. It's about constant innovation. The core product or service may not be new, but the entrepreneur will always find a way to improve it, streamline it, and reinvent it for a new era. And this isn't just any era. Today, the consumer places more expectation on a product, service and business than ever before. Why? As awareness grows of the climate emergency, buyers and users increasingly want businesses to contribute to solving the problems of people and planet. They want them to be responsible agents who don't profit from engaging in harmful practices. And they want the brands they buy into to care about the issues they care about. This has kick-started the rise of a new type of company, called purpose-led. More of that later, but first I want to look at where entrepreneurs get their ideas from.

From conscious consumer to entrepreneur

When I look at most entrepreneurial start-ups, one thing stands out: almost all entrepreneurs who bring an idea to life have developed their product or service because they have understood life through the eyes of a consumer. In the past, this may have been a consumer who simply couldn't find what they were looking for on the market, but didn't care much about the material that product was made from or the provenance of its supply chain. Today, a major shift has occurred. Entrepreneurs are having to respond to a new breed of 'conscious consumer'. In fact, it is likely that entrepreneurs will be conscious consumers themselves.

So what is a conscious consumer? Simply put, it's a person who demands more from what they buy. They want to make ethical, environmentally friendly choices, whether it's in grocery, fashion, or even when it comes to the pension fund they choose. The chances are that they've committed to buying less, but they want brands to have integrity, and for a company to be truthful and transparent about its credentials. They are probably willing to pay more for goods, but they want those goods to be of quality. And these consumers are a growing tribe: a 2021 survey by Deloitte found that one third of UK consumers now look for brands with strong sustainable and ethical practices. Meanwhile, environmental awareness has surged in the past year, with 85% now making more sustainable lifestyle choices.

But how does this translate into a business idea? To give an example, one of the modern pioneers of conscious consumerism was the late, great Anita Roddick. When she opened the doors to The Body Shop in Brighton in 1976, she was considered a rebel within the beauty industry – an industry known for its exploitation of workers from whom its raw materials were sourced, and an industry where testing on animals was commonplace. At the time, ethically sourced, cruelty-free natural products were not available on the high street and this was a gap she wanted to fill.

At its inception, The Body Shop embodied the spirit of activism and 'fair trade' a good 15 years before any official Fairtrade accreditation had ever come into existence. Now, that has become an easily recognisable stamp seen on many everyday goods from coffee to chocolate (and there are also many more accreditation schemes, some better than others). But back then the notion that business was part of a larger ecosystem – that should take into account the livelihoods of farmers, workers and suppliers, often in far-flung corners of the globe – was anathema. In fact, traditional companies rarely dealt directly with producers, or prioritised negotiating a fair price for goods, or even considered that lives and livelihoods were important. As for saving the planet, it was an afterthought, if it was ever a thought at all.

And there are many other fantastic examples of entrepreneurs whose companies date back to around the same time. One of my favourites is the US clothing company Patagonia, formed in California in 1973 that continues to be at the forefront of innovation today. What started in 1971 by climber Yvon Chouinard as a business selling steel pitons – the metal spikes climbers use to anchor themselves when rock climbing – has grown to be a billion-dollar clothing company. Ironically, though highly profitable, the pitons were soon abandoned by Chouinard when he noticed the damage they did to the cliff face. In the face of much resistance, he replaced the pitons with aluminium chocks that could be wedged into crevices rather than hammered in, thereby minimising damage. Since then, whatever product the company has made – from jackets to T-shirts, wetsuits to socks – its founding vision hasn't changed: to build the best product, cause no unnecessary harm to the environment and use business to inspire and implement solutions to the environmental crisis. This has been done through endless trial and error as techniques and materials have developed alongside. It's perhaps no surprise that Patagonia was recognised by the UN in 2019, who awarded the company its Champion of the Earth award.

What's also unique to every entrepreneur is how they tackle finding a solution to a problem, and there will be many stories throughout this book of entrepreneurs using their specific set of skills. I come from a physics background so I used my understanding of the scientific effects of climate change on the planet to understand how technology can help harness climate-friendly solutions. Others, like the fashion entrepreneur Mart Drake-Knight, who we'll meet later on, comes from an engineering background, and so to start his T-shirt business, Rapanui, he drew on those skills to build an operation using precision technology to produce a sustainable item of clothing. And the chances are you are starting your business because you asked the questions: why can't I find this product or service? How can I create it? What skill can I bring to the table? And can I build this proposition to have a wider societal impact? From the outset, your business will have a higher purpose.

The evolution of purpose-led business

Over the last 60 years, markets have emerged for corporate control and the idea of maximising profit as the sole purpose of business has prevailed. Yet it is widely predicted that the days of profit alone as the marker for business success are over. Focusing solely on maximising shareholder return will, in the future, be obsolete. Business as usual is no longer possible.

Often citing the UN's Sustainable Development Goals, designed as a blueprint to achieve a better and more sustainable future for all, more businesses have already embraced a universal call to action to address the social, political and environmental challenges that we face today and begun the process of creating a sustainable company. But what does sustainability actually mean? It's a word that gets bandied around often. It's a word that has arguably lost meaning, or seems too passive. Where is the 'action' in sustainability? For simplicity, it's a word I'm going to use throughout this book, but I want to be clear from the outset that it's not a straightforward concept. And getting to a quality level of sustainability isn't passive. It's all about climate action and believing we have the agency to 'do' something.

According to the UN, whose sustainability goals date back to 1992 and the Rio de Janeiro summit from where they evolved, sustainability touches everything related to people and planet. In their 2015 iteration, the UN's goals totalled 17 and they are worth repeating to show the remit. What will also become apparent throughout this book is how interconnected many of them are:

Goal 1: No poverty

Goal 2: Zero hunger

Goal 3: Good health and wellbeing

Goal 4: Quality education

Goal 5: Gender equality

Goal 6: Clean water and sanitation

Goal 7: Affordable and clean energy

Goal 8: Decent work and economic growth

Goal 9: Industry, innovation and infrastructure

Goal 10: Reduced inequalities

Goal 11: Sustainable cities and communities

Goal 12: Responsible consumption and production

Goal 13: Climate action

Goal 14: Protection of life below water

Goal 15: Protection of life on land

Goal 16: Peace, justice and strong institutions

Goal 17: Partnerships for the goals

Of course, it would be impossible, not to say grossly unfair, to place the burden of achieving any of these solely at the door of business. It's going to take national governments and international bodies, regulators and non-governmental organisations and many, many more people to drive forward change, plus a focus on how we act as individuals. For me, what's been encouraging is that the push towards increased responsibility has, as I've mentioned, been driven by consumers. It is us who are demanding that companies make a positive contribution to society. It is us who are shopping elsewhere if a brand falls short of the mark. Social media has made it far easier for people to share complaints and call out irresponsible behaviour. This pressure, combined with growing awareness around sustainability, has contributed to a shift towards purpose-led businesses.

That said, the relationship between business and purpose in itself is not new, but it has taken decades for it to filter into the mainstream. In the UK, I could cite two early examples. There was the pioneering work of Joseph Rowntree – the nineteenth-century philanthropist and chocolatier who didn't just build a confectionery business. He also built a village in York to house people on low incomes, many of who were his employees, and he gave them access to decent homes and affordable rents. Global confectionery giant Cadbury hailed from the same roots: in 1824 John Cadbury didn't just sell cocoa and drinking chocolate in his small Birmingham-based grocers; he went on to produce chocolate bars and his sons created the Bournville estate – a model village to give workers better living conditions. These, alongside some other entrepreneurs of the time, understood that successful business worked hand in hand with social responsibility to the extent that it did so in the community where the business was based. However, the extent to which both businesses were built on the exploitation of labour in the colonised countries they sourced raw materials from, is a subject currently being researched by Rowntree's own philanthropic society in the wake of the Black Lives Matter protests. Meanwhile, Cadbury, whose cocoa was sourced from Portuguese colonies, has issued an apology for its part in the historic injustices of slavery. In this era 'purpose' was localised.

Back then, the world was less interdependent and barely industrialised in comparison to some of our technologically advanced societies. There was an awareness of population growth and environmental degradation – and some very early eco-warriors – but people or planet hardly figured. Fast-forward to the 1970s, and we hear the first mention of 'global warming'. This, combined with a broader activism developed throughout the 1960s' civil rights movements, paved the way for more socially minded entrepreneurs, just like Anita Roddick and Yvon Chouinard. Then, in the 1980s when rapid globalisation occurred and we witnessed the rise of big business, 'purpose' shifted again with the rise of what is called corporate responsibility, which we'll come back to shortly. And today, purpose has evolved even further.

In an ideal scenario, purpose should sit at the very heart of a business and inform everything that business does. From a brand's reason for being to the people it employs, from how it treats those people to its marketing campaigns and to the causes it aligns itself with, purpose should be the core of a sophisticated nexus of internal decision-making and external communication through the stories a brand tells its customers.

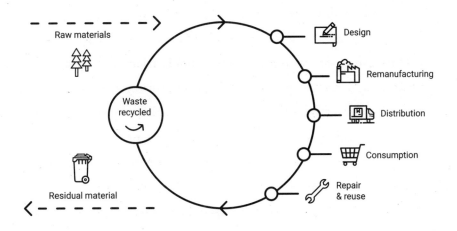

The Green Start-Up

The kinds of purpose-led businesses springing up are also evolving. Growth in the circular economy whereby goods are shared, leased, reused, repaired, refurbished and recycled to keep existing materials and products in circulation for as long as possible, has also sparked new ideas. Ocean Bottle, for example, is a UK company that makes fully recyclable and reusable water bottles, but each purchase also pays for the collection of 1,000 ocean-bound plastic bottles before they reach the sea. Its army of local collectors in coastal communities around the world then exchange this plastic for money or goods. Its mission is to stop 7 billion plastic bottles entering the ocean by 2025.

A business may not be making a physical product, but be a digital service or tool, and that service may have been conceived of to deal directly with a sustainability issue. Take Olio, a UK food waste app. Co-founder Tessa Clarke had the idea when she was packing up her home in Switzerland to move back to the UK. She couldn't bear the thought of throwing away any of the leftover food in her fridge, and the usual people she gave surplus food to weren't around. That was her light-bulb moment – if only there was a tool that could link a person getting rid of food to someone willing to take it. Can I create one? What's the market? How can I drive my idea forward?

Prior to Olio's incorporation in 2015, Clarke teamed up with a business partner and began researching the problem of food waste. It turned out it was a societal problem. A third of the food we produce globally is thrown away, and in the UK, households are responsible for more than half of all food waste. The average family throws away £700 worth of food each year, which adds up to £12.5 billion of food going straight to landfill. A shocking statistic, yet two entrepreneurs developed a food-saving app which has now helped share more than 5 million food portions. It couldn't have happened without mobile technology, and now Olio doesn't just work with communities. It works with hospitality, schools, corporates and retailers, to name a few.

But let's not get complacent. Although purpose-led companies are becoming more visible, and I'm going to be featuring some brilliant examples throughout this book, there is still a long way to go. What's bubbling away in a start-up or a small or medium-sized business (SME) that has the advantage of being forward-thinking and agile, hasn't yet significantly shifted the dial. Granted – large, established FTSE 100 corporates certainly have a harder job of unpicking decades of outdated practices and structures and convincing stakeholders that they have a higher reason for existing than delivering on a balance sheet. Plus, many of the national and global legal structures within which big business operates have not kept pace with this fast-changing landscape. But there is also an infuriating lack of will.

I know from experience the uphill struggle it has been for renewables to achieve any traction in the face of the multibillion-pound oil and gas extraction industries. According to one 2019 report, which brought together the work of climate experts, the 20 largest investor-owned and state-owned fossil fuel companies, including household names such as Shell, ExxonMobil, BP and Total, produced carbon fuels that emitted 35% of the global total between 1965 and 2018. Yet their willingness to shift into renewables has been glacial. The global pathway to achieving net zero – the point at which there is a balance between the amount of greenhouse gas emissions produced and the amount removed from the atmosphere – by the UK's target of 2050 hangs perilously in the balance. The target had been set at an

80% reduction by that date, but was amended in 2019 to achieving net zero. Currently the UK government's Climate Change Committee has highlighted that the UK is not on track to meet its goal.

Despite this, there are encouraging signs. Research in 2018 shows that 72% of companies now mention the UN's Sustainable Development Goals in their annual corporate or sustainability report, with 61% identifying climate action as a priority. But talking the talk is not the same as walking the walk – a point that I will come back to repeatedly. Purpose has to be meaningful. It's no longer good enough for a business to dabble in some recycling here or some renewable energy there, or sign up to a charter that calls for an end to modern-day slavery and shout about it on their website. Indeed, the goal of this book is to inspire a complete step change in thought and to embed a holistic green mindset into anyone wanting to take their first steps in creating or moving towards a sustainable business.

The limitations of corporate social responsibility

Many businesses will already be familiar with some of those first steps. As I mentioned, embedded within some may be a corporate social responsibility strategy (CSR) – a way of encouraging businesses to think about wider societal goals. This could be about the environment, inclusion and diversity, or alleviating poverty. A smaller business may not have an official strategy, but perhaps has a localised programme of 'giving back to society'.

Again, CSR is not a new idea. It has its roots in the writings of US steel magnate Andrew Carnegie at the turn of the twentieth century, who believed that the goal of a businessperson should be 'to do well in order to do good'.

Sparking Change

In the UK there is no single piece of CSR legislation setting out specific obligations for businesses, but many points, such as environmental protections and human rights, are covered by a vast array of existing laws such as the Equality Act 2010 or the Climate Change Act 2008. In the UK CSR also remains voluntary – a form of business self-regulation.

While there's no doubt that CSR forms part of the evolution to purpose-led, it has been limited in scope. It can be achieved through incorporating actual sustainable business practices or through extracurricular philanthropic initiatives, but therein lies the problem. I might run a small fashion business that sponsors a community football team and gives thousands of pounds each year to the local charities I am passionate about. In another business, CSR might be a commitment to reducing energy usage as part of a drive to be more environmentally friendly. These are all worthwhile goals but, in my view, they don't go far enough.

Too often, a business will choose programmes that play well with their brand image and help it create efficiencies and improve its bottom line. What constitutes 'socially responsible' can also differ wildly from company to company. But it is the lack of joined-up thinking that is the real enemy of transformational change. CSR is still rooted in the notion of the benevolent businessperson, not as business as an agent for change. My fashion company might give philanthropically to local causes, but I might also source my material from a supplier that uses child labour to dye it. I might install solar panels on my new factory roof to meet my environmental goals, but the makers of those solar panels might be dumping silicon tetrachloride, a highly toxic by-product of polysilicon used in solar cell production, into fields or rivers somewhere on the other side of the world.

The temptation is that some businesses wanting to move towards purpose-led and a more sustainable future will simply consider repackaging their CSR strategy. Yet we have to treat sustainability not simply as an add-on. If it is our core purpose, then it must authentically inform everything we do. Its tentacles must spread throughout every part of the business. It must be the driver that creates a constant momentum. If consumers are looking to place their trust in a brand, to affirm their values and create change in their own lives and the world, then a company must stand for something and do its utmost to stick to those values. It must employ people who buy into those values and be a genuine reflection of how a company needs to evolve.

Of course, we shouldn't pretend that any of this is easy. To live and breathe the higher values on which your company has been founded is a tricky balancing act. When it comes to attracting investment, or moving into growth, or even simply deciding how best to transform your fleet of vehicles, there will always be trade-offs. There will always be compromises you are faced with, and there will always be tough decisions that you have to make, and I'll discuss possible ways of managing these throughout.

What is clear is that being a purpose-led company will, in the future, be the difference between getting ahead or languishing behind or even becoming obsolete – the difference between bolstering the status quo or being a genuine force for good. Simply put, purpose-led is becoming good for business.

The sustainable future

The Covid-19 pandemic has put untold stress on health and the economy. As it has added to the climate emergency and increasing levels of social inequality, there has never been more need for entrepreneurs to develop new solutions and for business to think radically about how it can adapt to help the country's recovery. But while start-ups and purpose-driven SMEs can provide solutions, they are also going to need ongoing investment. Short-term backing will only limit businesses' ability to deliver social and environmental impact.

What's encouraging is that many of the businesses I talk to are already reporting that investors are looking for greater accountability and transparency around sustainability from the outset, even if the current regulatory framework is messy, outdated and, in my view, not fit for purpose.

Currently, reporting on sustainability comes under a regulatory umbrella that covers environmental, social and governance (ESG) issues. Although often interconnected, disclosure is only mandatory around certain metrics covered by existing laws and for certain sizes of businesses. For example, gender pay gap reporting is mandatory for any employer with a headcount of more than 250 employees. Meanwhile greenhouse gas reporting has been mandatory under the Companies Act 2006 for publicly listed companies since 2013.

To date, there is no one overarching piece of legislation covering all the touchpoints of ESG. That said, there is a direction of travel. At the UN's COP26 summit in Glasgow in 2021, the British government announced a plan to make sustainability reporting mandatory for investment products. Other larger companies have already started to publish ESG reports, despite this not being a legal requirement. Why? Away from compliance, potential investors are now looking at environmental and social risk because they also have a desire to invest their money responsibly. They want facts and figures about energy consumption, supply chains and how businesses are creating efficiencies. They want to invest in companies that are passionate about building a reputation around a commitment to sustainability, though it should be noted that investors are also not going far enough either. They, too, need to dig much deeper to understand whether a company is walking the walk and not just talking the talk. They need to shift their mindset away from simply managing financial or reputation risk and start asking searching questions, not because it's good for business, but because it's the right thing to do. And, in my mind, companies who embrace change for the right reasons will be streaks ahead in the future.

According to a 2015 global study by Harvard University, this competitive advantage is already visible. It found that a firm's level of commitment to purpose influenced its growth and broader success. Businesses where purpose was clearly articulated and understood were more likely to achieve more than a 10% growth between 2012 and 2015 than businesses where purpose was not well understood or communicated.

And it's not just increased profit where the benefits of being purpose-led lie. A business's operating costs are also affected. The point at which economics and the environment meet is when wasteful practices are designed out, creating efficiencies and cost savings so more can be spent on doing good stuff. Plus, employee churn within a business wastes money that could also be spent more positively. It is estimated that employees who believe a company has a higher purpose than just profits are 27% more likely to stay working for it. Of course, if a company values its people, then it will also work hard to listen to them and retain them.

If all this sounds daunting, then don't worry. In the next nine chapters, I'll guide you through the areas to concentrate on if you are making steps to be truly green at heart. If you are anything like me, you'll feel the exhilaration of the challenge alongside the nerves. The point is to feel the fear and act anyway.

But enough of the theory, let's get down to business . . .

Chapter 2
The Green Workspace

Whenever I'm in need of a dose of optimism I talk to friends, businesses and organisations who inspire me. The environmental challenge can feel overwhelming, but I've got a community of people who see opportunities and understand the hurdles to jump. Most of all they keep me 'doing'.

One go-to is Justin Albert who heads up the National Trust in Wales. The organisation, established way back in 1895, is now a climate-change champion. Yet running a portfolio of more than 50 stately homes, historic houses, castles, abbeys and museums in Wales alone, many of which are listed buildings, is an extra tough job, and Justin knows a thing or two about challenges.

'We've never before put a planet in an oven and turned it up to eleven. We have to force ourselves to solve this, but I think we'll get there,' he told me when I last called him. 'It doesn't matter what your business does. If someone asks you what your priority is, the answer should be that you are part of the fight against climate change. You could be running a widget factory but that should be your basic commitment.'

Justin is a guy who, with his brilliant team, brought solar PV, electric car chargers and micro-hydro plants to National Trust sites when people thought he was a 'weird ass'. He hates the word sustainable: 'Sustaining is often sustaining a level of rubbish,' he says, adding that he would much rather use the word 'regeneration'.

Nationally, the National Trust's goal is to reach net zero by 2030, and between 2017 and 2022 it has invested significantly in renewable power and measures such as plastic reduction, but when it comes to bricks and mortar, regeneration is like opening a Pandora's box. Damp, leaky windows and draughty roofs are all difficult to resolve. This is especially so given the plethora of planning red tape around heritage buildings that the Trust has to work through. But the same can be said of many other buildings across the UK – they all come with unique challenges.

It may surprise you, but the built environment – that is, the human-made environment – contributes to 40% of all UK carbon emissions, with 23% of that in non-domestic stock. Offices, retail space, industrial buildings, health and hospitality contribute to 71% of total non-domestic energy consumption. Staggering when you think that, by comparison, UK air travel accounts for 7% of the UK's total greenhouse gas emissions overall.

The usual culprits are creaky gas boilers and non-renewable sources of energy, but ageing buildings, substandard structures and poor fittings are a major contributing factor, not to mention environmentally unfriendly construction materials and techniques.

In this chapter we'll be talking you through some of the ways you can improve the energy efficiency of your physical workspace. This could be as simple as moving into an office where the landlord has prioritised sustainability. But, if you have some control, you can be more ambitious.

The Green Workspace

Of course, for complete control, one scenario would be to purpose-build your own space. We're not going to cover that in this book. Businesses are not usually in a position to embark on this kind of project until much further down the line. However it may be something to aim for when you start to grow. And there are some stellar examples. For inspiration on a modest budget look to buildings such as the Soil Association's headquarters in the UK designed by Max Fordham LLP. The building minimises energy consumption with features such as LED lighting and increased natural ventilation to reduce reliance on the existing refrigerant cooling systems. Suspended ceilings have also been removed to let in light and improve the views to the outside. Plus, there are both communal and quiet spaces inside.

Or, there's sustainable building specialists PYC Group who have built their own office in Welshpool, Powys in Wales constructed with a timber frame to a budget of £350,000. It uses recycled newspaper insulation within the frame. However, it's also worth knowing that some buildings created for low operational impact often require a high-impact build, and when it comes to CO_2 emissions the whole lifespan of a building needs to be considered.

Lastly, I'm going to talk about how workspaces sustain people. When I think about the workspace, I see it far more holistically. In fact, energy efficiency is often just the start of the journey. Just like how National Trust buildings are places of reflection, enjoyment and inclusion, workspaces are living, breathing entities. They support communities. And, if we look at sustainability through this lens we take people into account: who they are, how they use those spaces, how they feel in those spaces and what those spaces say about a business. In other words, we create working environments that sustain both planet and people.

The evolution of the workspace

Before we look in detail into how to create workspaces fit for the future, it's interesting to look at how the workspace has evolved. We're going to focus on office space, as everyone usually works from a base. The hierarchical office design of the 1950s, the likes of which you see in TV series such as *Mad Men* with managers in large offices lording it over others, has since given way to much more freedom.

The 1960s saw the advent of the 'work cubicle', which morphed into open-plan spaces by the 1980s. Employees might sit on one floor, or a number of floors grouped by department, and this is often still the case. Chances are the walls were grey, the people looked grey and the whole atmosphere seemed even greyer. Even the fun part – a café – might sit in an annexe.

But this silo space has become as outdated as silo thinking. In the 2020s, businesses can be much more fluid, open-plan and integrated. If creativity and innovation is at their heart, then the physical space reflects this. Rapid technological advancement has paved the way for agile working, giving employees a choice as to where they work, depending on the task and who they are collaborating with. Although many workspaces have yet to catch up, now it's not unusual to see a café as a central element of the workspace with everything else orbiting around. Workspaces have also become less static and more ad hoc: communities that come together as and when.

And the Covid-19 pandemic has altered this landscape yet again. Almost overnight millions of workers adjusted to remote working. As we take steps into a post-pandemic world, employers will need to fashion safer spaces with increased flexibility, perhaps spaces where employees come for two or three days a week. As for the truly sustainable workspace, this is a revolution happening as we speak . . .

The shared space

Unless you are working from home or taking over a unique space, many start-ups will begin life in either a shared office or a leased industrial unit. At first, you are on a hamster wheel of decision-making. Your business needs a home, but you may not have thought about that home as being a tool for climate action. What might that even look like? Anyway, you are constrained by time, your location, your budget and what's available.

The brilliant news is that some providers are also thinking about sustainability, although many more need to follow suit. And just like the conscious consumer who pushes change from below, you can also ask questions of landlords and providers before you move into a building, or make suggestions to improve a building that you are already inhabiting.

Not all landlords and providers are progressive enough to consider how to make their buildings more environmentally efficient, but an increasing number are. It's also worth remembering that, just like Justin at the National Trust, a landlord may have the will but hasn't yet found a way to alter parts of the building as this will depend on certain planning constraints.

One business that I think is streaks ahead when it comes to sustainability is Huckletree who run a number of shared office spaces in London, Manchester and Dublin. What's interesting about the company is that it doesn't just see the physical space as contributing towards saving the planet, it also speaks of an ecosystem of people – a network of users who it helps to form a community – which is another key element of sustainability.

It is exactly this momentum that Huckletree has harnessed: built into its operational structure are weekly meetings with its members so it can help them grow their businesses, plus it hosts events and talks. Through leveraging its 'intelligence network' it can connect a business with a specific need to someone who can help. This way the company adds value to its community, enhancing identity and trust alongside enjoyment and participation, elements which we'll return to in the last section of this chapter.

To understand the elements Huckletree considers when choosing a space, I met up with Patrick Keogh, Huckletree's director of programming. I was interested in how it thinks about physical space and how it balances opportunity with limitation – something every business has to do.

Huckletree's Soho space is curated mainly for the investor community who inhabit the area. Housed within a new-build run by Westminster City Council, it comprises two floors that include an upstairs open-plan and hot-desking area with a café. Downstairs there are private pods of varying sizes designed for meetings. There is even a meditation room!

To create this space, Huckletree worked with the local council to carry out a complete refurbishment to include new windows, doors, floors, a new ventilation system plus an interior furnished with chairs and tables mainly sourced from sustainable and recycled materials. Its eco-friendly design makes it highly energy efficient with low operational costs.

'When we consider spaces we are always looking to work with responsible landlords and builders,' says Patrick, 'but we also have to make compromises. Because we see sustainability as more than just a physical space, we balance limitations in one area with sustainability in another.'

A great example of this trade-off is to compare Huckletree's Soho space with another building it runs near Westminster called Public Hall which is a Grade II listed building. This space caters primarily for challenger brands pitching to government. While the location is perfect for Huckletree's clientele, the choice of building was limited in that area and few changes could be made to the building's structure because of its listed status. Yet when Huckletree considered overall sustainability one location balanced the other.

'The environmental impact of the refurbishment at Public Hall was far less than at our Soho hub,' explains Patrick. 'Because we couldn't change the building, we kept the internal structure, the original flooring, the windows, and we couldn't alter the ventilation. From an operational perspective it leaks heat, but because there was minimal construction we used less CO_2 in the build. And it works for the community we wanted to serve.'

To put this in context, globally the construction industry is responsible for 11% of all carbon emissions. In the UK, in 2021, the Royal Academy of Engineering called on the construction industry to radically improve its decarbonisation targets. This included creating more holistic and efficient building designs but also adopting measures such as reusing building materials and using non-fossil fuel powered machinery. For this reason, wherever possible, Huckletree uses developers and builders who adhere to BREEAM standards – an independent organisation that measures and rates the sustainability of infrastructure projects.

For me, Huckletree is a perfect example of a company striving to live its purpose while juggling the day-to-day reality of commercial viability, the choice of building stock available, cost and planning constraints. Yet I consider its most important achievement to be its relentless pursuit of that purpose. No business is perfect but what we can't do today, we can improve on tomorrow. And, as it has taken on more shared offices, Huckletree itself has amassed more knowledge, created better structures, found better building materials, used more efficient building practices and found new ways to nurture its community of users.

Green-proofing your workspace

As you start to grow you may want to, or need to, expand out of the space you are in. In the same way that you are hostage to location and availability in a shared space, it's exactly the same story when you look around for a space you have more control over. Unless you buy your space, you may still be faced with an unsympathetic landlord so try to align your goals with someone who is at least willing to listen. And, as we saw at Huckletree, every building has its unique benefits and drawbacks.

You may be a business who has taken over a disused church, a Methodist hall, a listed building, a draughty office block, a warehouse or a factory. A home office operation could have just as many challenges. To help us understand more of the basic structural alterations you can make to create a more energy-efficient space, and how this can spark further thought, I've sought the help of Julie's Bicycle, a charity that started in 2007 by advising the music industry, but that now works across all arts sectors.

What was interesting about talking to Alison Tickell, founder and CEO of Julie's Bicycle, is that organisations who first sought advice from them about building or energy efficiency have gradually started asking more profound questions about social justice through climate action.

The Green Workspace

'Climate action isn't about thinking, it's about doing. It's about having agency and nurturing and feeding good practice,' says Alison. 'Wherever you start from, you can't help but end up on a journey. We work in the arts but our work has never just been about artists. We wanted to create models for the whole sector that assist venue owners, tour managers, production and lighting companies and anyone else in the supply chain. It's about creating an ecosystem where people can thrive free from anxiety or reputation risk.'

Alison adds that the arts sector became more galvanised around climate change after 2012 when The Arts Council in England made action on the environment a requirement for funding. Not only did this make it a critical business concern, but it has also been the catalyst for people asking deeper questions such as: who has access to the arts? Who tours and for whom? Can we reach audiences in new ways? 'Climate literacy often starts with a business wanting to find a way to conserve heat in a building, but that is so important because it opens up so many other conversations,' says Alison.

So, if climate literacy often starts with building basics, what might those basics look like? To improve on any building's efficiency you will need to understand where energy is being lost. An initial energy audit will help you identify the best options for energy-efficient improvements, and this can be done professionally or through a self-audit. The Centre for Sustainable Energy is a great place to start and it features a checklist on its website. What's really important is to assess the whole building. Dependent on its position and unique structure, some works may be more effective than others.

In an ideal scenario, you should carry out all the works you need to do at the same time, as this causes less upheaval and is more cost effective.

But the capital investment required to do this doesn't always make the cost manageable. However, what's worth bearing in mind is that when it comes to structural alterations, some elements are more difficult to retrofit than others. Creating an action plan will focus priorities on work that will make the most impact. If you can't do it all at once, splitting the project into phases will help you understand the best sequence of works to be carried out.

Before you start, you will also need to check with your local council to see if planning permission is required. And, when it comes to sustainability, choose partners, such as developers or builders, to work with who understand your specific needs, who properly assess your building, and who can advise you on the best environmentally friendly materials to use. In other words, work with people who align with your mission. And, always choose the best materials that your budget will allow.

There are several sustainability standards you can look out for when working with partners:

- *BREEAM*: Launched in 1990, by the Building Research Establishment (BRE), a BREEAM rating sets standards for the environmental performance of a building through its design, specification, construction and operation, and can be applied to new developments and refurbishments. Its markers range from carbon emissions to pollution to health and wellbeing. On any project, try to partner with a firm that adheres to BREEAM standards.
- *LEED*: a global building rating system which assesses energy and environmental design. It is used for all building types and building phases including interior fit-outs as well as new constructions. It

is run by the US Green Business Council but there are accredited professionals in the UK.

- *The Passivhaus Standard*: an international design standard focused on slashing energy from buildings but also on comfort and health. Building performance is taken into account alongside reduced running costs, but the social impact of a building – involving, for example, productivity levels of employees and reduced absenteeism – is also assessed.
- *The WELL Building Standard*: a ratings system launched in 2014, for buildings and interior spaces that supports and advances human health and wellness. Although it is US-based, it does operate within the UK. Its assessment remit includes thermal comfort, movement, light, air, sound, as well as promotion of community and good mental health.
- *SKA Rating*: an assessment method that helps landlords and tenants of non-domestic buildings to fit out the space in an environmentally sustainable way. It is run by the Royal Institution of Chartered Surveyors (RICS).

Insulation

A lack of insulation in non-domestic buildings, just like millions of homes throughout the UK, is contributing to vast energy inefficiency. Remember the Insulate Britain protesters who stopped traffic on the M25 in 2021 with demands for home insulation to combat the climate crisis and end fuel poverty? The problem in commercial buildings doesn't cause the same hardship, but the solution is exactly the same. Insulation placed into roofs, ceilings, walls and floors is a great way to make your business heatproof.

So how does heat loss happen? Most people understand that heat rises, but it's not always the case. Thermodynamics teaches us that heat moves from areas of high temperature to low temperature, which means it can move in all directions. Insulation materials essentially resist the ability for heat to move from one place to another, and a material's thermal resistance value is known as its R-value. The better the insulation, the higher the R-value. The overall rating of a building with a combination of materials – including bricks, flooring, roofing and windows – is called its U-value. So the lower the U-value, the better a building is at holding on to its heat.

Roof, loft and ceiling insulation

In standard, leased office space, it is unlikely you will ever be faced with insulating a roof. However, if you take over a town house, for example, or a factory building, then it could be a decision you are faced with.

How you insulate a roof will depend on whether it is pitched or flat. The work will also depend on the current condition of the roof, the building's material frame, or whether it has existing damp or condensation. Always start with a full professional survey.

○ *Pitched roofs*: These can be insulated in one of several ways. The first decision you'll need to make is whether to insulate at ceiling or at rafter level. At ceiling level it's a simple job of filling in the joists with insulation material and boarding over if necessary. At rafter level, insulation sits between or below the sloping beams and a space is left between the roof and the insulating material so air can travel freely. Insulation can come in blanket form or in rigid boards and for neatness and extra warmth the insulating material can be boarded over.

○ *Flat roofs*: An average commercial building with a flat roof that is not properly insulated can lose up to 25% of its heat. As a rule of thumb, flat roofs need to be replaced every 10–15 years, so it will be more cost effective to combine any insulation work with replacement work. And there are two types of insulation: warm roof and cold roof. Warm roof consists of laying insulation materials on top of the roof and covering with a layer of asphalt. Cold roof insulation involves placing the insulating material between the joist spaces that support the roof structure. For this work to be carried out, it is likely a contractor will need to take the ceilings down. Remember that with any insulation project, air still needs to flow in and out of the building, and a good installer will be careful not to block vents, grilles or air bricks.

○ *A green roof*: Another more radical option for a flat roof is a green roof. There is often little space for greenery in urban areas and a flat green roof can offer temperature regulation (both in summer and winter), sound insulation and air purification, as well as encouraging biodiversity. For this you really need a specialist installer who can consider the space and the type of green roof that will work for your building. Different types of plants can hold different amounts of water content and therefore be more resilient to various climate and weather conditions. The vegetation blankets can be placed on all types of roofing, assuming they are waterproof and root-proof and they support both the BREEAM and LEED scores for a building.

○ *A suspended ceiling*: You might also consider fitting a suspended ceiling and insulating in between. This will make the volume of space you need to heat smaller and the work will also be cheaper.

Floor insulation

Underfloor insulation is especially appropriate for older buildings. Many have suspended floors which means there are gaps underneath the floorboards. These gaps can be filled by removing the floorboards and laying the insulation. With floor insulation it is important not to block ventilation points, as floorboards will rot without adequate air circulation.

Another easy and inexpensive way of preventing heat loss through a floor is to fill the gaps between the floor and the skirting boards. If you are using caulking or sealant to do this, source an eco-friendly product. A quick search will find you no end of eco-caulks!

A further alternative way of insulating a space is to carpet or refloor. But before you source new flooring companies, be mindful of the embodied carbon in the product – that's the amount of CO_2 it's taken to manufacture it. There are some great companies out there innovating in this space, but probably the giant amongst them is still Interface, set up by the visionary Ray Anderson in the early 1990s, who are way ahead of the curve on carbon-neutral flooring – so do research the product that best suits your purpose.

Cavity and solid wall insulation

When it comes to wall insulation, there are several factors to consider. If the building is pre-1920s, it is likely to have solid walls rather than cavity walls, which feature a gap that can be filled with insulating material.

○ *Solid walls* can be insulated from the outside or inside, though remember that insulating from the inside will reduce the floor area of any room. Also, work cannot be done until any underlying problems, such as rising damp, are fixed. Internal insulation can be done by fitting rigid insulation boards to the wall, or by building a stud wall to be filled with insulation material. For this work, all skirting boards and door frames need to be removed and reattached.

- *External wall insulation* can be carried out with no disruption inside and involves fixing a layer of insulation material to the exterior wall which is then covered in render or cladding. An assessment of the outside walls will determine whether the work can be done, and planning permission may be required.

- *Cavity walls* are insulated by injecting or blowing insulation material into the cavity from the outside. Holes are drilled in the walls and filled back in once the insulation is complete. Again, air needs to flow in and out of the building, so a good installer will not block or seal any ventilation.

Insulation materials

A number of eco-friendly materials can be used in insulation, ranging from loose chips to semi-rigid and rigid materials. There are many on the market, but the following materials have the lowest carbon footprint:

- *Sheep wool* comes in blanket or chip forms and is a natural alternative to mineral wool, which has a higher carbon footprint. It can be used in roofs at ceiling level, internal partition walls and under floors.

- *Cellulose* is blown-in insulation produced from either natural plant fibres or recycled paper products and can be used in roofs and cavity walls.

○ *Hemp blanket* is also produced from plant fibres. It can be used in roofs at ceiling level, internal partition walls and suspended timber floors.

○ *Hemp board* is compacted and less flexible, but has good thermal performance. It can be used in roofs at ceiling and rafter level, and under suspended timber floors, as well as in walls.

○ *Cork* is a rigid material sourced from the bark of the cork tree with excellent thermal performance. It can be used in floors, roofs and walls.

Windows

Ill-fitting doors and leaky windows are the enemy of energy efficiency, and unless you are working in a building situated in a conservation area or you occupy a listed building, then it's an easy problem to tackle.

In conservation areas there may be restrictions on what you can do to windows, as any work carried out must preserve the character of the area. Similarly, listed buildings will require permission to make changes to windows and specialist materials and methods may also be required. For guidance, contact your local council's conservation officer.

Otherwise, the most common window replacement is double- or triple-glazed windows. The energy performance of a window depends on how well these materials stop heat from passing through, as well as how much sunlight travels through the glass and how little air can leak around the window. The most energy-efficient type of glass for double or triple glazing is low emissivity (low-E) glass which has a special coating that reflects heat back into a room but still lets light in from the outside.

The energy performance of a window is complicated but there is an independent rating system to help you decide. Run by the British

Fenestration Rating Council, the scale runs from A++ to E, the latter being the least efficient. Seek advice from your installer and invest in the best according to your budget.

Lastly, make sure you arrange to recycle old windows. Wood, aluminium and UPVC can all be recycled. Window glass has a different composition to a glass bottle and needs a different treatment, so do speak to your installer or nearest recycling centre about how best to recycle window glass.

Doors

Like any other part of a building's fixtures and fittings, both external and internal doors are important when it comes to energy efficiency. You could be operating from a draughty warehouse that needs constant access or a standard office block, so again seek advice according to your needs.

That said, there are some very low-cost measures you can put in place when it comes to conserving heat. For example, make sure that doors are not propped open for convenience. Self-closing doors may help, but make sure this doesn't cause accessibility problems for employees or visitors.

Another simple way to reduce draughts is by fitting draught excluders around the door frame. You may also want to investigate fitting doors with drop seals, which do exactly as the name suggests – when the door closes, a seal drops down to cut off air passing underneath.

Secondary glazing, shutters and blinds

Secondary glazing is a great way of discreetly fitting a secondary pane of glass or other transparent material inside an existing window. This can be more cost effective than installing double- or triple-glazing, and it's also perfect if the building is in a conservation area, is a period property or a listed building. As well as providing thermal insulation it can also reduce noise pollution from traffic or street noise.

However, one of the easiest ways to prevent some heat loss is to install blinds or shutters. In some settings, such as in hospitality, heavy draped curtains may also do the job in winter. Shutters and blinds also have the added benefit of reducing heat gain in summer.

Thermal energy loss will differ between shutters, different types of blinds and curtains, so do seek proper advice applicable to your building. You should also be mindful of the comfort of your employees and choose a system that controls light levels and harvests natural light.

Ventilation

As the world heats up, so does our need to keep cool. Currently, there are around 1 billion single-room air-conditioning units operating in the world – that's around one for every seven people on earth. But predictions put the number needed by 2050 to be as high as 4.5 billion. When you pause to consider this, it's not only the materials needed to manufacture units that will be required in staggering amounts, but the vast energy needed to power them. On average, a home air conditioner uses around 3.5 kW of electricity. Compare this to a laptop which on average runs at 30 watts per hour. This means that you need the same power to run 100 laptops as you would one air conditioner. Multiply that to billions of homes and businesses around the world and the devastating impact becomes clear.

That said, there is nothing worse than working in oven-like temperatures or in a stuffy office. And most people spend more than half of their day at work, so it is important to consider an energy-efficient ventilation system. In newly constructed or refurbished buildings there is now a minimum requirement on ventilation dependent on how big the space is and how many people inhabit it. Poor air in buildings can affect concentration, productivity and make people feel stressed out and unwell. But before replacing or installing an air-conditioning system, consider the following environmentally friendly options first:

- *Natural ventilation*: As simple as it sounds, natural ventilation and cooling relies on a natural flow between openings on opposite sides of a room or building, or rising warm air being replaced with cooler air sucked in through windows and doors. However, don't forget to evaluate your security when considering opening vents, doors and windows.
- *Night cooling*: This is where cool night air is passed through the building to remove heat that has accumulated during the day. When the building fabric is cooled it will absorb more heat the following day, meaning lower internal temperatures. This can be fan-assisted, although if done naturally with automated venting you will save money and use less power.
- *Evaporative cooling*: If you do install a ventilation system, work with your supplier to find the best for your building. In the right circumstances, one low-energy alternative is evaporative cooling. Unlike air-conditioning systems which use recirculated air, it circulates cool, fresh air through a building and forces out stale, hot air. Fresh air from the outside is then cooled by passing it over water before it is directed around the building by a fan.
- *Ventilation efficiency*: Whether you stick with an existing system, upgrade it or replace it, there are some dos and don'ts that will

save energy and money. For the best energy efficiency, all doors and windows should be closed when a system is running. Also, don't run the system when no one is in the building and operate it on a timer. Some buildings operate a 'mixed mode' whereby a combination of natural ventilation and mechanical ventilation is used when needed. In addition, set the system on 'auto' so that when it reaches the desired temperature it cuts out at that point.

Interiors

Refitting an office is one of the most cost-effective changes you can make to a workspace, and mindful refurbishments take into account what you put in as well as what you take out. Nearly 1.2 million office desks and 1.8 million office chairs end up in landfill every single year in the UK. Yet so much of this is avoidable.

End-of-use programmes can bring furniture back into the supply chain. Plenty of companies offer this service but there are also charities in need of unwanted office furniture. For example, Relieve Furniture connects not-for-profits and schools to businesses. Always try to find a recycling scheme local to your area, as transporting furniture over longer distances will impact carbon emissions.

When it comes to sourcing chairs, tables, shelving and any other office items, there are also a growing number of suppliers creating products using recycled materials such as plastic bottles, car batteries and old wooden pallets, to name a few. There are even cardboard chairs on the market! And one company, Unwasted, has developed a recyclable substitute for conventional Medium Density Fibreboard (MDF). The material, called Neverwaste, uses waste cardboard packaging without any of the glues, resins and toxins used in MDF to create an eco-friendly fibreboard.

When we refitted the kitchen at Good Energy we sourced recycled wooden worktops and cabinets as a cost-effective and environmentally friendly alternative and refurbished old chairs with wool to give a more eclectic feel. Always think about the end of life of whatever you purchase. Can it be reused or recycled when you come to refit again? If a contractor is clearing the office to be refurbished, ask them what they will do with the debris. Waste can be tracked and a reputable company will provide you with documentation to show where it has been recycled.

For more specialist machinery, for example machinery used in food production, again use the reuse and recycle mantra, although, when it comes to heavy machinery, if you can buy well and maintain well then this is by far the best option.

What your space says about your business

So far we have looked at the workspace mainly through the structural and decarbonisation lens, and we will expand on this further when we cover green energy in Chapter 3. But, as companies like Huckletree have demonstrated, sustainability is more than just a commitment to reducing CO_2 emissions.

We must ensure that a building works in harmony with the network of people it supports. Huckletree report that many of its members choose the space because they align with its sustainable ethos, and this feeds into identity and trust. In turn, they want their clients, or whoever they bring to a space, to understand that these are their values, too. Another key element of sustainability is the notion of enjoyment: a space that is pleasant to be in and aids wellbeing as well as encouraging participation. Good Energy's original office, which it has since returned to, was on the top floor of the local council building. The far-reaching views over the town gave you a sense of wellbeing every time you looked out of the window.

Inclusive spaces

It is impossible to design a workspace that caters for the needs of every single individual, but there are some obvious ways in which the physical space can be adapted to take difference into account. Not everyone is the same or works in the same way and it is vital to understand your employees, and constantly check in with them to find out if the space is working for them. As an example, Huckletree reports many more requests for mixed spaces that encompass open-plan and private rooms. In the post-Covid era, good, improved technology is also highly sought after. Fast internet speeds, monitors that work and good video conferencing facilities are all part of bringing communities together, whether they physically share the space or not.

The green canvas

When you move into a new space, one of the easiest and cheapest ways to make it enjoyable is to paint the walls. But don't forget that many conventional paints contain harmful chemicals and plastics. So-called volatile organic compounds (VOCs) in paints are impossible to eradicate completely but choosing paints that have low percentage levels are better for the environment.

That said, I can't stress enough to read the small print on paint. Some companies will highlight low VOC levels but may use synthetic pigments or bind paints together with vinyl, acrylic or PVA to create a certain finish. Choose a company that doesn't greenwash its eco-credentials. Today, there is a much wider range of eco-friendly paints on the market. There is a growing range, including: plant-based paints; clay paints; limewash paints; paint made with milk proteins called casein paint and mineral paints. We painted the Good Energy offices in 2008 with eco-friendly paint. The decorators told us they found it more difficult to apply but the benefit to employees was that it was odourless. We didn't have to sit with a 'new paint' smell polluting the office for weeks.

But paint isn't only about creating a pleasant environment for people to work. We used brightly coloured paint to colour-code each floor to make them easier to remember and identify. Plus, one in four people of working age in the UK are registered blind or have some form of visual impairment, so paint can also be used to highlight areas to make workspaces safer and more navigable. For example, door frames or skirting that contrast with walls can be used as guidance. Other areas to consider are stair handrails and other obstacles such as radiators. The Royal National Institute of Blind People (RNIB) is a great place to start your research.

Space, light and plants

The Covid-19 pandemic has been a double-edged sword in terms of the workspace. Employees who lived in a shared house suddenly found themselves squeezed into a bedroom typing on a laptop. There were parents perched on their kitchen tables working while simultaneously home-schooling their kids. Others were home alone, suddenly feeling the isolation of a life on Zoom. But there were benefits, too . . .

Not being in an open-plan office and being able to control your work environment can increase productivity and improve employees' wellbeing. This doesn't mean that employees want to work at home forever. Interaction is also a crucial part of employee satisfaction but there are lessons to be learned that can be transferred to the new working environment.

Creating multifunctional spaces is one way to achieve a balance. While open-plan offices can encourage interaction, creativity and a sense of togetherness, they can also be anxiety-inducing. Open-plan can also affect concentration. High noise levels affect certain people more than others, and also a lack of privacy can be a real work killer. If you can build in both open-plan areas and private spaces where people – particularly when they are working long hours – can meet, concentrate, make calls and attend virtual meetings, then this provides choice.

If you have the budget and space, also think about a quiet zone, chill-out room or meditation room where employees can unwind. If you have outdoor space you can adapt, think about putting seating in so people can take a break, eat lunch or hold a meeting outside when the weather is nice.

Natural light is also a big boost to employee wellbeing and productivity. If you can, choose a space with good light and move desks as near to natural light as possible. Plants are also known to reduce stress levels, but be aware that certain plants are allergy-inducing, so always choose carefully. There is a brilliant US company called Sempergreen who lead the way in living walls and green roofs, and a tour around their website should give you lots of inspiration.

Another option is to consider a living wall. These can be complicated to have the right irrigation systems and guttering, but technical developments mean that they are becoming more of an option for offices. They don't have to cover a whole wall, as a compact version can have a big impact. A free-standing, moveable wall divider may be a better option for a small workspace, having a positive effect on wellbeing and acoustics.

The kitchen or café

Most workspaces will have a kitchen area or even a café. Believe it or not these areas can say a lot about your values. Aligning yourself to brands that chime with your sustainable heart can create a healthy symbiosis. What's the point in embodying a clean, green message but serving coffee sourced from a company that doesn't value fair trade? What if you have a recycling bin in your kitchen to collect plastic, but use teabags that contain polypropylene – a sealing plastic to keep the bags from falling apart?

You may also find employees or users asking questions of your food waste. Do you encourage the recycling of teabags, for example? Do you use a coffee machine that uses fresh grounds? How do you dispose of them?

Admittedly, I had no idea of the amazing things you can do with coffee granules! Take the Cambridge-based business bio-bean. It picks up coffee grounds from a range of businesses and turns them into fuel briquettes, a great eco-friendly alternative to burning kiln-dried wood in domestic burners.

Although this list is not exhaustive, here are some further elements to consider when it comes to a kitchen or café in the workplace:

- If you offer your employees free fruit, make sure it is organic, seasonal and sourced as locally as possible.
- Choose washable and reusable cutlery, plates and mugs in the kitchen.

- If you can't offer reusable, use fully compostable containers.
- Avoid unnecessary packaging that contains plastics.
- Offer plant-based milk alternatives, and ethical tea and coffee – Pukka teas and Ethical Addictions coffee are my favourites, but there are lots of local, sustainable companies popping up too.
- Avoid buying or selling bottled water by offering tap or filtered water.

Your loo

It's not a phrase I ever thought I'd be writing, but loos really do matter. Everyone uses the facilities, whether they are employees or guests, and believe it or not your loos say a lot about you and your business. Simply put: you snooze, you loos, so there are some simple ways to improve:

- Accessibility is key for bathrooms. Wherever possible source premises where you can offer a disabled toilet. Remember that heavy doors or self-closing doors are a barrier for disabled people. Also choose handles that can be operated by people with limited dexterity.
- If you are able to refurbish your bathroom, source recycled tiles and recycled fixtures and fittings wherever possible.
- Offer recycled toilet paper – it's an absolute no-brainer! And there are some great brands out there. For example, Australian company Who Gives A Crap not only produce recyclable toilet paper but 50% of their profits help to build toilets and improve sanitation in the developing world. Also, the soap and air freshener you use says a lot about you. We kitted out the toilets on our first wind farm with natural products made on site in a nearby herbery, so our loos also told a local story.

⊘ Offer free tampons and sanitary wear and source these from a company who also puts sustainability at its heart. Companies such as DAME and Here We Flo produce vegan and cruelty-free sanitary products using materials such as bamboo and organic cotton.

Waste

One thing I did at Good Energy was to remove all waste bins from under senior manager's desks – it almost caused a riot! At the time, lots of employees championed recycling, but there were a few sticklers who were impossible to shift. One bin sat under their desks and the temptation was to throw everything into it. I confess, the mischievous side of me did enjoy their rage, but with hindsight I should have sought everyone's buy-in and helped them to understand the importance. Besides, as recycling has become more commonplace at home, it's become easier to communicate the message.

All businesses are legally required to collect waste and dispose of it responsibly but having a visible waste strategy can also help build your business's reputation. Whether you operate from an office or run a park café, it's important to show employees, clients, investors and any other user that you are proactively reducing your impact on the planet. It's also increasingly likely that you will also be asked to report on your waste strategy by clients.

We're going to be exploring waste in more depth in Chapter 7 when we look at supply chain, but the first action to take in any workspace is to measure waste. Once you know what waste your business generates and how much it generates, then you can understand how best to collect your waste, dispose of it and set targets for waste reduction.

Typical office waste comprises of:

- Food waste
- Paper
- Cardboard
- Glass bottles and jars
- Tins and cans
- Plastic bottles
- Printer cartridges
- Electrical equipment
- Laptops and desktop computers
- Batteries

When it comes to the physical workspace, the most important factor is where to position waste bins:

- Set up bins for paper near desks, but also examine if your business could go paper-free.
- Bins for food waste, food packaging, plastic bottles, cans and tins should be positioned around areas where employees tend to prepare and eat food.
- Recycling bins for batteries, printer cartridges and electrical equipment should sit in a central location. You may also consider switching to rechargeable batteries and buying refurbished electrical goods and IT equipment. Large corporates typically replace their IT systems every three years and so there is an established marketplace for discounted, refurbished laptops, desktops and mobiles.

The green workspace . . . in a nutshell

See the workspace as a holistic whole rather than just bricks and mortar. If you are using shared office space, try to find a landlord or provider who aligns with your values. If you have more control over your space, look at ways you can make the space more energy efficient and people friendly. If you are carrying out work to create energy efficiencies, remember to factor in CO_2 emissions generated by the work itself.

Quick wins

- ◌ Choose an office space or shared space with a provider that also cares about sustainability, but be mindful that they may be working under landlord and planning constraints.
- ◌ Try to choose a space with the best accessibility for your employees and guests.
- ◌ Paint your office space with eco-friendly paint and consider how you could use colour to guide visually impaired employees or guests.
- ◌ Make sure you have clear, well-placed recycling points.
- ◌ Offer recycled toilet paper and eco-friendly sanitary products in your loos.
- ◌ Align yourself with a tea or coffee brand that reflects your values.
- ◌ Have a recycling plan for food waste such as teabags or coffee grounds.
- ◌ Fit blinds, shutters or curtains to minimise heat loss.

Moving up a gear

⊘ Plan a series of works that will save energy in the building. If you can't do everything at once, create a phased programme and carry out works that will have the most impact first. However, do consider that some works cause more upheaval than others.

⊘ Refurbish your office with second-hand furniture or furniture made with recycled materials.

⊘ Fit double- or triple-glazing to conserve heat.

⊘ Fit secondary glazing as a cheaper alternative or in buildings with planning restrictions.

⊘ Ensure doors are draughtproof.

⊘ Insulate floors and walls, whether solid or cavity.

⊘ Insulate the roof or ceiling.

⊘ Fit a new ventilation system.

⊘ Install a green wall.

Going for it

⊘ Plan to build your own purpose-built space using eco-friendly materials and green roofs, and using builders committed to sustainable practices. But remember that builds themselves can be carbon heavy and this must be factored into your plan. Whatever work you carry out, make sure your construction partner adheres to at least BREEAM standards.

Chapter 3
Powering the Future

There are some moments in my career that stick in my mind like a line from a bad film. It was around ten years ago when I was invited to a round-table discussion hosted by Vince Cable MP, at the time then Secretary of State for Business, Energy and Industrial Strategy for the then coalition government. He was looking at opportunities for growth in the energy market.

Before then, I had barely dipped my toe into politics, but having worked at the European Commission and the European Parliament, I understood how energy companies, rooted in fossil-fuel revenue, used their well-funded lobbying to influence energy polices. This lunch was no different. Some of the CEOs from Britain's largest energy suppliers were guests and I called them the 'walruses' of the industry.

The conversation covered the gamut of energy sources before moving on to renewables. At the time, 13 gigawatts of renewable power was about to be added to the system in the UK within two years, which would take total power generated by renewables to 25% by 2015.

'What are the opportunities for solar?' was one question posed by the Secretary of State to the group. Naturally, I had a lot to say, but before I could even take a breath, the then CEO of one of the UK's largest energy firms leaned forward. 'Well . . .' he said, 'It's just not that sunny in the UK, is it, Minister?' Suddenly, my internal bullshit-o-meter started clanging. It was a classic political move to dismiss technologies to ministers behind closed doors. Not being as polished as my counterparts, I couldn't help blurting out, 'What utter rubbish!' before making sure that Vince Cable was in no doubt about the potential benefits of solar, something that still holds true today.

Of course, I understood that those energy giants had vested interests in fossil fuels – they still do – but what also struck me was the lack of awareness about renewables from people who ought to take an interest. By then I had been running Good Energy for ten years, but I realised how tough it would be to shift entrenched mindsets and also bust pervasive myths.

By 2012, solar power had come a long way. It wasn't a Cinderella technology, and while the UK is not best known for its balmy temperatures, there is more than enough sun to power a system. But the problem with this kind of misinformation is that it filters down. It filters down through business, to the politicians and eventually to the consumer . . . and it sticks.

In this chapter we're going to be busting some more myths around renewables while also guiding you through some simple changes you can make to create an energy-efficient business. From knowing what energy supply to switch to, to saving energy and even generating your own power, these are all actions to embed a cleaner, greener electricity or heat supply. In the last section, we'll also be looking at how to reuse energy, with a particular focus on recycling heat.

To get started, though, I want to make the case for renewables. After all, it's the business I've dedicated my life to.

Why renewables?

In 2022 we have witnessed a global crisis in the energy market, with prices predicted to soar in the years to come. It's a perfect storm of market forces: China's post-Covid economic recovery coincided with an uptick in demand across Asia and Europe, whose long, cold winter drew on gas reserves. Flows of pipeline gas from Russia also failed to make up the shortfall, culminating in a limited supply. And now the war in Ukraine is creating a triple whammy. In the UK, around half of electricity is generated from burning fossil fuels – oil, gas and coal – in gas-fired power plants, but decisions made in this country in 2017 to cut costs mean we also lack gas storage facilities, leaving us vulnerable to price shocks and energy shortages.

The fallout continues to be devastating. At the time of writing, 2022, millions of households are already having to choose between heating and eating. Understandably, businesses will look to create efficiencies, and the more they save, the lower the prices for everyone. But, if you're just starting out then it may be tempting to put off switching to, or investing in, renewables. Let me try to persuade you otherwise.

Every business must prioritise, but I would argue that this is a cost worth absorbing. Greening your business overall will create cost efficiencies elsewhere. The planet wins with renewables every time. Nuclear aficionados will disagree, but my analysis is based on cost and long-term benefit.

In sum, nuclear plants take longer to build, are more expensive and costs often spiral due to delays compared to an equivalent-sized renewable project. It takes just three months to build a solar park, and six to nine months for an onshore wind farm. Given that renewable schemes are often smaller and more widespread, this gives quicker and more cost-effective returns. Plus, the climate emergency is now – so do we have time to wait?

Moreover, large-scale nuclear projects do not necessarily equal lower carbon emissions, yet renewables do every time. And what about a plant's afterlife? It takes six months to dismantle a renewable system and often the parts can be reused. Nuclear, on the other hand, takes around 60 years to decommission and the site can be off-limits for up to 10,000 years.

Of course, when the sun isn't shining as much or there's less wind, then renewables do need back-up. But my answer is always to balance energy efficiency with increased storage facilities and increase the mix of renewables to include hydro, tidal, wave and biomass. In the case of failure, nuclear needs back-up, too, and we can't afford for that to be fossil-fuel driven. So, how does power actually work, and what actions can you take to reduce consumption?

How UK power works

Energy in the UK is made up of a complex network of high voltage cables, gas pipelines, interconnectors and storage facilities. While its energy mix is always fluctuating, dramatically so during the Covid-19 pandemic, pre-pandemic figures show that around 2.1% of the UK's electricity supply is from oil, 2.1% comes from coal and 40.9% comes from gas. Nuclear accounts for 17.4%, while renewables, which includes solar, wind, hydro and bioenergy, accounted for 36.9%. Half of our gas comes from the North Sea, while we import the rest. From this data alone, you can see the pressing need to shift.

Both gas and electricity have transmission and distribution systems. Transmission systems carry power around the country while distribution networks take power into homes and businesses. Run by the

National Grid, the transmission system is balanced second by second to match supply with demand.

Most power companies buy energy in the wholesale market, meaning they buy a mix of power from fossil and renewable sources, but a genuine 100% renewable company will buy its power directly from renewable sources. The more people who buy power directly from renewables, the more investment there is into them, and the more renewables feed the network.

Switching your energy supply and avoiding greenwashing

One of the easiest moves you can make in your business is to switch to a renewable electricity supply. If you are based at home or run your own office, then this is a simple switch to a new tariff. If you are in a shared office space, it's worth asking whoever owns or manages your building. The more workers who want this, the more persuasive the argument. It may also be a factor which informs the space you choose in the first place.

But how do you know which supplier to switch to? Are the energy companies who claim to be green, as green as they say? And how can you spot which companies are not telling the truth about where they source their energy from? In other words, who is 'greenwashing'?

Energy greenwashing involves companies claiming to be 100% renewable despite not buying power directly from renewable generators. Or, in the case of fossil fuel giants like Shell, promoting renewable services while continuing to invest in fossil fuel extraction. In the UK around a third of tariffs marketed as 'green' are not the real deal.

The practice doesn't only happen in the energy industry. It happens across every industry, so I hope some of what follows makes you look more closely at every purchase you make for your business. I got so incensed by energy companies greenwashing that in 2019, Good Energy ran a campaign to highlight the problem. We also wanted the energy regulator Ofgem to tighten its rules around transparency. Greenwashing is not only dishonest; it's dangerous to climate-change goals.

Primarily, greenwashing is a consumer protection scandal – people aren't getting what they think they're buying – but it has a larger impact, too. If the greenwashing suppliers were actually buying green electricity, it would create a transformational amount of investment into renewables. And if they were more honest about their fuel mix then more customers who wanted to support a 100% renewable supplier would switch.

In the energy sector, greenwashing became more prevalent after 2015 when the government pulled a tax incentive for renewable generators. This allowed suppliers to no longer have to buy directly from renewable generators to be able to claim their product was clean. At the same time, Ofgem dropped the entry barriers to the energy supply market. This paved the way for more energy companies and an era of greenwashing.

But spotting greenwashing claims is not easy. The point about the practice is that it is evasive and confusing. However, there are some tell-tale phrases to look out for. If a supplier talks about 'buying green energy from the wholesale market', this should ring alarm bells. The wholesale market is a mixture of everything, and the only way you can buy renewable energy is direct.

Another key phrase to look out for is if a company claims it supplies 'electricity backed by renewable certificates' but does not go on to list which renewable generators it buys from. Across the energy market, there are three ways of certificating green tariffs: long-term power purchase agreements (PPA); traded UK renewable certificates without an accompanying PPA; and tariffs based on certificates purchased outside the UK. Only tariffs based on PPAs contribute significantly to supporting renewables.

The UK certificates are called Renewable Energy Guarantees of Origin (REGOs), and renewable generators can acquire them from the regulator Ofgem for every unit of electricity they generate. Any excess REGOs are retired at the end of the year rather than traded with other energy companies. Because of this, a bona fide renewable power supplier will aim to match supply and demand. However, a greenwashing company will have no process in place to match in real time. Instead, it will calculate how much power has been supplied over the past year to customers and buys REGOs from the open market to claim this power as renewable. This further detaches the customer's choice and energy usage from the renewable energy generated.

If in doubt, talk to the company you want to switch to and ask:

- Can you provide me with a breakdown of your fuel mix?
- Is your tariff PPA-backed and which generators do you buy from?
- Do you match supply with demand and how?

If a company is truly 100% renewable, it will only be too pleased to offer you the information you need.

Using less power

If your business is in a building that you have control over, there are a number of easy ways you can minimise energy use. Shared office spaces can be notorious energy-wasting spaces. Again, prompting whoever runs the building can embed a new, green culture and pay dividends.

Here are five areas where you can take action:

- The most obvious energy-saving tip is to turn off equipment when it is not in use. This includes light switches and computer monitors. Turning off a computer can save up to £5 every year and turning off one that would have been on screensaver mode can save up to £45. Laptops also use less power than desktops, so consider switching to a laptop with associated flat screen rather than a desktop and screen. The former will use 25W of power whereas the latter will consume 200W. Companies such as Sheffield-based VeryPC make a range of energy-efficient laptops. Because desktop computers pump out more heat than laptops, if you have a room where desktops are housed you can heat it less.

- Lighting often works on circuits that isolate different parts of a floor. If these are labelled properly then it can help employees to only turn lights on in the areas they need to use. A reminder sign to switch off all lights when not in use can also help shift behaviour.

- Energy-efficient light bulbs are another way to reduce consumption, and LED lights are the most energy efficient. Not only do these last around 20 times longer than standard bulbs, but they waste less energy. Fluorescent bulbs, for example, convert around 95% of energy to heat and only 5% to light. Standard fluorescent lighting also contains the highly toxic metal mercury which, when disposed of incorrectly, can cause harm to wildlife and water supplies. LEDs contain no hazardous materials.

o Air-conditioning units are energy-guzzling monsters and often get left on at weekends or at times when no one is in the office. Installing a timer is a simple way to cut usage. Ensuring air-conditioning vents are not blocked by office equipment will also increase efficiency. If you have a server room, housing that within a colder, north-facing room will cut down on the air conditioning needed. And don't overestimate the amount of cooling a server room needs. Most IT equipment can operate with no adverse impact up to 27°C.

o Placing heating on a timer, or turning it off when it is not needed, especially at weekends, will also help reduce your carbon footprint. Turning heating down by just 1°C cuts 8% off an energy bill. There is no law for minimum and maximum temperatures at work, but as a rule of thumb the minimum temperature for a typical office should be around 16°C.

Generating your own power

If you have control over your space, you may want to consider generating your own power. For electricity, this will most likely be done through installing solar PV units. Renewable heat is available through solar thermal and heat pumps, and the latter is gaining in popularity. Again, if you are working from a leased office or warehouse space, then approach the freeholder to ask if they have considered these installations. It is unlikely you will be able to purpose-build your own space yet, but if this is something that you aspire to do in the future, embed it in your plans. Building in renewable power sources from the outset causes far less upheaval and are cost effective in the long term.

To help us understand more about the concerns entrepreneurs have when considering generating their own power, I asked the advice of

Gareth Williams, founder of Hereford-based Caplor Energy. Gareth has always been a passionate environmentalist, and for the last 15 years the company has been installing solar panels and heat pumps with commercial clients as his fastest growing sector. Funnily enough, he still has to bust some of the same myths which I am all too familiar with. Here are a few:

- It's not sunny enough in the UK for me to install solar (that classic is still doing the rounds!).
- My roof won't be strong enough to accommodate solar panels.
- It's too cold in this country for a heat pump.
- I want a secure green energy supply – going off-grid is the answer.
- The technology is still developing – it's not the right time to invest.
- The layout costs are too high.

All these concerns are perfectly valid so, with Gareth's help, I'm going to address them in each section covering solar and heat. What was also interesting about talking to Gareth was how many more of his clients are being asked to provide proof of their green credentials to the companies or organisations they supply to. And when it comes to reporting on carbon reduction, renewable power is a big win.

Going off-grid

Going off-grid means that you would have to produce enough electricity through solar or wind, and heat through a pump, to be completely self-sufficient. In terms of carbon reduction this is fantastic, but it's far from straightforward. Many people underestimate how much kit they need to power a small business, especially one that uses a lot of electricity. So, layout costs are high and it's heavily dependent on the space you have.

In terms of energy security, you would also need a back-up and storage facility for when there is less wind and sun. Off-grid sounds very attractive, but unless you are a farmer in the wilds of Scotland whose business can function if there is a power blackout, then I'd say it's seriously ambitious today. However, there are other actions you can take to make an impact.

Installing solar panels

Solar panels are a great way to reduce your carbon footprint in terms of energy generation. The technology is advanced and, as demand has increased, its cost has decreased by around 80% between 2012 and 2022. This alone should dispel the myth that's it's not sunny enough – solar panels work based on the amount of light hitting them, so it doesn't have to be warm. In fact, they work most efficiently when up a mountain where the air is clear. One major benefit for a business is that, just like solar on domestic properties, the energy produced on site can power the site.

Panels can be fixed to any roof facing south, east or west – and sometimes even north. South-facing is best for maximum yield, but the technology works on any, albeit with varying yields. Gareth compares the weight of the unit to a dusting of snow, so it is suitable for most roofs. However, if a roof is old and needs repairing then this may be an extra cost to factor in. It also helps cost-effectiveness if this work is done together.

An initial assessment will be made based on your roof space, its pitch and direction, what access you have to the grid, how much power you use and the ownership of the building. And some businesses will also have specific usages. If you are a seasonal business that experiences high demand at certain times, it's worth highlighting this to your supplier as you could benefit from a more nuanced solution.

When choosing a supplier there are a couple of checks to make:

- Ensure your supplier is MCS accredited. The Microgeneration Certification Scheme is the industry mark of quality. However, be aware that some subcontractors working for MCS suppliers may falsely attach the accreditation to their own business. Check the accreditation is attached to whoever is carrying out the work, not an umbrella company.
- Choose a supplier that you can build a long-term relationship with and who will help you with maintenance and troubleshooting. Ideally your supplier should be a recommended business who you can call on for the lifespan of your purchase – solar PV is guaranteed for 25 years but will usually work for much longer.

As this work falls under the remit of a capital project, tax relief is available so do seek advice applicable to your business from your tax advisor. It's worth noting that in March 2021 the government announced a super-deduction capital allowance scheme to run until March 2023, allowing companies to cut their tax bill by up to 25p for every £1 they invest.

Some suppliers also offer buy-back schemes whereby they fund the upfront cost, and you pay them out of the savings to the business. Some businesses recoup the outlay in energy savings in as little as three years. There are other options for investment, and Atrato Onsite

Energy, launched in 2021, will pay for the installation of the panels on a reasonably sized roof in exchange for a long-term power arrangement. This will not be for everyone, but it's worth taking a look if you have larger warehouse-type space.

Planning permission is not required below a 1MW system – that's pretty big! – but if you are a listed building or operate in a national park or conservation area you should check with your local council planning office as requirements may vary.

Solar PV

Solar PV (photovoltaics) is the most common way to generate your own power. Commercial rooftop solar systems can range routinely from 20 kilowatts to several megawatts depending on how much space is available and how much electricity you need. At one end of the spectrum you might want to run a printer and a few laptops. At the other, you may need to store food at low temperature in a distribution centre, or power a server farm.

The solar panels themselves consist of cells made from layers of semi-conducting material, most commonly silicon. The cells don't need direct sunlight to work so they can work on cloudy days.

Solar technology works by absorbing the energy from photons from the sun, and using a semi-conductor to convert that to an electrical current through the photovoltaic effect. The current is created as direct current (DC) and to convert it into the type of electricity most appliances use, an inverter is needed to create the alternating current (AC). It is possible to use DC directly with a separate wiring system, as all USB ports are 5 volts DC, which accounts for most mobile phones. However, if you want to charge a laptop directly you will need to get a separate DC connector. Setting up this type of wiring or charging system tends to be a little complicated, so probably one for the electrical engineers among you, and would need a battery on the system to manage times when there is no power. For most of us, the inverter does the job of syncing the power and allowing us to use the existing wiring in an office.

Solar thermal panels

Solar thermal panels work by absorbing the radiative heat from the sun, producing hot water feeding directly into your heating system. With these, there's no possibility to feed back into the grid! Installing them can be a great addition to your business, but the system must work in conjunction with your existing heating system, for example, a boiler, collector or an immersion heater.

The technology works when the solar collectors absorb the sun's energy. This heats a highly conductive fluid which is pumped around a sealed circuit, through the collectors and into a coil within a specially designed hot water cylinder. The hot water is then stored in the cylinder until it's needed.

The system is ideal for high usage in spring, summer or autumn, at locations such as shower blocks or campsites, or for businesses that have routine hot water demand, such as dairy businesses or food processors. However, the technology is good enough to work all year round.

Roughly speaking, a 3kW system would produce approximately 3,000 kWh of heat per year. To see what that means for your business, check the energy bill to see how much energy is being used to heat hot water and this should provide an estimate of what you can generate yourself (an average house uses around 12,000 kWh of heat a year for heating and hot water).

Most systems are roof-mounted, but if you are planning a purpose-build or re-roof you may opt for an in-roof installation. South-facing will give you maximum yield and, as it's all about heat radiation, an area free of shade will also improve efficiency, so overhanging trees won't help. Running and maintenance costs are low.

Installing a heat pump

Before we explain heat pumps, let's bust a third myth: it is too cold in this country for a heat pump to work. To put this falsehood into context, a 2022 report by Imperial College in London shows that respectively Norway, Finland and Sweden have the highest number of heat pumps installed across Europe – not exactly the warmest countries on the planet! Norway boasts 517 heat pumps per 1,000 households compared to the UK's mere seven.

Heat-pump technology is still relatively new which means it remains expensive. While the main growth area for installation is domestic, Gareth is getting many more calls from commercial outfits who are beginning to ask the question for their businesses. This is only set to increase.

In 2021, the British government announced a £450 million scheme to begin the upgrade of domestic gas boilers as part of its strategy to decarbonise heat and buildings. It also made a commitment to reduce the cost of buying and running a heat pump by 2030 as the market expands and the technology develops. As of mid-2022, there is no help available for business, but it's always worth checking to see if any grants or subsidies come on stream. Again, your business will be able to claim against tax.

Which heat pump you choose will depend on a range of factors that includes where your business is situated, how much outside space you have, your existing heat source, and what your budget is. Efficiency can also be dependent on factors such as existing levels of insulation. An initial feasibility study by a trusted supplier will give this information. And while most heat pumps do not require planning permission, if in doubt do check with your local council planning office as criteria is often complex.

Overall, heat pumps can significantly reduce carbon emissions, although they are only carbon neutral if you power them with renewable electricity. They are easily maintained and have a decent lifespan similar to a gas boiler of between 8 and 15 years.

There are three types of heat pumps:

- *An air-source heat pump* is by far the most common installation and works by drawing in outside air. Using electricity, the pump then compresses the air and releases it at a higher temperature. This hot water is then circulated through the building and stored in a hot water cylinder which can be used as and when. The pump, or pumps, sit flush on an external wall, making it cheaper and easier to maintain or repair. Suitably set up air-source pumps can also be run in reverse in the summer, as a form of cooling.

- *A ground-source heat pump* requires greater outdoor space. Heat from the ground is absorbed at low temperatures into a fluid inside the loop of a pipe or borehole which is buried underground. The fluid then passes through a compressor that raises the temperature, which can then heat water for the heating and hot water circuits of the building as with an air source or any boiler system. The collector loops can be laid horizontally in an underground trench around a metre deep or, if there is less space, these can sit vertically in boreholes. Ground-source tends to be more efficient at transferring energy, and you don't have the inconvenience of the outside systems. However, the cost is higher, there is more disruption on installation and long-term servicing may involve digging up the outside space.

○ *Water-source heat pumps* are more specialist and only applicable for a building based near a body of water. There are two types of water-source heat pumps: open- and closed-loop systems. An open-loop system works when water is pushed through a pump to extract heat for the system before releasing it back to its source. In a closed-loop system, a collector extracts the water which is then filtered and passed through a heat exchanger before being circulated back through the system. This system is best for smaller projects, is cheaper to install, and requires less maintenance.

Installing a wind turbine

If you go to the Outer Hebrides, you'll see lots of mini wind turbines perched on hills, spinning gracefully in the breeze. Wind is a fantastic source of energy but it's all about location and it does tend to work better at scale. Large offshore wind farms, or wind farms set high on mountains, produce vast amounts of electricity. However, as soon as you scale down, the turbine will produce less, as generation is determined primarily by the height of its tower and the diameter of its rotor. Height is really important because once you position a turbine near any trees or property, wind becomes turbulent or blocked and results in a lower output.

The technology is pretty amazing, though. As the blades rotate, a rotor captures the kinetic energy of the wind and converts it into clean electricity. You only need to stick your hand out of the window of a moving car to feel the power of the wind. A small wind system can be connected to the grid, or it can stand alone off-grid, making them great for rural areas. Finding a small-turbine manufacturer is a little trickier as small turbines are not mass-produced in the same way as, for example, solar PV. But don't let us put you off. If you are situated in the right place and can position your turbine in an exposed area, then it's a great addition to powering your business.

Installing a biogas plant or a biomass boiler

While many businesses get caught up in cost-cutting through energy reduction, taking your business a step further in self-generation can make it even more cost-efficient and robust. One untapped potential in the UK is biogas, whereby plant and other waste is broken down by bacteria in an oxygen-free environment in a process known as anaerobic digestion.

To find out more, I spoke to Richard Clothier, managing director of family-run dairy business Wyke Farms, whose three biogas plants help run its cheesemaking operations at its Somerset site of Bruton.

For the last 20 years, the business has kept in mind a phrase that Richard's grandparents handed down through the generations: 'If you look after nature, nature will look after you.' And it's been a guiding principle for the business, through good times and bad.

'We started looking at lean manufacture to make our sites as energy efficient as we could, including reusing water and using heat recovery,' Richard explains, 'but this led us to look at how we could become a more environmentally responsible business. Lean manufacture is inward-looking whereas being environmentally responsible is outward-looking.'

In Richard's view, measures to become energy independent are under-utilised in the UK, but it's something manufacturers should look to become, especially in the food sector. While Wyke chose to install its own biogas plants, other businesses might think about becoming energy co-dependent – partnering with someone in close physical proximity who runs a generator.

Previously, Wyke generated gas from its own factory waste, but it now buys waste from surrounding farms and a number of other sources, with the price paid based on its calorific value. 'We take in apple pomace from cider mills, bread waste from supermarkets around Bristol, silage from surrounding farms and activated sludge from other dairy companies,' he lists. The business even buys ship cleanings – waste brushed from the holds of cargo vessels. And recently it processed around 400 tonnes of grain infected with weevils and unfit for human consumption. In the past, this waste would be land-spread, releasing quantities of harmful methane into the air.

Richard describes the process itself as 'very simple', once it is up and running. Organic matter is broken down with methanogenic bacteria and goes through a four-stage process including fermentation and oxidisation before the organisms convert to methane and carbon dioxide, which is then harvested. At Wyke, some of the gas goes to the site's combined heat and power plant which generates heat for the farm's cheesemaking process. Meanwhile, Wyke has also invested in a plant that cleans the gas, some of which goes to its boilers or is sold back to the grid. Wyke is now a net producer of energy, generating 20,000 cubic metres of green gas per day.

'We've shown that if we incorporate a biogas plant into a dairy farm then we can reduce our carbon emissions by around 25%,' says Richard. But the process also has some other surprising benefits. Once the relatively low-grade waste is broken down and the gas is extracted, what's left is an organic fertiliser rich in nitrogen, phosphorous and potassium, and the business has now started working with farmers to displace artificial fertiliser.

'The organic fertiliser produced is very liquid,' says Richard, 'and runs down the foliage and straight down to the root, making it more useable and a better alternative to organic slurry which, when spread on a field, sticks to the crop and renders the field unworkable for around eight weeks.'

But a biogas plant needn't be as extensive as the one at Wyke Farms. The technology can range from small-scale generators to much larger operations. For example, several small breweries now use a biogas to process spent grain and effluents perfect for anaerobic digestion. Wyke has the advantage of using its engineers on site, but for smaller businesses, maintenance costs should be factored in.

Also highly scalable is installing a biomass boiler as a renewable energy source. While a boiler, sometimes known as a wood pellet boiler, doesn't eradicate CO_2 emissions, it uses considerably less than fossil fuels. Biomass heating systems burn wood pellets, chips, logs or plant material grown for fuel and can provide heat through central heating or hot water boilers. Wood burning also becomes a carbon neutral fuel source when new plants are grown in place of those that are burned. However, you need to be mindful of how the wood is managed and where it comes from. If wood is imported then this is already a climate fail, so make sure it is certified by the Forest Stewardship Council (FSC) and sourced from the local area.

The boiler itself needs some space and usually includes a grate to support the fire bed in a combustion chamber, a hot air ignitor to light the fuel, fans to supply the combustion air, and a system to collect and remove the ash. It will also need a chimney or ventilation system.

The system works best when a business produces waste wood on site to be burned, or when wood can be sourced locally and stored in large quantities, reducing delivery and transportation costs. When thinking about a biomass boiler it is always best to check with your council if there are local air quality limits. Larger boilers may also require a permit and the chimney height needed should be checked with the local authority.

Heat recovery

While businesses look to energy reduction and methods of self-generation, recycling energy is, again, an under-utilised process in the UK. Yet for businesses using energy-intensive processes, it could also be a way to reduce emissions. Cement, ceramics, iron and steel, glassmaking, chemicals, paper and pulp, and food and drink account for two-thirds of all industrial emissions in the UK. You can recover heat from any process that involves heating or cooling and this includes processes such as distilling, pasteurisation, refrigeration, drying and finishing, and heating ovens.

Larger operations will typically be able to monitor, measure and put resources behind heat recovery, so investigating possibilities may be something for the future. Technologies differ depending on the type of manufacturing process, but in food production heat exchangers can transfer gas or steam to hot water instead of it dissipating into the air.

Heat recovery from computer servers is also a growing technology and to find out more I spoke to green IT consultant John Booth who advises business and data centres on sustainability through his company Carbon3IT. 'If you have a server room, fitting a rear-door heat exchanger will cool the server racks,' he says, 'and is more energy efficient than a conventional air-conditioning system, but do seek assistance from specialists in this field.' Typically, the system captures heat from the back of the servers through a liquid-filled coil. The heat is then transferred through the liquid, bringing neutralised, cool air back to the heat source. 'Technically you could heat a building with a rear-door system that is connected to radiators,' he adds. 'However, heat recovery from small server rooms is still an embryonic phase.'

Of the technologies that are emerging, one developed by French company Qarnot places a server within a wall-mounted radiator which is used to warm a room. In the summer, when no heat is needed, the IT load is shifted to a cloud service. Small-scale server-powered heat boilers are also being piloted. 'In the future it may be possible to warm rooms in winter with a computer radiator and then move the IT load to a hot water boiler in winter,' says John, adding that for hotels or businesses in need of constant hot water, this could be a game-changer.

However, it is most likely that start-ups and SMEs will use a cloud provider for storing data. Certainly, the Covid-19 pandemic has seen more migration to cloud-based IT. According to Deloitte analysis the sector saw more than 30% annual growth in 2019 and predicts this will continue until at least 2025, citing Covid-19, lockdowns and work-from-anywhere policies as the reasons for increased demand, whether it's a homeworker or business storing data in a public cloud, private cloud or a hybrid cloud that combines both.

But while cloud computing cuts a business's emissions, questions are being asked of the providers who build, power and operate cloud IT data centres. The big three – Amazon, Google and Microsoft – all claim to be powered by renewable energy, but according to successive Greenpeace reports, big tech firms greenwash their environmental credentials by buying renewable energy certificates that are not tied to specific renewable energy projects as offsets or 'credits' to compensate for emissions. Moreover, all three are aiding the fossil fuel industry with lucrative contracts with oil and gas companies offering AI and data analytics to maximise both production and profit for the fossil fuel sector.

That said, there is increased pressure on companies to act, and some positive steps are being made. Apple, Google and Facebook have all made meaningful long-term commitments to be 100% renewably powered. And Facebook has teamed up with one local heating company in Odense in Denmark to heat the town. The heat is transferred via copper coils filled with water which link heat pump facilities to the 176 cooling units in the company's data centre. While rankings are fast-changing, a good place to start researching is Greenpeace's 2017 report 'Clicking Clean', which will give you an indication of who is showing leadership.

In the meantime, ask your cloud provider about their green credentials, but, as with the energy industry, be mindful of greenwashing claims.

Carbon offsetting

For businesses not able to plan methods of energy self-generation or in an interim stage, one way of countering CO_2 emissions may involve

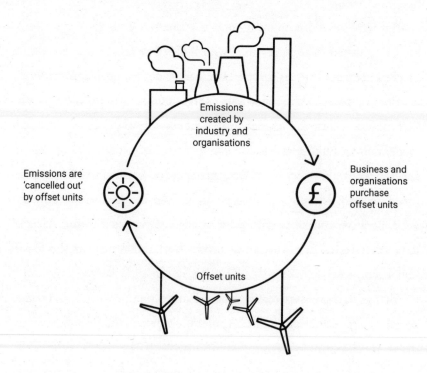

waiting for a time when they can move into a building and control more of their energy supply, then contributing to a carbon offsetting scheme.

There are many offsetting schemes, ranging from tree-planting to clean-energy programmes. Typically, these work by calculating a business's carbon footprint, then offsetting it through projects either in the UK or globally.

When thinking about offsetting you should consider what it is you are offsetting and try to find like-for-like projects. For example, we debated long and hard about how to set up a green gas proposition whereby a percentage of our supply would come from biogas. Knowing that we could realistically only source 10% at that time, we decided to work with offsetters ClimateCare (now known as Climate Impact Partners), one of the more reputable companies in the market, and focused on finding other similar projects to support to make up 90%. One of those was Xuyong Biogas, which helps communities in one of China's poorest provinces by installing household biogas digesters and providing training to maintain them. This allows farmers to use animal waste to generate clean fuel, reducing the need for households to spend money on polluting coal.

Also, by looking at the UN's Sustainable Development Goals (SDGs), you can quite often find projects that don't just offset your carbon but also provide other key attributes to a community so your contribution has a bigger overall impact, whether that's towards gender equality or health and wellbeing. The Climate Neutral Now Initiative run by the UN is a great place to start researching. It helps you to calculate your business's carbon footprint, then helps you to work out how to reduce it. Finally, through its Carbon Offset Platform it recommends a range of projects to engage with, from wind power in India to hydropower in Brazil. Elsewhere, look out for projects that are certified through either the Verified Carbon Standard (VCS), the Gold Standard Verified Emission Reductions (VER) and Certified Emission Reductions (CER) programmes, as these will give some reassurance about quality.

While carbon offsetting has been around since the late 1980s, over the past few years the market has grown and it can feel like a minefield. Tree-planting schemes in particular have been criticised for displacing indigenous people and being hard to maintain, so it is worth asking questions about projects you want to support. Clearly, this is easier if a project is closer to home. UK organisations such as Carbon Footprint promote transparency by encouraging visits to the community projects it works with, such as its range of solar-powered schools.

But offsetting should never be used as a sole mechanism. Many corporates have come under fire for using offsetting schemes as a PR tool rather than seriously looking at ways to reduce emissions within their own business. Any business who wants to be green at heart should put into practice the following mantra: measure, reduce, offset. This reinforces the need for a business to firstly calculate, then look at its own practices and earmark areas where CO_2 emissions can be reduced. If you only offset unavoidable emissions, ensure that the offset comes with other SDG type benefits. Of course, offsetting extends way beyond energy usage, although that is a good place to start. For example, if you are a paper-heavy business, look at areas where you can reduce paper consumption or go paper-free before you sign up to a tree-planting scheme. Similarly, if travel in your business relies on domestic or international flights, then look at ways to reduce air travel before you look to jump on a plane and offset.

Power and the circular economy

However positive a shift to renewables is, it does threaten to cause a negative feedback loop, and it's one we must remain conscious of. The more people switch to self-generation through renewables, the more raw materials are needed. This problem reflects the perennial environmental conundrum. Do we solve a problem in one place only to create a problem in another? This is a topic we'll discuss further in Chapter 7 when we look at supply chain and in particular electric vehicle batteries.

But when it comes to renewables, we can't ignore the fact that many of the materials needed in manufacture have to come from somewhere, and that somewhere is not our backyard. For example, solar panels use aluminium, cadmium, copper, gallium, indium, iron, lead, nickel, silica, silver, tellurium, tin and zinc, the mining of which harms wildlife and biodiversity if not planned or regulated properly – not to mention its impact on humans, including issues of child labour. Mining companies are notoriously blind to the environmental and social impacts of their businesses, and it will take a lot to shift certain practices.

With a problem like this, we should remember: the planet comes first. Why? Because without a planet we don't exist, and if we don't exist we can't innovate and solve any of these problems. Moreover, none of us can carry the whole weight of the world on our shoulders. As eco-entrepreneurs, we can't necessarily influence regulation in parts of Africa or China. What we can do, though, is do our best to examine our supply chain, strive to be better and help to achieve a wider impact by campaigning on these issues. When more people are mindful and want to do the right thing, it creates a tipping point and that's when transformative change happens.

What we should find encouraging is that there are already purpose-led businesses who are seeing opportunities. Many small companies are innovating around recycling. They have asked the question: how can we reuse this material? What can we do with it? Copper piping in solar is already reused, and so is a panel's aluminium casing and the underlying glass sheet. More difficult to crack is the recycling of solar cells, but it is hoped that in the not-too-distant future this will also be standard.

When it comes to wind turbines, again positive steps are being made. Some components, such as the tower, already have established recycling routes, and in 2021 tech giant Siemens launched the first recyclable wind blade. Previously the blade's glass, carbon fibre, wood and foam were bound together with resin, which meant its components were impossible to separate. So, amazingly, materials that automatically went to landfill will begin life again as car parts or suitcases or phone casings. These should all be reasons to be hopeful.

Powering the future . . . in a nutshell

There are a number of ways to reduce your carbon footprint by focusing on power. These include: switching your existing supply to a renewable source, reducing your usage, or generating your own power through solar, heat pumps, wind turbines, biogas or biomass. Carbon offsetting schemes can also be used to counter any unavoidable emissions.

Quick wins

- Switch your energy supply to a renewable provider but look out for greenwashing claims.
- Reduce your usage by turning off equipment, putting equipment on timers, and changing to LED bulbs. If you are in a shared space, then embed a culture of reducing usage.
- Measure your carbon emissions, reduce them and look to offset unavoidable emissions through a reputable carbon offsetting scheme.
- Ask questions of your cloud IT service and choose the most environmentally conscious provider. A good place to start your research is *The Good Shopping Guide*, which regularly updates its IT recommendations.

Moving up a gear

- ⊘ Generate your own power by installing solar panels: PV panels will cater for electricity while thermal panels will heat water.
- ⊘ Install a heat pump: there are three types, but air-source is the most common.

Going for it

- ⊘ Install a wind turbine.
- ⊘ Install a biomass boiler.
- ⊘ Install a biogas plant for anaerobic digestion.
- ⊘ Install a heat recovery system.
- ⊘ Say goodbye and go off-grid.
- ⊘ Crack a recycling problem and start another business.

Chapter 4
Purpose, Mission and Values

Tom Kay stands by the original commitments of the clothing brand, Finisterre, which he set up in 2002. In fact, he has them painted on the wall of his cliff-top headquarters, minutes from the St Agnes coastline in Cornwall: *Finisterre has always stood by three guiding commitments – to people, environment and product. We undertook these commitments knowing it would be a journey.*

I first interviewed Tom some years ago for a YouTube series I hosted, and his story never ceases to amaze me. Finisterre was born from his childhood love of the sea, instilled into him by his parents, and his passion for surfing. The company, which began in his bedroom, has another motto: *Born for the sea, built for adventure, sustainability as standard.* The first item Tom created was a waterproof and windproof fleece for surfers to warm themselves as they stepped from the waves. While the original was made from polyester with some strong seams, he now uses recycled wool as standard. Finisterre even sells clothing made from recycled fishing nets.

Yet running a fashion business with environmental stewardship at its heart is not for the faint-hearted. Crafted clothes made from recyclable fabrics aren't cheap. 'Communicating longevity in a world of fast fashion has not been an easy narrative,' Tom admits. While the brand always had a core following, it is only since awareness of the climate emergency that more consumers have embraced Finisterre's reduce, repair and recycle ethos.

What's so inspiring about Tom is his relentless pursuit of those original commitments. Take his quest to find a natural jumper fibre that didn't itch the skin, for example. He started out by importing superfine Merino wool from New Zealand, but mindful of the environmental impact of sourcing from overseas, he searched for a supplier closer to home. Enter Lesley, a Devonshire farmer who kept a remnant flock of Bowmont sheep – a cross between a Merino and several British breeds that had fallen out of favour.

'When I eventually found Lesley,' says Tom, 'she was the only UK farmer who could supply superfine wool. She had 29 sheep and we worked for five years to create the jumper. Through our partnership, Lesley's flock has now grown to 350. The journey has been about creating a beautiful product, but it's also about British sourcing, bringing back a rare breed into existence and building a long-lasting relationship.'

Has Finisterre's commitments been tested at times? Absolutely, he confesses. The company was profitable in its first year, but not for the next 14. Being commercial and ethical is a tricky balancing act. 'We had rent to pay and mouths to feed,' he says. 'One mistake was when we went off-brand and created a line of yoga outfits, rather than sticking to our roots – but like every journey we have learned and evolved and grown,' he says.

In so many ways, Tom's story illustrates perfectly the challenges that all purpose-led brands face. The traditional bottom-line business was so much easier: product and price were king. Factoring in people and planet adds layers of complexity. It's no wonder that Tom calls those original commitments his 'North Star' – the guiding light that he comes back to time and time again. As I know, there are times when a purpose-led business threatens to get blown off course and some soul-searching is required. Yet building a clear set of principles from the out-set creates a solid foundation from which to operate – a way of focusing the business's emotional heart.

In this chapter we'll explore how to find, articulate and evolve your business's emotional heart. It's one of the most powerful tools you have to galvanise your company and prevent it from losing its way. It's also the best tool you have to reach out to your customer or user. But when is the best time to formulate your purpose? Is your purpose the same as your company values? And how are you going to live those values? These are simple questions that often require complex answers, but coherent statements and credible actions matter when we consider how the conscious consumer connects.

How the conscious consumer connects

We touched on the conscious consumer at the start of this book. This is the new breed of consumer who wants the products they buy to mean more. They want the brands they buy from to consider people and planet as well as offering great products. But the conscious consumer doesn't only buy from a brand – they buy *into* a brand.

This phenomenon is brilliantly discussed by Mary Portas in her book *Rebuild: How to Thrive in the New Kindness Economy*. In it she describes the shift from passive consumer to active buyer. To become an active buyer, she says, people want to buy into brands that reflect their own identity and status – to care about the things they care about. The relationship is no longer transactional, it's personal. It's what she calls 'Status Sentience' – the act of spending money with a brand that demonstrates care, that is intuitively connected to their customer and whose values aren't faked. As we've already established, virtue signalling only goes so far. If we have purpose and values, then we have to live by them.

How brands demonstrate status sentience has changed dramatically. Today, brand loyalty isn't only nurtured in stores through the act of buying. It happens on platforms like Twitter and Instagram. As Mary says: 'Brands are now being built on the soft stuff that previously had no place in business.' It's about tone, empathy and alignment. Building on the work The Body Shop's Anita Roddick began, brands have also become campaign warriors, entwining themselves with social and environmental causes close to their hearts, and all of this connects back to purpose.

As this book shows, squaring all these circles is a non-linear process. There are tensions and trade-offs, and these become more complicated as you grow. Suddenly, it's not just you, but a team of employees. You have more customers, suppliers, investors. In other words there are more stakeholders in the business to pull you in different directions. But a solid foundation – your own North Star – will keep bringing you back to why you began on the journey.

When to formulate purpose, values and behaviours

Hands up – when I started Good Energy I did a lot of trying to 'get things right'. Coming from a scientific background, my journey had been largely around the technical and economic practicalities of our proposition: how did you buy and sell renewable energy? And how did you explain why you were doing it to a customer? Our purpose felt obvious, grown out of the people who joined us with a passion for the environment, but as the company expanded it became harder and harder to make the assumption that we all had the same purpose when we came to work!

This hit home when, a few years in, we merged with our outsourced service company, whose culture was fundamentally different. We needed to figure out how to create a cohesive narrative to bring the teams together. I'll never forget that when we started to discuss this, one of my then directors announced: 'We don't have to think about values. We follow Juliet's.' The weight of that responsibility, and the concern that if we didn't share the same purpose and values we could end up pulling the company from pillar to post, suddenly dawned on me.

Up until then, any emotional underpinning of the business had gone unspoken, and the business had been small enough to touch every point. Our company purpose to 'keep the planet habitable' had been developed – a rather dry statement which probably only had relevance to the few rather than the many. Our reason for being did have a pulsing heart in its proposition – 100% renewable energy sourced directly from independent generators – but that wasn't really enough to help us through our day jobs. How did that translate to how we answered the phones, dealt with our suppliers or collected our debts? Moreover, I began to ask, is mine the only vision?

Thankfully, talking to other business leaders, I have realised I am not alone. When entrepreneurs start out, many get consumed with the setting up of the company and the nuts and bolts of delivering the product, not to mention trying to keep their financial head above water. But perhaps we should have chiselled our purpose, values and behaviours from the outset?

For a fresh perspective, I rang Giles Gibbons, founder and CEO at Good Business, who works with start-ups, SMEs and larger businesses on formulating company purpose, values and behaviours. According to him, today's small businesses can go too far the other way and become consumed by all three actions before they've properly got started.

'When you begin, it's really important to have purpose – to under-stand what your reason is for being and then to do it – rather than adopting a clear set of values,' he says, adding that too often start-ups look to the corporate world believing they have to replicate what it does. 'It's important not to overdo it. There will come a time when values and behaviours have a really important job to do, but if you articulate them too early you may fall into the trap of these just becoming a marketing exercise.'

In fact, company values only become crucial when you grow and take on more employees and there is a need to shape the culture of the organisation and drive its purpose forward. Behaviours naturally follow on from this: it is values that guide people, but habits that define how people put those values into practice. So, if the most important aspect of the start-up business is its purpose, let's start there.

Keep purpose simple yet flexible

Purpose (sometimes also called mission) defines what you are provid-ing to your customers or users, how it improves their lives or improves a current process or product. The old way of doing business defined purpose simply: we're providing this product or service because there's a gap in the market and we want to make money for our shareholders. But in the new business landscape you'll want your purpose to have a positive impact on the world.

Purpose, Mission and Values

For this reason, purpose doesn't warrant a superficial approach. We've spoken about 'greenwashing' throughout this book. Well, there's 'purpose-washing' too. Purpose must be genuine and realistic – a purpose you can live by and evolve with – not one that reaches for the stars but can't deliver.

If I go back to Finisterre's purpose, it is realistic. Tom recognised from the outset that his commitment to product, people and planet was going to be a journey. What's more, Good Energy's mission of 'making the world a more habitable place' *was* a purpose we could live by and grow – we weren't promising an energy revolution on day one! I guess the problem was that 'making the world a more habitable place' appealed more to the head than to the heart. So how can we encapsulate a compelling purpose?

When thinking about purpose, the most important question you must ask is: why does this business exist? This is crucial because it is the 'why' that will expose a truth about your business and guide you to make better decisions. In other words, it will give your business its personal, emotional core to connect with the outside world, whether that involves customers, investors or employees. If we return to our conscious consumer, remember that they will buy *into* a brand not because of how it makes them think, but because of how it makes them feel. They will look beyond price and functionality and look to what using or having a brand says about them.

Finding your 'why' might take a bit of self-reflection. I find writing my ideas down on a whiteboard, or drawing some pretty poor diagrams to try and encapsulate what is going in my brain a really useful exercise, and this should help you begin the process of teasing out your purpose. Three areas that you might think around to reach your purpose are:

- ○ What does the world need?
- ○ What skill are you bringing to help change the world?
- ○ What are you passionate about?

Once you've discovered your 'why' it should remain the same. In fact, even as you evolve as a company – perhaps you will add new products or services – if you have a well-thought-out and authentic purpose, it should only become clearer as you progress. That said, your purpose should be flexible enough so your company can grow around it.

Imagine that you are a company bringing an electric vehicle to the mass market. You might be tempted to say that's your purpose, but ultimately that may become self-limiting. If your purpose becomes 'to accelerate transport for a greener, fairer world', then this is wide enough for you to adapt without fundamentally altering your core. Perhaps you'll start selling EV chargers or electric scooters or branch out in other ways, in which case your purpose is open-ended and aspirational enough to allow for evolution, yet remains narrow enough to stick to your principles and keep your business on track. And it has an emotional heart. You are not just manufacturing and selling electric cars – you are doing it with people and planet in mind.

A business that changes its purpose all the time only demonstrates that it is not working from a secure foundation and it won't inspire trust. It is better to develop a purpose that is truthful, flexible and has longevity.

Furthermore, before you finalise your purpose, it's a good idea to make sure that it resonates with people outside the business. Your own personal echo chamber can sometimes be a little limiting. This could be potential customers, investors or other stakeholders. Talk to them and ask them their opinion. You'll soon get a sense of whether your purpose is compelling and whether it grabs people through its emotional appeal.

Creating a purposeful narrative

Finding your authentic purpose will have got you thinking about who you are, why you exist and what got you to that place. In other words, you may start to crack open a narrative around your business. Surprisingly, this isn't obvious when you are dealing with the day to day and many entrepreneurs find it difficult to step outside of themselves to even understand what their story is, or the value of that story. Yet it is your story that will allow you to build on your purpose to connect with others. The majority of people touched by your business will be attracted to you not only because of what you do, but also because they believe in your story.

That story does not need to be complicated. I mentioned the US clothing brand Patagonia in Chapter 1 – a company born from its founder's passion for climbing and his observation that the metal chucks he sold damaged the cliff faces he so loved to climb. Tom Kay built Finisterre on his enduring passion for the sea – the name Finisterre itself is taken from the shipping forecast which Tom used to listen to in the back of his parents' car as the wind lashed the coastline. For generations the shipping forecast has provided trusted information and safe harbour to sailors.

We'll talk more fully about creating and developing a compelling narrative in Chapter 8 when we explore marketing, but it is worth having this in mind from the outset because building a purposeful narrative that is reinforced over time is vitally important to building a brand that people trust.

Embedding purpose within your business

It's one thing understanding and articulating your purpose, but it's another to live it. But formally embedding purpose within your business could also be an actionable way to keep your North Star on course. One way you might want to do this is to set your sights on high environmental and social performance through a form of certification. Embarking on this from the outset, or at least being aware of what certification requires, will give your business a purpose-led framework which, if you leave it too late, may be harder to retrofit. It's one of my regrets that I didn't formally note our purpose in our articles of association from the outset at Good Energy. It has meant that, although the purpose is core to the business, it isn't protected, and the brand and the customers have to carry that responsibility to keep it on track.

One of the fastest growing schemes is the B Corp certification, and I talk to so many entrepreneurial businesses who are either moving down the B Corp route or who are certainly amassing knowledge about it. The B Corp movement began in 2006 in the US with the aim of making business a force for good, but it now has impact globally. At the time of writing, around 5,000 companies across 155 industries and 70 countries are certified B Corp.

To discover more, I spoke to Luke Fletcher, a partner at the London law firm Bates Wells who leads the firm's purpose and impact strategy. Not only was the company the first B Corp law firm in the UK, but it has also helped design the legal requirements for UK B Corp and advises others on becoming a B Corp. In Luke's view, purpose shouldn't simply stop at articulation. Rather, the sooner you can embed it in your constitution the more aligned all parts of your business will be from the outset.

'The very fact that you are a business with higher purpose suggests that you are already thinking about doing less, or no, harm in the world,' he says, 'but perhaps you are also looking at something bigger and more transformative. That can spill over into your leadership and your systems and wider advocacy that breaks new ground, and very often these form part of the entrepreneurial vision. If you fail to articulate and capture purpose at an early stage, you run the risk of setting up a structure where there is likely to be some misalignment of intention among different stakeholders in the future – for example as you build employees, widen your brand or reach out for investment. If purpose is in your constitution, then you signal what kind of business you are and embed it, protect it and nurture it over time.'

The majority of existing B Corps are SME businesses. Start-ups can't attain full B Corp status until they have been operational for more than 12 months, although this is nuanced according to your set-up so do check with B Corp when you would qualify. That said, a start-up can work towards B Corp by becoming a Pending B Corp. This signals to future investors that a company measures and manages its social and environmental performance, and also shows strong governance as the process requires companies to adopt a legal framework to protect its mission and brand equity.

The five areas that B Corp assesses across are governance, community, workers, environment and customers.

1. Governance

This is one of the most crucial parts of the B Corp journey as it requires you to adopt or change your articles of association to include a commitment 'to promote the success of the company for the benefit of its members, and through its business and operations have a material positive impact on society and the environment, taken as a whole'. Legally, this means that you have to make decisions that consider people and planet alongside profit. In practical terms, Luke believes doing this creates a fluidity around decision-making that can be harder to reach otherwise. 'Ordinarily, if you want to bring a matter that concerns a social issue to the management board, you may assume it's not legitimate. However, if the business already has a pre-agreed purpose, it means that strategically everyone is already thinking in more ways than just financial. Those questions become a normal part of business.'

Formally embedding purpose also becomes important when a director leaves a business or the business grows to a certain size when it can't rely on traditions or mindsets being passed down, like Good Energy. 'B Corp is a way to bottle a different outlook and set of values that says you are in business for different reasons,' adds Luke.

Even if you don't go down the formal B Corp route you could embed these into your company articles from the outset to focus around purpose. If you are an existing business, you will have to decide whether you are ready and able to take that step.

2. Community

Community evaluates a company's engagement with, and its impact on, the communities in which it operates, hires from, and sources from. Assessment topics include diversity, equality and inclusion, economic impact, civic engagement, charitable giving, and supply chain management. In addition, it recognises business models that are designed to address specific community-oriented problems, such as poverty alleviation through fair-trade sourcing or distribution via micro-enterprises.

3. Workers

The work environment, ownership structure and compensation, benefits and training are all assessed under this heading. Questions cover holidays, sick days, education opportunities, and whether your employees are satisfied and feel engaged.

4. Environment

Looks at impact to land, energy and water among other markers. It will focus your mind around CO_2 emissions, energy efficiency, the amount of on-site renewables you use, your waste collection and monitoring practices, plus your transport and that of your suppliers.

5. Customers

Evaluates a business's stewardship of its customers through the quality of its products and services, ethical marketing, data privacy and security, and feedback channels. Also recognised are products or services that are designed to address a particular social problem for or through its customers, such as health or educational products serving underserved customers, or services that improve the social impact of other businesses or organisations.

There are many pros to becoming a B Corp, not least that the process has a commitment to transparency. This means you must be willing to share your scores on the B Corp website and publish an impact report in between certification, all of which can keep your business focused.

Plus, it can help your bottom line. UK B Corps have reported above-average growth, and the mark itself can improve the saleability of your business, to employees, customers and investors.

However, before embarking on the B Corp journey be aware that it is a rigorous process and working towards it may eat up time and resources that you may not feel you can commit in the early stages. Once certified, B Corps are also required to pay an annual subscription fee which licenses them to use the B Corp logo among other benefits. There may also be additional costs dependent on the size and structure of your company, and certification needs to be renewed every three years.

If you decide certification is something to work towards in the future, one good interim digital tool that B Corp has developed is the B Impact Assessment. It's worth signing up to it just to see what kinds of questions B Corp is asking on the road towards certification. Of course, if you have the time and resources to work through the assessment more formally, then receiving a verified score of 80 points out of 200 counts towards becoming a fully certified B Corp when the time comes.

Every year B Corp also holds events, so signing up and taking in a range of talks and masterclasses can also set you on your journey. Through engaging in the wider B Corp community you can share tips and ask questions with like-minded people, and even access investors aligned to your purpose. The B Corp website is a great place to start your research.

Also developed by B Corp alongside the United Nations is the SDG Action Manager, another really useful self-assessment tool that helps businesses focus purpose around the UN's Sustainable Development Goals listed in Chapter 1. You do not have to be a B Corp to use the tool and through it you can learn which goals are most relevant to your business, assess what you are currently doing and find out what actions you can take. You can also set goals and track your improvement with the added benefit that your whole team can access a dashboard to participate and collaborate.

And lastly, if you want to change your company articles then a step-by-step toolkit developed by the internet platform Purposely will guide you through the necessary steps needed to embed purpose into your DNA.

Looking at the criteria around other accreditation schemes applicable to your business may also give you a lighter framework for purpose. While none has the holistic or broad scope of B Corp, the Fairtrade Foundation, for example, is a certification label for products sourced from the developing world. By adhering to its rigorous process, you will be ensuring safer working conditions, fair pay and local sustainability for farmers and workers. Other industry-specific accreditation schemes are also available, several listed in the directory at the end of this book, although these will usually focus on one aspect of a business, for example, food provenance or animal welfare rather than an overarching standard.

How purpose and vision intersect

Alongside understanding why you exist, it is equally important to understand where you want your business to be in the future. Closely related to purpose is vision. Some companies do use the terms interchangeably, but they have slightly different uses. If your purpose or mission defines who you are, what you do, and who you do it for, your business vision is an aspirational statement that feeds into your strategy going forward.

It asks, where are we going? And, how do we get there? In a traditional business, this could be an ambition to be the bestselling brand in a certain category. In a purpose-led company it's likely your vision will have a little more depth.

It also differs from business to business as to where a vision statement is seen. Some businesses use it in their consumer-focused literature, while others embed it in their investment material or share it internally with employees to help drive the business forward. Often, key employees will contribute to shaping the business vision and this is important because everybody needs to understand it and align with it. Wherever you choose to display your vision, we would recommend chiselling one out from the outset. Without a clear vision you will not be able to create coherent strategies to achieve your purpose.

A business vision could be, but need not be, wholly measurable in numbers. Let's look at two examples of purpose-led start-up visions to demonstrate:

- I previously mentioned the UK company Ocean Bottle, who have developed an eco-friendly reusable water bottle. Its core business helps fund people across the world to pick up plastic from coastal areas. Its vision is a clear, measurable goal: 'to stop 7 billion plastic bottles from entering our oceans by 2025'. The plastics collected are weighed and measured by the equivalent weight of a plastic bottle. As of 2022, the company has collected almost 4.5 million kgs of plastic, a number clearly visible on its website, so consumers can chart its impact.

- On the other hand, the company Here We Flo, who make organic sanitary wear, aims for a destigmatisation of periods. Their goal is:

'to make products that inspire people to feel crazy confident and empowered about their messiest bodily moments'. It's not numerically measurable, but it's a goal that encapsulates the social impact the company is aiming for. Its goal is about opening up a conversation.

How you define your goal will be directly related to the business you are in and what it is you want to achieve, but whatever you decide, your vision should be:

- Clear and concise: it should say a lot in a few words.
- Passionate and memorable and helps build a picture in people's minds.
- Realistic. There's nothing wrong with being ambitious, but at the same time understand your resources, capabilities and growth potential. Don't claim you are going to be the world's number one brand in the next three years if you haven't yet launched.

Of course, as you evolve your vision may change. For this reason, your vision statement is not something to be written down and never referred to again. Unlike your purpose which should remain relatively static, your vision statement needs to be constantly revisited and updated. It should be seen as a much more dynamic part of the heart and soul of your business – a living, breathing statement.

Understanding your values

When your business is small enough for everyone to be connected and easily communicated with, having a set of defined values is not crucial, but when the business grows, values start to have a really important job to do.

Remember my director who announced to the team meeting that everyone followed my values? That was my wake-up call that, as an organisation, we had never debated or decided on a coherent set of values. Up until that point we hadn't needed to, but because we had suddenly grown, that made the need to formulate a more urgent set.

But what are values? And how do we get them right? Values naturally follow on from purpose and vision, although they are not the 'why' you are doing something but rather the 'how' you are going to achieve it.

We would advise you, if you can, to include key employees in the process of deciding values. Not only will others highlight values that you hadn't considered but the debate around values may also reveal the strengths or shortcomings of particular values. For example, different values can mean different things to different people, whereas what you are aiming for is a defined set of values that can be easily understood by everyone and acted on.

When we first started looking at values at Good Energy, it was around six years after the company was founded. We certainly learned by trial and error, so it's been interesting to look back and see how we changed those values once we understood how they worked in practice. Good Energy's current values are fair; inclusive; straightforward and determined, but they started out as innovative; ethical; fair; inclusive and honest. To help you understand values better, let's explore each one in turn and describe how they evolved over the years:

○ *Innovative*: This made perfect sense when we first decided on it. To the outside world, Good Energy is innovative. We started out as a business with a progressive, democratic approach to the problem of climate change because we empowered small-scale generators. However, over time, this value became problematic because it became an objective rather than a value, as not every department had the scope to be innovative. We eventually dropped it because it created conflict as the value could not be adapted to every part of the business.

O *Ethical*: With hindsight, ethical is a value that was too vague, and we soon discovered that it meant different things to different people. For example, not long after we named it as a value, members of our debt collection team said they didn't feel it was ethical to collect unpaid bills from customers. This highlighted a tension about what it was to stay commercial yet purpose-driven. In my view, a business that didn't stay afloat wasn't going to exist in the future. In the end, we dropped ethical as a value given it was too open-ended. Words such as 'sustainable' often fall into this trap too.

O *Fair*: This is a value that Good Energy still keeps to this day. This value evolved from an idea about fair distribution of wealth. We wanted to treat everybody equally – for example, we aimed to pay every partner or supplier the same market rate. For customers, we tried to offer all payment types, including cash, cheque and even local currencies (although this did become more challenging as payment types were phased out). Fairness also extended to our employees who we wanted to pay fairly for the same role regardless of gender. And, over the years, we've grown fairness further: once we became profitable we wanted to be fair to our shareholders so we began paying a dividend. We wanted to apply fairness to our employees, so we looked at how we treated employees, how we could serve them better through honest feedback, self-development and employee benefits that aligned with our goals. Fair is a value that works across every part of the business. Whatever change we wanted to make we asked: 'Is this fair?'

- ○ *Inclusive*: This grew from an idea about societal inclusiveness. The ethos behind Good Energy was that we included ordinary people in the energy market which up until that point was exclusive, dominated by the big six through a top-down mechanism of energy supply. It is a value we have kept but evolved to include both customers and employees. We now apply inclusive to every decision: 'Does this include everybody we cater for?' This even extends to our company benefits – for example, when we developed our green travel bonus we looked at everybody in the organisation and the different ways they travelled to work to ensure no one was left out of the scheme.

- ○ *Honest*: Initially, honest seemed an obvious word to use because it was how we wanted to do business both externally and internally. Again, honest turned out to be too vague and open to interpretation. What is one person's idea of honest may not be another's. In the end we changed honest to *Straightforward*. We wanted to communicate clearly both with our customers and internally with employees.

- ○ *Determined*: We added determined many years later and it is a value that emerged through our experience of trying to change the status quo. As a purpose-led company we always had big ambitions – for example, to buy and run renewable energy-generating projects such as wind and solar farms, but to do this it is essential to continue to generate profit. To achieve this, we had to be determined in often challenging times. From the outset, we also wanted to change the energy market, namely through better regulation. Good Energy continues to campaign for change. This is, at times, a frustrating struggle and determination must run through all parts of the business.

Purpose, Mission and Values

When the time comes for you to adopt a set of values, you may choose a completely different list of guiding principles. These could range from being curious to collaborative, accountable to passionate, bold to empathetic. In the process, it will be helpful for you to think about how a value connects to every part of the business. This will allow you to eliminate values that are too woolly, open-ended, risk being misinterpreted, or do not translate to all of your business functions. Once values are embedded, then every decision you make should be seen through the values lens. They will determine how you hire and treat employees, how you interact with customers, how you drive the business forward and so on. The following illustrates some methods to help you develop a set of values:

- A good starting point is to look at the values of other businesses you like or aspire to, regardless of whether they are in your space. This will start you on a journey of understanding what chimes with your own values.
- Go back to your purpose and think about what values naturally arise from this. A good question to ask is: what values are important to the business over and above profit?
- Create a list of values from the above and around your own values and by discussing values with key employees. I would advise you adopt no more than five core values that really mean something rather than ten that people will forget. Internally, if people don't understand values, then you will spend a lot of time telling people what to do.
- Think about all the functions of your business and who your business touches. List these as categories such as: employees; customers; customer service; suppliers; environmental impact; future growth;

community impact and so on. Write down the values that spring to mind when you think of each function.

○ Once you've come up with a list, stress-test it. Ask: what is this value about? Why is it important and what do you really mean by it? For example, if one value listed is 'respect', drill down into what that really means. Do employees understand it easily? Do customers understand it? What overall picture is created when the value is said out loud – is it clear, positive and tangible, or bland and too vague?

○ Lastly, think about whether the value can be applied to every part of the business. If a department cannot enact the value because its function doesn't allow it to, this will create tension. This is especially so if some of your key performance indicators (KPIs), which will measure performance over time, correlate to company values.

Translating values into behaviours

Once your values are decided on, you have to be able to turn these into actions – in other words you have to live your values, not just talk about them. Values will underpin certain standards of behaviour within your organisation. A good way of understanding this stage by stage is by taking one value, then thinking about its guiding principle. After that, start to list behaviours that embody this guiding principle. I'll return to Good Energy's value of 'Straightforward' and show a process of teasing out behaviours from it.

Value: Straightforward

Guiding principle: to make the energy market easy to understand; to make sure our dealings with customers, stakeholders and employees are clear and transparent.

Behaviours: We wanted to be honest with customers for whom energy price changes are always a difficult time. Over the years, Good Energy has always tried to be transparent, detailing exactly how the energy price is made up and being clear what the costs are, including the company's own costs.

When it came to our stakeholders, such as suppliers, we steered away from 'horse trading' wherever possible. If we were embarking on a deal, we didn't start from a ridiculous position with a view to negotiating. Instead, we agreed a price or a deal and then stuck to it as fair and reasonable, thereby reducing time and effort.

When dealing with employees we were clear about our company targets and about how the individual's contribution to those targets or plans is incredibly important. We spent time with employees to explain how the business runs and makes financial returns – aspects of the business that people on the front line might feel excluded from.

Once you have teased out behaviours from values then you must reinforce them over time. This can be done in a number of ways:

- Display your values publicly – for example, on your website – but also internally, perhaps on a wall or in a common area or on your intranet site or employee code of conduct. Talk about values when you induct new employees.
- Talk about your values constantly and stress-test every new idea, policy or venture around them.
- When recruiting, talk openly with potential hires about your values to see if they align and include them on any job advert.
- Train employees in key values. If one of your values is 'inclusive', for example, train people to be actively inclusive in everything they

do. This could be holding workshops in teamwork or unconscious bias training, or training your customer service team to feed back on customer interactions so the service becomes more inclusive.

- Promote employees not just on their ability to do their job, but also on their ability to live the company values through their behaviours. Include a discussion of this in any appraisal or employee evaluation.
- Reward employees against how well they live the company values through behaviours.
- Encourage employees to speak out when they see or hear a clear breach of company values.

Through communicating a clear set of values from the outset and training employees in how those values should be lived, over time you embed a set of behaviours that reflect and reinforce your company and its purpose.

Purpose, mission and values . . . in a nutshell

Purpose is the reason why you exist and so you should spend time chiselling out your clear purpose. See it as your North Star that you come back to in every decision you make. Your vision encapsulates your goals and is a more moveable statement. It should be ambitious but at the same time realistic and evolve over time. Values and behaviours have an important job to do once you start to grow. These should be meaningful, tangible and easily translatable into actionable employee behaviours.

Quick wins

- Formulate your company purpose by asking why you exist.
- Create a clear vision for your company – where are you going?
- Understand the principles of accreditation schemes such as B Corp and use the framework as a way of embedding purpose in the business from the outset.

Moving up a gear

- Establish a set of values.
- Understand how you can turn that value into action.
- Create a set of behaviours that will guide your business to living its values.
- Communicate values to your employees.
- Formally work towards an accreditation such as B Corp to ensure you are focused on your purpose in every part of your business.

Going for it

- Understand how values translate to behaviours.
- Look at every part of your business and see how a value can be adapted to benefit it.
- Provide training to employees to show them how to live the company values.

○ Find ways of rewarding employees who demonstrate best practice.

○ Review values regularly and update if necessary.

○ Showcase your accreditations and become an influencer in the market to bring wider acknowledgement for purpose-driven businesses.

Chapter 5
People First

It was in the fledging years of Good Energy when disaster struck. In the autumn of 2005 the UK energy market started to see a price shock in a market that had been calm for a few years. A cold winter collided with the late onstreaming of several nuclear sites, and spiking gas prices across Europe culminated in the skyrocketing cost of wholesale gas and electricity.

We'd managed to weather the storm relatively well at Good Energy, insulated in part by our position in renewables. Cash was tight, but we could make it through. But then I got a call that is every CEO's worst nightmare. In the fallout, our back-office company was teetering on administration. It was the nerve centre of our operations – the company ran our call centre that signed up new customers, dealt with problems, fielded power-cut enquiries, and most importantly billed our customers. It became quickly obvious that we had to take them over. Now, all I recall is the frantic conversations, and the furious paddling under the surface to keep the show on the road: transferring the building, IT systems and suddenly managing a company five times the size of our own. What I hadn't predicted was the culture clash of people that was to follow.

Before that point, Good Energy was a gender-balanced team committed to combatting climate change. Overnight we went from a tight operation to a workforce of around 40. Our sister company was largely run by male management with a completely different ethos – driven entirely commercially. The culture wasn't collaborative; rather, it was confrontational. If I'm honest, this didn't sit well with me. Suddenly I watched as the team we'd grown were faced with stand-offs closer to a reality TV show than a purpose-led business. It came to a head when one male employee approached me for a pay rise. 'How can I justify paying you above market rate?' I asked him. His answer left me speechless: his wife was having a baby and he felt he should be paid more so that she could stay at home.

Thankfully, attitudes like that are less common these days, and certainly not at Good Energy, but reflecting on that period, I do wish I'd been better equipped to deal with the transition. In the end, knowing the culture clash was damaging our business, we brought in outside help to unpick the company's DNA and glue us back together. That said, it wasn't an easy time. We didn't have built-in resilience to manage a change we hadn't planned for.

Over the years, I've come to understand that if you don't get people right, nothing in your organisation works. And if you are a progressive company that talks of a people-first policy then you have to walk the walk. Of course, back in 2005 ideas around inclusion and diversity were hardly embedded in the employment lexicon. The Equality Act, that brought together 116 separate pieces of anti-discrimination legislation, didn't come into force until 2010. With hindsight, the will was there, but we were finding our way.

In writing this book, I started to think about what a purpose-led, people-first company might look like from the outset. How can you build in resilience to attract, engage, motivate, nurture and reward your employees? So many companies get some way down the line and then find it difficult to untangle limiting behaviour. Or perhaps a company *wants* to be a people-first organisation, but instead of penetrating the heart of the business, it tinkers around the edges with token gestures like placing a lone woman on the board – a start, but not progress enough. And is nurturing your employees more than simply understanding what they do at work? How can a workplace better understand the experiences they have as people?

I do appreciate that putting some of these ideas into practice is not as easy as it sounds. It takes a mature organisation to lift the lid on its practices and peer inside, expose its vulnerabilities and challenge itself to be better. Yet if you think that people are your biggest asset, they can also be your biggest weakness if you don't get it right. Companies often see human resources as a necessary evil, yet if you do take the time to think about what a good culture looks like, it can pay dividends in the future.

In this chapter, I'm going to be looking at every aspect of people, from the people you employ to the relationships you build externally; from instilling meaningful change around inclusion and diversity, to employing sustainable support services. If people are the lifeblood of your mission, then you need to take them with you on every part of the journey.

People, diversity and planet

Growing evidence points to a diverse workforce as being instrumental to company performance and growth, although more research does need to be done to understand the link. A 2019 report by global management consultancy McKinsey found that corporates with more than 30% women on the executive team were 25% more likely to enjoy above-average profitability compared with those with the lowest. When it came to ethnic and cultural diversity, those companies at the top outperformed those at the bottom by 36%. As we'll discover, diversity is more than just factoring in gender and race. However, the research suggests that companies who embrace diversity attract and retain employees more easily and are more likely to foster healthy debate which leads to innovative and more effective decision-making to better challenge established thinking. Plus, they are less likely to take uncalculated financial risks, all of which lead to increased profitability.

While that link between diversity and profitability is being explored, the link between diversity and tackling climate change is less discussed. Yet, a 2017 study found a connection between gender diversity in business and increased carbon disclosure and enhanced performance on carbon emission reduction. Moreover, in the run-up to COP26 in 2021 there were calls for increased representation for women in decision-making roles if companies are to achieve net zero targets. Rupal Kantaria, partner at the Oliver Wyman Forum, who was involved in compiling research from more than 20 companies exploring the link said: 'As our research and interviews progressed, it became clear that not only are women often excluded from many high-level government and corporate discussions on climate, their role as climate-action change-makers is largely unrecognised and underestimated. Yet businesses need to include female colleagues, customers, and investors if they are serious about meeting net-zero carbon emissions by 2050.' The report is well worth a read.

And when you think that climate action is going to need widespread public participation and a shift in behaviour, then representation at all levels is needed. Indeed in 2021, research carried out for the UK government cited that inclusivity is vital to public engagement on reaching net zero. 'Different societal actors have a key role to play with public engagement with net zero . . . these all have an important and different role to play in overcoming key barriers to action on climate change and in empowering different groups of citizens,' the report read. I see business as one of those key actors but how a business communicates with the outside world can only be a reflection of who we are within our own organisations, and this is where the hard work begins.

Who do you want to be?

We all have a way of being – a way we like to be treated and a way we think others should be treated. And if we start a business, and take on employees, we should look to build a reciprocal relationship based on respect.

The days where employers could squeeze every last drop from their workforce, with little thought given to employee satisfaction, are gone. Millennials especially vote with their feet. The average person spends two years in a job before moving on. In the early days we had a turnover rate of less than 5%. Today, employers are lucky to keep it under 25%. The impact of high turnover on both the culture and the bottom line is altogether real. People want to work for a company that has values and who values them – a company that fosters a culture where people can evolve and grow. In return they want to give their all. If I were to pick a word, I'd call it 'fairness'.

To help us understand how organisations might build in 'fairness' from the outset, I've asked Greg Jauncey, a human resources expert who focuses on diversity and inclusion. Greg works with arts organisations and is the co-founder of his own business Theatre People, and I love the way he shifts an often dry conversation around 'human resources' to being a launch pad for 'human opportunity'.

'The real quality of people is not that they simply fulfil the function of their job description,' he says. 'It's about discretionary effort – the extra value people give you, rather than the work they have to give you. You are more likely to get to that magical "other" if you create an environment that's inclusive and that gives people a space to thrive.'

Ideally, you'll want to be thinking about people from the earliest point, even if you don't have any 'people' to manage. If you are two or three people starting a business, you should discuss how you want to behave towards each other. Then, you should think about how you want to operate with your customers. Are you going to be straightforward? Transparent? Empathetic? Determined? Efficient? You'll probably settle on a combination of behaviours. And remember, if you say who you are, you have to authentically be who you say. And the best way of understanding this is by measuring.

Measure and keep measuring

In so many businesses, understanding your relationship with people happens through trial and error, after something goes wrong, or a customer complains. 'Measuring from the outset can establish a framework whereby you are constantly reflecting back,' says Greg. Externally, this could take the form of a regular customer survey that asks people: are we meeting expectations by doing what we say? Internally, this should be, at the very least, knowing who your employees are and what they want.

I remember sitting around a table with the senior leadership team just after a hectic period when Good Energy had grown to more than 100 employees. You may think I would have noticed before, but suddenly I realised there were no senior women. It wasn't until the evidence was in front of my nose that I asked for our data on diversity. Sadly, the person who led on HR at the time took this personally and we had a fraught conversation about equality, but data should never be personal. Understanding it leads to finding out what is going on unseen.

Even now, I know of established companies who still do not measure. In my view, this is a missed opportunity. They don't know why, when women leave the business to have a family, they don't return. They don't know why there are only men sitting around the boardroom table. They don't know why they are not attracting culturally and ethnically diverse people to their organisation. They don't know why employee churn in their company has tipped from a healthy amount to one that is disproportionately high. They don't know why, because they have never analysed the pinch points in their processes. And, if you don't know, you can't be responsive, and you can't adapt and improve.

I'll expand on what and how to measure as I continue, but if there's one mantra to repeat it's: measure, measure and keep measuring.

Build without gates

'Start-ups have the perfect opportunity to build without gates,' says Greg. His analogy of 'gates' is a very useful one, not least because it's a visual way of thinking about the invisible barriers businesses often put in place for people. Yet once a company is aware of the societal barriers to attracting and nurturing a diverse workforce, it can build in structures to combat any inherent structural disadvantages that marginalised groups may face.

For companies already up and running, the challenge is to recognise that gates may exist within the organisation. The questions then become: where are those gates? Who are the gatekeepers? And what can we do to remove those gates or, at a minimum, wedge them open? If you don't recognise or remove gates, then you remain complicit in perpetuating inequality.

To give an example, structural racism is a concept that reached public consciousness after 1999 and the Macpherson Inquiry into the death of the black teenager Stephen Lawrence, killed by racist thugs in south London. The report specifically looked at structural racism within the police force, but Macpherson's findings rippled throughout many institutions. He recognised that structural racism persists 'because of the failure . . . to recognise and address its existence and causes by policy, example and leadership'. The death of George Floyd in 2020 and the Black Lives Matter protests have reignited debate around what structural racism is and how to combat it.

When it comes to racism, I would sincerely hope that no one would argue it is a good thing, but how businesses often unknowingly maintain it requires a much more nuanced analysis – this is where measuring really helps.

Placing an anti-racist statement on your company website and telling potential applicants that you are an equal opportunities employer is meaningless if, when you analyse your talent pipeline, you are only employing ethnically diverse people in lower-paid customer service roles. Unless you monitor this, you will never discover it, and if you don't discover it you will never find ways to support people to move through the ranks. In other words, your diversity strategy is always going to be skin deep.

It's the same story for gender parity. If you say you welcome women to your company and offer them equal opportunities, then you need to do more than pay lip service. Offering tangible benefits like maternity and paternity care, flexible working, childcare support or contact days for women on maternity leave will not only help you to attract talent, but also retain talent. You will be walking the walk, not just talking the talk.

Attracting employees

So, let's begin where most businesses begin. If you are a start-up it's unlikely you are going to be employing many people yet, if any. Rather, you may be paying people to work for you on an ad hoc basis. This could take the form of engaging freelance contractors or consultants to carry out certain functions or to undertake short-term projects. As an employer you will have different levels of statutory obligation towards employees depending on what basis they are employed. Even though contractors do not have the same rights and responsibilities of a permanent employee, it pays to have a policy in place that helps you build relationships with reliable contractors.

In the future, you may want your contractors to become full-time employees, or you might bring them in recurrently to work on projects. So, it's worth noting that they have specific needs. For example, a freelance worker will have booked time out to work with you, so cancelling at the last minute, especially on work booked months in advance, is inconvenient not to mention potentially financially devastating. While many will have established terms that includes a cancellation fee, it's worth discussing this before work starts. Also, contractors don't bring in regular salaries, so you can help their cash flow by paying on time. Some companies prioritise contractors' pay, but the majority do not.

After some time, you may want to flex and grow your human resource, and you'll want to attract the best and brightest to your business. If you are a progressive company, this will mean looking to a diverse and inclusive workforce. To build without gates, some thought will need to go into your recruitment process. A good starting point is the Equality Act 2010. Under the Act, it is against the law to discriminate against someone because of: age; disability; gender reassignment; marriage and civil partnership; pregnancy and maternity; race; religion or belief; sex; or sexual orientation. As Greg says, 'No business gets bonus points for adhering to the law. Instead, be ambitious from the outset: know it's not enough to say that you are an anti-discrimination employer. To build without gates you have to be a *proactive* anti-discrimination employer.'

The job advert and application process

Who you attract to your business starts with the call-out for talent. Yet so many employers unknowingly put off underrepresented job seekers. Being aware of limiting language in your recruitment literature, for example, and knowing how to change this can open you up to a wider talent pool.

Understanding that people face a range of barriers will also create a level playing field for applicants. For example, offering an application in different formats such as Braille or large type will immediately aid blind or partially sighted applicants. Also, do ask potential applicants to contact you if there are any other reasonable adjustments that can be made to the application process to make it accessible for them.

One very useful resource is the Disability Confident scheme, available through the Department for Work and Pensions. It takes employers through three levels to eventually become a disability-confident employer and provides checklists along the way.

And remember, many people have invisible disabilities. In fact, around 7 million people in the UK of working age are disabled as defined by the Equality Act, yet only a small percentage are visible wheelchair users. Disability covers a range of physical and mental health problems and also includes people on the neurodiverse spectrum which covers disabilities such as autism and Asperger's syndrome, as well as learning difficulties such as dyslexia and attention deficit hyperactivity disorder (ADHD).

You may also want to widen your talent pool by bringing in people from a variety of socioeconomic backgrounds – even though this is not a protected characteristic – each with their own set of experiences. So how do you best appeal to this cross section? Take the following excerpt from a call-out for the role of marketing executive:

Experience:

- A graduate with minimum five years' relevant experience.
- Superb communication skills.
- Comfortable with Excel, Word and PowerPoint.
- Self-starter with drive who can thrive in a competitive environment.
- Ability to prioritise and plan effectively.
- Assertive with a go-getting attitude.

Benefits:

- Chance to make a significant impact within a dynamic company.
- Competitive salary dependent on experience.
- Modern, flexible company: all employees given the option to work a four-day week.
- Employer pension contribution.
- EMI share option scheme.

Now, compare it with this rewritten version that is unbiased and inclusive:

We are an equal opportunity employer. All applicants, especially minority groups and disabled people, are encouraged to apply.

Experience:

- A great opportunity for an ambitious marketer who wants to apply their experience within a purpose-led business.
- You will be confident working with people at all levels of the organisation alongside external audiences.
- Would be a distinct advantage to have experience of Excel, Word and PowerPoint, but it is not essential.
- Self-starter with the opportunity to learn, grow and test yourself in our collaborative and fast-paced environment.
- Ability to prioritise and plan effectively.

Benefits:

- 25 days holiday plus bank holidays and the option to buy more.
- Flexible working for everyone.
- An annual working allowance – supporting the costs of working from home or travelling to the office.
- A green allowance that rewards our people for travelling to the office in a green way and generating energy.
- Chance to be part of an active personal development community with an annual learning and development allowance.
- Enhanced maternity, paternity and shared parental leave, with family-friendly return-to-work coaching.
- Healthcare cash-back plan for support with everyday health costs.

Notice that in the second example:

- The advert actively invites people in protected groups to apply.
- It does not use words like 'assertive', 'go-getting', 'drive' and 'competitive'. These words are male-gendered and have been found to put women off. Equally, feminine words include 'support', 'understanding', 'reliable'. Always use gender-neutral words. To help, use a gender decoder such as www.gender-decoder.katmatfield.com.
- There is no specification that the applicant has to be a graduate with a set number of years' experience. People who are not graduates may have taken an apprenticeship route or amassed experience another

way – it doesn't make their experience less valuable. Asking for a set amount of years' experience leaves you open to accusations of age discrimination.

⊘ The second advert makes clear that if a person works hard for the company, it will invest in that person's development.

⊘ The work benefits show that the company is committed to environmentally friendly policies, equal opportunities and flexible working for both sexes. Even if you are at a stage when you can't offer a whole range of benefits, work out what you can offer that will benefit all your employees.

Equal opportunities monitoring

If you are serious about diversity and inclusion you can start measuring from the moment people reply to a job advert by including an equal opportunities monitoring form. It is a good idea to explain why you are asking for this information as it will include sensitive information on gender, race, sexual orientation, disability and/or religion. If you say it is because you are committed to being fair and an equal opportunities employer then people are more likely to fill out the form, although they are not legally obliged to do so. The charity Stonewall has produced a great resource called *What's It Got to Do With You?*, outlining ten reasons why people should tick the boxes.

If you are collecting data from the outset, then you must also make sure you are compliant under General Data Protection Regulation (GDPR) legislation. New laws came into force in 2018 that require all employers to treat personal data fairly and responsibly. This puts the onus on you to think about how and why you are using data. GDPR regulation will depend on what kind of business you are and what data you collect. A good starting point for guidelines relevant to your business is the Information Commissioner's Office (ICO).

Another opportunity to collect data is when a person joins your business if you have not asked them to fill out a monitoring form before. Subsequent employee surveys will also keep you in touch with who your employees are and how best you can support them, and you can make this fun by offering a benefit if the survey is completed. However, anonymity should always be ensured when seeking responses.

When it comes to the application format itself, it is your preference whether you ask applicants to send a covering letter and CV, fill out an application form, or show their credentials in another way. Today, some businesses even ask applicants to send in a video blog – a vlog – of themselves, perhaps for a customer service role. Whatever you choose, think about how you can assess job seekers in the fairest way. Basing decisions on assumptions, beliefs or attitudes that you may hold in your subconscious is called unconscious bias. Yet if you want to build a diverse workforce it is something you must avoid. One automatic way of doing this is to standardise the questions you ask people. 'An application form can be fairer than a CV and covering letter,' says Greg, 'simply because application forms require applicants to answer the same questions. CVs, on the other hand, take more effort and skill to mine for information and you may end up not comparing like with like.'

Sharing your company values

Unconscious bias can also occur when you recruit in your mirror image. Most people don't set out to do this – it's often just human nature. Employing people who look like you, think like you and hold your values may sound attractive, but by doing this you are limiting your talent pool. Businesses perform better in an atmosphere of healthy debate, and this only happens when people join from a variety of backgrounds and hold a variety of viewpoints.

That said, always be transparent in the application pack about who you are and what your company values are. And if you are a new company without the luxury of being a trusted brand, do include as much information as you can. Ideally you want to reach a sweet spot of attracting a person who fits the business but also challenges the business to be better.

Moreover, as you are sifting through applications be mindful of the job on offer. A green technology company recruiting for the influential position of marketer is unlikely to want to employ a climate-change sceptic. However, if you are recruiting for the role of administrator you may find that, even if someone doesn't align 100% with your business's higher purpose, they are still committed and have the potential to do a great job. Perhaps that person is more attracted by the flexible working on offer than the company's environmental credentials. In this case, you have an opportunity to grow and nurture those values while that person is employed. And there is always an opportunity during the interview process to further explore values.

Shortlisting and interview

Fairness can also be built into the shortlisting and interview stages. If you can, devise a mechanism whereby names, gender and educational establishments are screened out from people shortlisting. By doing this, you are further limiting unconscious bias by removing information that could connect an appointee to a potential hire. For the same reason, screening out the names of referees is also preferable. Excluding these details allows you to concentrate on an applicant's experience, talent and how well they have answered the questions rather than who they know. The so-called 'old boys' network' thrived on this kind of bias, but it can no longer be currency within a progressive business.

When it comes to shortlisting, having two people working through applications is the ideal scenario. And, if you can, there is an opportunity to build in diversity here. By having a male and female shortlisting, or by including a person from a minority ethnic background, you immediately widen your perspective. It's not always possible, but it's something to aim for.

Establishing a system of assessing how well applicants have answered questions is also key to a fair process. You may devise a scoring system, but whatever you choose, think about whether the system assesses people equally. Again, during an interview process you can mitigate unconscious bias by having two or more people on the panel. Asking all applicants the same sequence of questions naturally creates a level playing field, as does asking applicants to carry out the same competency test.

If any applicant does have additional needs, offer alternative pathways for them. For example, if a person is dyslexic, they may need extra time to complete a test. Or perhaps someone has special access needs. Whatever the request, letting potential applicants know you will do your utmost to support them automatically demonstrates you are a responsive employer. That person will still have to perform well to get the job, but it's important to understand that they may need some extra help to put them on a par with other job seekers.

Creating psychological safety

Fostering a workplace atmosphere that empathises with employees, but at the same time positively challenges them, can be a difficult balance to achieve. Yet businesses that encourage employees to bring themselves to work and support them to perform at their best build trust – it's what's called psychological safety. When I think about it now, this was missing when Good Energy subsumed its sister company, and it was that lack of safety that meant we were working on rather shaky foundations for a while.

In collaborative workplaces, building psychological safety can be a driver of high-quality decision-making, better interpersonal relationships and increased innovation – and in a fast-paced, responsive workplace it is this resilient foundation that can unlock flexibility and dynamism.

Psychological safety starts when people can share ideas free from bullying or humiliation. This could be during team meetings, but it's also about creating an open door whereby if someone has a problem, they feel empowered to raise it. Giving employees direct, constructive feedback further develops a culture of mutual respect, and there will be more on this in the next section. Encouraging people to take responsibility also helps build respect – a fear of making mistakes created by a blame culture will only stunt personal growth and development. Everybody makes mistakes – the key is to allow a person the opportunity to learn from their mistakes.

And it involves seeing your people as people. In the past, the personal and professional remained separate, but understanding who employees are is crucially important in supporting them to do their job.

Some may have specific pressures. For example, a person may care for an elderly parent and it would help them to work from home two days a week. Another may have childcare issues and needs to leave on time on certain days. And let's not forget the single person who may consistently get work dumped on them because they are perceived to have no other responsibilities.

Whatever an employee's challenges, building solutions that show empathy but also require accountability creates clear boundaries around how you as an employer can work alongside employees yet let them know what's expected from them in return.

Developing and assessing your employees

Psychological safety also extends to how you value your employees' development and give feedback to your employees. This can be done through informal check-in meetings, formal appraisals, peer reviews or a combination of all three. However you decide to performance manage, feedback should be direct and positive, but not shy away from where improvements can be made.

At Good Energy, we discovered one very useful resource, a technique developed by ex-Google employee Kim Scott called Radical Candor. In her book of the same name, Scott breaks down a variety of employee interactions into four subsections. 'Obnoxious aggression' is feedback where a person challenges directly but doesn't care about the impact personally. 'Manipulative insincerity' happens when a person might try to smooth over a relationship by saying something they don't mean. 'Ruinous empathy' is when a direct challenge is needed but a person ends up being 'too nice' and avoids conflict. To reach a place of Radical Candor, various techniques can be used. They include:

praising publicly and criticising privately; not saving criticism up for an appraisal but doing it quickly and lightly when the situation demands; not tearing down personality but giving reasoned criticism, and involving the person in a solution. Through clear, direct but empathetic feedback, you can further build psychological safety. It's not always easy, but awareness and reflection are key and I recommend Scott's book as a launch pad for thinking about how to manage feedback and relationships in a fair and positive way.

Employee development is also about proactively identifying areas where extra training would help a person. Offering a good training package may only be possible once your business is more established but bringing in a trainer from the outside to work with a cohort of employees may be a more cost-effective way. Supporting employees on their own personal development journey will also help retain them. Perhaps a person wants to take a weekday course, in which case you may be able to work with them to build in flexibility around their job, or even help pay for the course, should it be of value to the business in the future.

Inclusive networking events

Everybody in your organisation should benefit from networking opportunities, yet still so many of these favour certain employees. It's easier for someone who doesn't have to rush off at 5:30pm to collect children from the childminder or have other commitments to attend an evening event, but this does automatically place limits on who attends. Think carefully about how to include all employees in these events – it could be a once-a-month breakfast meeting or a lunch rather than an evening event. An evening out at a football match, that might not be to everyone's taste, could be replaced. A good idea is to ask your employees what they might like to do and have events on a rotational basis, perhaps picked by separate departments.

Unlocking gates through micro-inclusion

Earlier, we mentioned unlocking gates in your business, and so far we've explored ways to build without gates. Yet for existing businesses for whom gates already exist, finding them and opening them can be a difficult process. 'Many employees will believe the solution lies in the decisions the senior team make,' says Greg, 'such as who it hires and what provision is put in place for protected groups, yet it doesn't have to be a top-down process. As your business grows, each department will have people who, through awareness building, can become proactively inclusive.'

Every business has what Greg calls 'gatekeepers'. These can be anyone in your business who finds themselves responsible for a structure, system or process that has the power to enable or hamper an individual's access, progress or development. This is obvious with something like recruitment, but think about all aspects of your people-management systems and your customer interactions – for example, a complaints handling process. 'Gatekeepers rarely construct the gates that they find themselves responsible for,' says Greg, 'and may even not recognise the power that the role in your business gives them. Gatekeepers aren't innately racist, ableist or discriminatory, but any closed or selective gateways have the potential to be just that. To be proactively anti-discriminatory you have to open or remove the gates that you find yourself with.'

One employer I know of instigated regular meetings with employees to discuss how they might foster a more inclusive culture in their company, through what it called micro-inclusions. These are small actions that people can carry out on a day-to-day basis to understand or help more marginalised groups. First, the company built awareness with employees by bringing in outside speakers to talk about issues such as structural racism or LGBTQ+. Then, it asked employees to think about what gates existed in the organisation and how they could help break them down. Subsequent actions ranged from people being more mindful of cultural and other differences to colleagues stopping certain behaviours that could be interpreted as discriminatory, to employees offering to become a mentor if requested.

What also grew was a sense of solidarity among all employees towards protected groups, expressed mainly through regular celebrations or coming-together moments. For example, employees wanted to hold a bake-off competition to celebrate July's annual Gay Pride event. International Women's Day also became a convergence point. From there, other micro-inclusions grew organically, simply because awareness had been raised and a platform for discussion had been created.

Rewarding your employees

So many employees leave a job because they feel undervalued and unappreciated, so developing a performance-based reward system can enhance relationships. If you are in a position to offer financial benefits based on results then this is one way of recognising employees. However, rewards needn't cost a lot and they needn't be financial at all.

First off you will need to decide what you want to reward employees for and how. This could take the form of manager or company awards for performance at work, or even peer-to-peer awards which do more to recognise the unsung heroes at work. However, you may also want to reward employees who change their behaviour to align with your green ethos. Offering a points scheme for cycling to work so employees can clock up time in lieu is one idea, but be careful that this is not seen as discriminatory. Not everyone can cycle to work. And some people may not be able to walk, so think about how you can spin out that green travel reward to be inclusive, such as including a car-sharing scheme or points for taking public transport. You may also want to reward employees for recycling or even volunteering in the community. These rewards could range from a discounted gym membership to money-off vouchers towards products that align with your green ethos.

However, if you are just starting out, sometimes the simplest recognition of employees can go a long way. Knowing when people's birthdays are and sending them an e-card is a great and environmentally friendly way of telling your employees you value them. Work anniversaries and milestone moments such as births and marriages are also easy to mark. A set of babygrows is always helpful! Of course, do make sure that any present you give is ethically sourced. Where you can, use locally sourced suppliers for cakes and food and compile a list of ethical gift suppliers to buy from rather than rushing to send Amazon vouchers.

Adding value to retain employees

Earlier we briefly mentioned the need to develop a better understanding of your employees as people. Since 2020, the Covid-19 pandemic has accelerated this need. Suddenly, through technology, we have caught glimpses of colleagues' lives: their kitchens, their bookshelves, their children, their partners and their pets. Perhaps we've also come together to support a colleague who has lost a loved one. We've understood that people are people inside and outside of work, and that what keeps people working for a business is more than just a monthly pay cheque.

Of course, in its most basic concept a job is an exchange: people are paid in return for their work and commitment. While financial compensation is critical and an employee may move on because they can earn more elsewhere, what you want to do is avoid unnecessary churn for all the wrong reasons. Poor management, lack of support, lack of reward and job stress are all contributory factors as to why people leave their jobs. In fact, what retains employees is often company purpose, a positive environment and the added value an employer brings to a person's life.

There are numerous ways to add that value and some actions can be very simple. For example, acknowledging that employees have the right to enjoy downtime shows that the business respects a work-life balance. Many of us have our faces pressed up to our smartphones hour by hour, and employees often feel an urgency to respond to an email, regardless of whether this is in the evening or at the weekend. Everybody deserves time to pursue their hobbies, spend time with their families, or just not be at work. Creating a signature that tells senders a person will respond at a time convenient to them outside of office hours can immediately alleviate anxiety. My own email signature was inspired by another CEO and says: *Please don't feel any need to respond until a time that suits you. My iPhone allows me to work flexibly so I've sent this at a time to suit me.*

Understanding the life challenges that many people go through is also a way of being responsive to employees and needn't come at a great cost. Many employees will embark on establishing their own family life and may need some extra support on that journey. Some will find it more difficult to conceive and may undergo fertility treatment which impacts emotional and physical health and which in turn can spill over into work. Women of menopause age may be suffering in silence as they navigate hot flushes, mood swings or hormone replacement therapy treatment. Men also may be struggling with invisible health problems that are rarely spoken about, such as mental health difficulties or physical conditions such as erectile dysfunction – often the sign of an imminent heart attack, not a personal weakness or loss of manhood, or a range of cancers that specifically affect men.

Of course, this does not mean that a business must hold a weekly meeting where employees share their sensitive health concerns, but a business may look at offering employees some fantastic, inexpensive tools emerging on the market. One company whose business has taken off over the past couple of years is Peppy Health who run a workplace app that allows employees to speak with health professionals 24/7 with no appointment necessary. The app also gives users access to a range of resources that can help them better understand whatever life change they may be going through.

When I spoke to its founder and co-CEO Max Landry, he highlighted the increased need for businesses to support health and wellbeing. 'We are not equipping people to do their job better,' he says, 'but we are giving people tools to be a better and fuller person and that makes them happier in their lives, and one aspect of that is being better at work.'

Peppy Health offer tailored support for people undergoing fertility treatment, advice for new parents and women returning to work, and has launched a men's health service. However, one of the most used services on the app is the menopause service, the reasons for which became clear when Max drilled down into the statistics. Around 25% of women consider leaving work because of menopause symptoms, while 63% of women who go through the menopause say it has negatively impacted their work, resulting in 30% of women taking time off work or simply leaving – shocking when you consider that this natural, but often challenging process affects every woman, yet the majority feel abandoned.

And when you see women's working lives in the round, you begin to understand how inequality is baked in. Life outcomes for women at work often change after they've had a family. 'Until women have children the gender pay gap doesn't exist,' Max says. 'Then women's pay drops off a cliff and often doesn't recover. When they hit menopause they may leave work earlier because of it, and that becomes the difference between a man retiring comfortably and a woman retiring poor. By addressing health you are also addressing structural inequality.'

What's most interesting about apps such as Peppy Health is that they don't make people's problems go away but what they can do is help people gain control of a situation through better understanding and through supporting them with a plan. 'The feedback we have had is that this has made people more positive about their lives, more productive at work and they also feel more positive about their employer,' Max says.

And it's not just health and wellbeing apps that are adding value. For example, Octopus MoneyCoach is a platform that assists employees in managing their personal finances. In the future, surely more businesses will offer these or similar services.

Employing support services

Naturally, the focus of your business will be your direct hires. These are the people who embody your business purpose and drive it forward. But what about your support services? Most small businesses don't embed a company lawyer or an accountant in-house but also contract these services ad hoc. While it's not always possible to unpick the culture of an outside business, there are questions you can ask of an auxiliary service to make sure your green values are aligned.

Advisory services don't fall neatly into a box with a defined supply chain – measuring the climate impact of advice is impossible – but there are enough practical markers to indicate whether a company is thinking in a green way and what their future climate change goals are. The company might not be perfect – neither will you be – but at least you can make an informed decision about who you want to work with, based on what they are doing now and what they plan to do in the future.

Employing a sustainable lawyer

It's unlikely you'll be in the market for a multimillion-pound merger or acquisition just yet, so you'll be employing a lawyer to help you with basic elements of your company such as structure, compliance, data protection, employment contracts, or more specialist services aligned to whatever business you are in, such as advice on intellectual property.

As a start-up or SME business it's likely you'll be calling on a small- or medium-sized law firm for advice. And coincidentally, these are exactly the firms who are themselves seeking advice on how to be greener.

The Legal Sustainability Alliance is a member organisation that advises a network of commercial law firms on how to reach net zero. The LSA's own growth area is currently in local and regional firms, signalling a shift towards a greener mindset. These firms are agile with a shorter decision-making chain, meaning they can implement change faster. And unlike the big corporate law firms, known as the 'magic circle', lawyers are less likely to be hopping on a plane every two minutes, automatically reducing a firm's carbon footprint.

There isn't yet a sustainability accreditation specifically for lawyers – a stamp of best practice – so unless a firm advertises its green credentials, or is part of another accreditation scheme, such as B Corp, the ball will be in your court to ask questions.

'Law firms are all on a different stage of the net zero journey,' says the LSA's Amanda Carpenter, 'but as members of the LSA this already shows they are engaged and interested and many see proving their sustainability credentials as giving them a competitive advantage.'

What's encouraging is that since 2007, when the LSA started sharing best practice, law firms have become more sophisticated in the advice they have sought. A decade ago, Amanda might have got a phone call from an operations or facilities manager who needed to know about recycling printer cartridges or paper. Now it's the board that often wants guidance on how to implement a well-resourced sustainability strategy.

A firm's selected client list might be visible on its website and can also give you an insight into its values. Corporate law firms have come under increasing pressure to cease working with clients embedded in fossil fuel activities. That's not a debate I'm going to have here, but the more green clients a firm works with, the more it works with green clients – call it a virtuous circle.

What's also good to know about law firms is that they have an unusual structure. Partners own the firm, but the managing partner rotates every few years. One sustainability visionary may be replaced with a less enthusiastic champion. As with all support services, my advice is to do a two- or three-year audit. If a company did align with your values but is now not delivering on its green pitch, you can decide if you want to continue the partnership.

When engaging with a law firm for the first time, there are a few basic questions you can ask:

- ⚪ Do you have an environmental and/or sustainability policy? Can I see it?
- ⚪ What is your policy on working with fossil fuel companies?
- ⚪ What is your carbon footprint and what are your targets to reduce it?
- ⚪ Have you set targets for reducing emissions based on your operations, for example, travel?
- ⚪ Do you have a paper-light policy and how do you manage paper and printer waste?
- ⚪ Are you a member of the LSA?
- ⚪ Do you have any green accreditation?

Employing a sustainable accountant

Despite the existence of the Legal Sustainability Alliance, unfortunately there is no equivalent sustainability membership network in the UK that covers accountancy. Nor is there any tailored green accreditation for accountants, although the charity Accounting for Sustainability reports that accountants are downloading resources on how to make their businesses greener – showing that, at the very least, there is an interest.

When approaching an accountant, similar questions to those posed to a lawyer also apply:

- ⚪ Do you have an environmental and/or sustainability policy? Can I see it?

⊘ What is your carbon footprint and what are your targets to reduce it?

Employing a sustainable cleaning and waste management service

Support services also include cleaning services, and you may need to hire a company yourself, or, if you operate from a shared office space, you can ask questions of the facilities manager.

Questions you should ask of a cleaning company can include:

⊘ Do the cleaners have an environmental and/or sustainability policy? (This would cover whether the company uses environmentally friendly cleaning products.)

⊘ Do they use reusable cleaning technology, such as reusable mop-heads?

⊘ Are the cleaners being paid in line with the National Living Wage?

Cleaning also feeds into waste management so if you employ a company to collect waste, there are certain criteria this support service must follow. Waste companies must have a waste carrier licence, so do check. Also, be aware that you may have the best in-house recycling system in place, but once it leaves your site you have no control. The main question you should ask of a waste company is:

⊘ How do you manage and track your waste? Can I see documentation?

People first . . . in a nutshell

People are everything in a business and if you get it right you will attract great people, develop and reward them, and ultimately retain them for longer. A progressive business should be looking to a diverse and inclusive workforce that values people as people, not just employees. Not only is this good for business, but increasing evidence shows that this positively impacts on meeting a business's environmental targets. When it comes to stamping out discrimination you should be proactive in your approach and encourage people to bring their true selves and values to work. You should also, where possible, assist them in their lives, not only their jobs.

Quick wins

- ○ Create a framework around how you want to handle relationships. Build in regular time to reflect on whether you are behaving in the way you say.
- ○ Measure everything so you understand your people and how best to support them.
- ○ Think about how you are going to work with contractors or consultants and create a policy.
- ○ Do the same around how you will work with permanent employees.
- ○ Understand diversity and inclusion in its widest sense and think about how you are going to build without gates.

- Check your job adverts do not feature language that excludes marginalised groups.
- Devise a mechanism to screen out names, gender and educational establishments from people involved in shortlisting and interview.
- Shortlist and interview with two people and build diversity into this mix.
- Create standardised applications and interview processes so all your candidates are applying from a level playing field.
- Understand that some applicants will need extra help. Let them know that they can ask, and that you will reasonably fulfil their request.
- Think about how you can celebrate and reward employees in a low-cost and on-brand way.
- Look to aligning with like-minded and sustainable support services, such as lawyers and accountants.

Moving up a gear

- Carry out regular employee and customer surveys to highlight where you are doing well and areas to improve.
- Build an atmosphere of psychological safety through strategy and training.
- Train your employees to get to a place of Radical Candor, as outlined by Kim Scott, to further build psychological safety.

- Offer added value to your employees through low-cost soft services such as a health and wellbeing app or a way to manage their finances.
- Step up your reward programme with financial and non-financial rewards based on job performance and the company's own sustainability goals.

Going for it

- Take the next steps to being a full disability-confident employer.
- Bring in outside speakers to help employees understand discriminatory behaviours, then hold regular meetings to discuss how employees can become proactively anti-discriminatory through micro-inclusions.
- Build in regular reviews to understand if and where your processes fail to attract a diverse workforce and how you can more meaningfully support people through the talent pipeline.
- Analyse employee churn to see whether it is healthy and in what better ways you could retain employees. Use anonymous surveys to receive honest feedback.
- Create regular time to reflect back on everything you do to make sure you aren't just talking the talk, but also walking the walk. And do talk to other business leaders to find out what they are doing.
- Become part of a support group, or set one up, where leaders debate how they can improve all aspects of their people practices.

Chapter 6
Finance and Investment

There's nothing more soul-destroying than sitting in a meeting with an investor a fraction of your age who spends the time shaking his head, then cutting you dead with a polite but firm 'no-way José' to your pitch. Yet that's exactly where I found myself in the early stages of Good Energy. Initially, the venture had been financed by a green fund from Germany and then, when it went bust, by high net-worth individuals in the business. We'd grown to 3,000 customers, but to drive forward the business and our purpose I needed to raise at least half a million more. I cringe now at how young and inexperienced I was. There's an art to attracting investment, and I hadn't learned the ropes. Pitches I've witnessed since are inspiring, and are often delivered with a flamboyant flourish. But I didn't have that confidence back then. I was brutally realistic and, with hindsight, a bit pedestrian in my analysis of where the business would be in three or five years' time. Also, at a time when climate denial was the norm, selling a proposition whereby customers were going to pay more to be part of a renewable revolution wasn't impressing any venture capitalist who was well versed in withering looks. After a while, it felt like all the colour was leeching out of me.

The Green Start-Up

Unsure of how many more knock-backs I could take, I had a light-bulb moment. The core idea behind Good Energy was democratisation of the energy market – so why couldn't I democratise finance too? After all, I'd often talked to customers who repeatedly wanted to invest in the business. Might they help us achieve greater impact? One investment document, a mass mail-out to our customers, and some anxiously chewed fingernails later, and we watched as 600 offers flooded in – a crowdfunding debut before crowdfunding was ever a thing. Of course, since then internet platforms have replaced the mass mail-out and crowdfunding is a common concept. Moreover, a whole new landscape of financing has developed for businesses of all shapes and sizes.

But before you skip off imagining a magic money tree spreading seeds of growth on your start-up, let's take a reality check. Start-ups face real challenges raising capital and no one wants to amass crippling debt at an early stage. Finance becomes one of the most difficult aspects of any business, not least because you have to wear many hats. You need to be a good marketer to sell your proposition; your business plan and financials need to stack up too. And it's only as you prove your worth that a greater choice of help will be open to you. Then, you need to understand who to approach and know the implications of each form of investment. And to top it all, there's always risk involved.

In this chapter, we'll examine the several different stages of funding and the variety of routes you can take. Of course, things may not happen in a typical sequence. You may have a chance meeting with a venture capitalist early on who chimes with your mission and can offer you expertise you cannot resist. Or you may go down the route that most start-ups do, which is to plough your time and effort in, harnessing the support of a close network before growing the business with outside help.

But if you want your business to be there for the long haul, you will need to be profitable and, since you're on a higher mission, you'll want to invest those profits to deliver on your purpose. So we'll also be looking at who you might want your business to invest in, namely through a pension scheme if you are in a position to offer one. Where you and your employees put their hard-earned cash is becoming a pressing issue and provides another lever in shaping a greener, better and fairer world.

Sweat equity

Starting any entrepreneurial business is an exciting but haphazard process. Remember that feeling of jumping off a cliff I described in the introduction to this book? Getting to the surface without drowning is a hard task and you'll find that much of your time and effort will be spent paddling to stay afloat. This might involve juggling a part-time job while you bring your idea to life, or living off savings or credit cards (not advised!). It could also mean living at home with your family, or – if you are a homeowner – remortgaging to free up some cash.

As well as the financial contortions you'll do, there is the mental and physical effort needed in the first few months, even years: the sweat equity. At the simplest level this could be your time spent writing a business plan, approaching partners, or building a website. More complicatedly, you may be developing a product or an app or testing a prototype. Sweat equity compensates for your immediate lack of cash which, in the fullness of time, you'll want rewarded back with when the company becomes profitable. But sweat equity is as valuable as cash equity, so all this time and effort should be logged and a value attached to it, as ultimately this will be part of the calculation of the value of the company when you do receive funding.

Depending on your proposition, you may also need to use the expertise of advisors, contractors or employees but, again, you may not yet be at a stage where you can pay them a salary. This becomes a way of developing the business faster when there's no immediate cash flow. If you are in a position to pay people then it may only be on the understanding that it is a subsistence salary, but that you will want to reward their valued contribution with a fair and legally binding commitment to be enjoyed later on. This sweat equity is usually paid back in a share allocation that places them equal to cash equity investors, or share options that can be bought for an agreed price and sold at a later date.

While sweat equity sounds very collaborative, if you are entering a sweat equity agreement with an outside employee, it will be money well spent to engage a lawyer to help you in this process as there are some risks attached. For example:

○ To allocate sweat equity, you must have a company structure in place, as agreements can't be used for certain types of business set-ups, such as partnership structures or sole trader operations.

○ You'll need to decide how much equity you want to give to an employee which will require a company valuation to determine the value of each share. You'll also need to decide how to structure the agreement. You may put in place a tiered structure whereby a person delivers a part of the job before they are granted equity, or shares may be granted incrementally. And you'll want to include a termination clause if either party wants to exit.

⊘ Check where you stand on employment law. Depending on the status of your worker, such as whether they are an employee or a contractor, you may have to, at the very least, pay minimum wage and this will also carry tax implications.

⊘ You may need sweat equity workers to sign up to a shareholder agreement which includes how decisions are made, how disputes are handled and what happens when a shareholder exits the business.

Friends and family funding

Other than your blood, sweat and very likely some tears, it's typical that your initial round of funding will come from friends and family. These are people closest to you, or perhaps a trusted network you've amassed along the way.

At this stage, you're asking people to support your venture, so try not to get too hung up on whether these people share exactly your values. The chances are they know you, like and trust you, believe in your idea, and want you to do well, so this should give you some peace of mind. Besides, you can make sure that early investors don't have a controlling stake in your business and so you will always remain in the driving seat.

But before you cast the net for initial funding, it's a really good idea to become registered with the government's Seed Enterprise Investment Scheme (SEIS). Under the scheme, a business can receive up to £150,000 through investments and it encourages investment into start-ups by giving private equity investors initial 50% tax relief on investments up to £100,000 per tax year, and no capital gains tax exposure on the investment after three years. It also means that if your business folds, an investor can offset losses against tax. Follow-on government schemes, such as the Enterprise Investment Scheme (EIS), are available when you start to grow and we'll discuss these later in the section on venture capital. Details of full criteria are available on the UK government website, but to qualify, your business needs to be:

- Less than two years old
- Established in the UK
- With no more than £200,000 in gross assets
- With fewer than 25 employees

Building an investment deck

To get friends and family on board, it's likely you will have put together an initial business plan, but when you move up a gear and look beyond this circle, you'll need a polished investment deck. This shouldn't be a regurgitation of your plan. Instead, it needs to be compelling presentation. If you are in the innovation space, my advice is to strip out the vast amounts of technical detail you may be tempted to include. Tell your story simply. Once you have worked through this thoroughly, you can build on it and repurpose the information for different audiences as you progress and cast your net, including all the technical information you want in the annexes.

As an eco-entrepreneur, you need to be very clear about your purpose. If you have already achieved B Corp status then your higher purpose will already be baked into your articles, or you may have done that independently. However, if you haven't got to that stage, then I suggest you shout about your purpose from the rooftops. Whenever I talked to potential investors, I pulled no punches in saying we existed to help solve the climate emergency. That was my way of saying to people: 'This is our reason for being. If you are investing in us, this is exactly what we are going to do.'

Your investment deck should reinforce this purpose, and while there's no right or wrong way to structure a deck, there are some pointers to ensure you are an irresistible proposition:

- Be clear about the problem you are trying to solve, and why your product or service provides a solution. Back this up with facts and statistics. For example, if you are a business trying to solve the problem of plastic pollution in the ocean, make investors aware of its serious impact by drilling into the numbers.
- Be open about who you are and what your values are, but remind them why this is a benefit for the business in attracting talent and taking the proposition out to market.
- Tell your story in a concise and compelling way. Remember that investors who love your offer will also look at you. Are you engaging? Credible? Determined? Can you take the business forward? And who else is in the team? They will want to see how any team works together.
- Outline where your revenue is going to come from. You may be manufacturing or selling a physical product, or you may be a tech platform. Is your revenue going to come from sales? Subscriptions? Advertising? IP licensing? Or a hybrid model?
- Have you tested your product or service, and how? This information will show an investor that you've done your homework, that there is a market for your offer and that its design and usability has been worked on.

○ List your competitors and say what gap your product or service fills. Spell out the reasons why you are better, and why you will succeed.

○ List who you have partnered with. Perhaps you have already received some sponsorship, grant funding, endorsement, or support in kind from another businessperson, brand, charity or organisation. This will show that others have confidence in your idea and want to come on board.

○ Detail how you are going to reach your market. This could be through existing partnerships or through advertising, communications and PR, or through a combination of these.

○ How you will scale your business is also key to future investment. So many entrepreneurs, particularly in the innovation space, have a great idea but have grown through grants or subsidies. Moving to a scalable, commercial proposition requires a different mindset and make no mistake that investors are looking for a return. Avoid saying things like, 'This space is really hot' or 'The market is ginormous'. Outlining future markets, plus the sources for your information and their potential size will reinforce your scalability and your credibility.

○ Build in a comprehensive profit and loss statement with realistic projections. Start-ups are a risk for investors and they need reassurance about how their money will be used and their future return.

Crowdfunding

Once you've worked on honing your proposition, you can use parts of it elsewhere to bring in different kinds of investments such as on crowdfunding platforms. Given that I haven't crowdfunded since I sat stuffing envelopes more than 20 years ago, I wanted to know how platforms had evolved in the intervening years and how entrepreneurs can best use them.

Karl Harder is a founder and managing director of the investment platform Abundance. His business crowdfunds long-term investors for large-scale green infrastructure projects and was the first UK platform to be regulated by the Financial Services Authority. It operates a niche in the crowdfunding space by behaving more like a bank offering interest-based lending. 'Crowdfunding has matured over the years,' says Karl. 'When we started it didn't really exist and we called it "democratic finance". Now there's lots of different types of crowdfunding offering capital for almost every type of venture and stage of the business life cycle from start-up to growth capital. Start-ups are probably going to be looking at equity crowdfunding, where people invest money and in return receive shares in the company. Your investors will not be looking for a regular cash return as such, but they will want their share to grow in value as you grow, and the ecosystem for this type of crowdfunding is very well established.'

While crowdfunding may sound like a fast, easy way to raise cash, it is not as straightforward as people think. That said, used smartly it can help you on your journey. The main platforms for crowdfunding are Seedrs and Crowdcube who have a sizeable number of investors interested in green-for-profit projects. Meanwhile, Triodos Crowdfunding and Ethex are exclusively purpose-led platforms. However, don't assume that if you post up your proposition . . . hey presto, it will get funded. 'If you're accepted, the investment community will be looking at what support a project has already attracted,' says Karl, 'so demonstrating friends and family support is key. Typically, equity crowdfunding is very useful for topping up the last 10 to 15%, getting the project over the line and raising a little bit extra, but entrepreneurs should see it as part of a solution, not the whole solution.'

While equity platforms typically have large communities of investors, the average investment amount tends to be low, primarily due to the higher risk of providing equity to early-stage projects. Furthermore, because the companies raising capital on the platform are diverse in nature, not all investors will back every project. More specialist platforms such as Abundance will tend to have smaller communities, but investor participation and average investment rates tend to be higher as the investor community is focused on funding a specific section of the market. In all cases, your business, and whatever project you're seeking finance for, will be rigorously assessed before it is offered through the platform. In the former, you won't always need a proven track record to crowdfund against, but it will put you at an advantage to have:

- ⊘ A compelling story, especially if you are a technology company. While an EV charging or a heat pump initiative might make sense in the public's consciousness, more experimental ideas will feel remote in investors' minds, so you need to communicate your proposition well.
- ⊘ An existing network that you can reach out to, who understand your proposition and perhaps have already supported the initial phases. These people may support you again or help spread the word. For equity crowdfunding you should know where at least 75% of your target amount is coming from before launching on the platform. For debt financing it is less important to have your own network to provide the capital.

⟋ The energy to build up interest before your product launches on the platform, and a follow-on. In other words, don't assume your work ends when your project appears. Getting it over the line will require marketing.

⟋ Protection over your idea, such as a patent or copyright. By opening it up to others you risk someone in your space stealing your concept.

If crowdfunding fits what you want to achieve, and you can make it work, then it has some great advantages. By putting your project out there, it's a good way to test public reaction to it, and even get feedback. Investors also get updated on your progress, which is a good way to promote your brand through their networks. However, if ultimately you don't reach your target the money will be returned and could cause you some reputation damage.

Innovation funding

For those working in the innovation space, which includes environmental innovation, there are numerous grants available to help bring your idea to life. Some funds are broad, such as the Smart Grant Scheme or the Open Innovation Fund, but there are hundreds of ring-fenced grants focused around certain technologies. While grant funding is a great way to kick-start a project or take it to the next level, it is always important to have a commercial sensibility focused on scaling up.

When I spoke to Simon Buckley from the Knowledge Transfer Network (KTN), an organisation that connects ideas to funding pots and expertise as part of the national innovation agency Innovate UK, he reiterated this point: 'People shouldn't apply for grants unless they plan to fulfil their projects without that money. If you spend your life in a perpetual cycle of winning grant money, you end up changing your business model to fulfil the contract, rather than following your commercial nose.'

That said, not every project is suitable for grants, and you may be advised to seek private equity as an alternative. And connecting with organisations like KTN isn't always about money. Another role it fulfils is to link entrepreneurs with commercial partners and also the academic community to share expertise. Such connections may turn out more powerful than funding, but they can also work in parallel. Once connected the parties may apply for funding together, de-risking collaboration while ideas are in their infancy. 'Engaging in the process allows you to work with some big organisations who may not want to take financial risk normally,' says Simon. 'Because the project is grant funded, it has support and is monitored and this gives them confidence to help shape it and be a part of it.' He adds that this often results in an accelerated time to market as the work is well resourced.

Free at the point of use, KTN also helps businesses through the application process through its open-source Good Application Guide and face-to-face service. According to Simon, there are four main pitfalls to look out for when applying for funding, and after a bid is successful:

- Applications contain a set of bullet-pointed questions. Many applicants become engrossed in technical detail and only submit partial answers. 'You don't need to employ grant writers,' advises Simon. 'Just read the guidance carefully and answer exactly what you are being asked.'
- Remember that while some grants will fund 100% of your project, typically a fund will support 70%, so it's likely you'll have to make

up the 30% shortfall. Funds are usually allocated on a one- to two-year funding cycle.

⊘ You are expected to pay for everything up front and claim back, so you'll need to ensure adequate cash flow in your business to cover the time lag.

⊘ Finally, every offer comes with an ongoing monitoring process. While funding will have been allocated around a tight scope, slippage and change occurs, so keep the monitoring officer informed to lock in support.

While many funding pots are UK-based, European funding is still open to UK businesses through the Horizon fund, although it is unclear for how long this fund will continue due to the UK leaving the EU. Plus, there are periodic bilateral funding calls from further afield. I highly recommend an initial call with KTN to help you understand whether your idea is a goer, which funds may be applicable to you, and how to put together a successful application.

Community Development Finance Institutions (CDFIs)

You may also look to the micro-finance market. Community Development Finance Institutions, otherwise known as CDFIs, are locally rooted social enterprises that can get finance to businesses who don't qualify for loans from traditional banks, who tend to be more risk averse. In 2021, the CDFI network lent £263 million to 6,000 start-ups, businesses and social enterprises across the UK, and it is estimated that for every £1 lent by a CDFI to a business, £7 is added to the economy.

Typically, the CDFI micro-finance market comprises of existing micro and small businesses that are commercially viable but cannot access the finance they need, either because of their size or their lack of security. Because CDFIs usually take a more flexible stance on security and access risk differently than high-street lenders, they also use their local understanding and relationship-building approach with clients.

There is significant diversity in the way that CDFIs operate in terms of size of funds and their different customer bases. However, borrowing usually starts at a lower amount than national lenders (some lenders start at £100), and CDFIs often operate in areas where there is poverty, unemployment and social isolation. The Finding Finance website, run by Responsible Finance, is a good place to start searching for a CDFI in your area.

Other alternative micro-finance organisations include the Prince's Trust. It runs a free enterprise programme which includes training and mentoring and workshops offering advice on business planning, marketing, sales, budgeting and tax. The organisation also works alongside the Start-Up Loans Company, who are part of the government-accredited British Business Bank, to offer low-interest personal loans up to £25,000 repayable across one to five years. A loan also comes with 12 months of free mentoring. To complement this loan scheme, the British Business Bank has partnered with The Open University to offer a fantastic range of free resources to start-ups, including: guides on entrepreneurship; finance and accounting; environmental decision-making; project management and leadership, to name a few.

Approaching a bank

The first contact you'll have with a bank will be to set up a business account. When it comes to deciding on which bank, your choice will be limited mainly to the high-street providers or challenger banks.

Finance and Investment

While none of these banks claim to be ethical, the Co-operative Bank have a partially ethical remit, as do app-based banks such as Monzo and Revolut. That said, there are encouraging signs that traditional banks are nudging into this space, although meaningful change is still a long way off. NatWest's Group Chief Executive Officer Alison Rose made a commitment to people, planet and purpose in the run-up to COP26 when she announced that the bank aimed to make £100 billion of climate and sustainable funding available by 2025. Less clear is the bank's commitment to phasing out its own investments in fossil fuels. In a 2021 report by Reclaim Finance, campaigners highlighted the bank's investments in coal giant Glencore and European company RWE, who currently has no real plan to shut down its coal assets by 2030, the date NatWest has said it will stop financing coal. Although, at the time of writing, full details of NatWest's policy are also to be clarified. Elsewhere on the high street, Barclays and HSBC are also leading providers of fossil fuel finance.

My advice is that in the early stages, do not overly worry about which bank you opt for. You must have a current account to trade, so choose the best bank for your needs and if it has an ethical stance then this is a bonus. Setting up an account normally takes between six and eight weeks, so make sure it's on your early to-do list.

At some point, you may have surplus cash to deposit into a business savings account. Here, you can be more discerning as the bank will use your money for loans to people, other banks or businesses, and it's worth asking who and what the bank invests in and what their sustainability goals are. Among some of the UK's largest banks, tax avoidance is also commonplace, so do check the bank pays its fair share. The Bank Green website also offers a quick-check tool that gives a rough overview of a bank's rating on sustainability.

As for the account itself, business savings accounts work just like personal savings accounts in that the more restrictive the account the higher the interest rate. There will also be variables such as a minimum balance and how to access funds, so again choose what suits your needs.

There are some ethical providers, such as Charity Bank, Starling Bank and Unity Trust Bank, although since the Covid-19 pandemic some business accounts have been axed, so ask for up-to-date information. Over and above holding business accounts, you may need a loan to boost your cash flow, grow your business, refurbish your building, buy new assets or pay for a one-off cost. Most banks will not consider early start-ups as you'll have no proven track record or credit history, but may look at a business after it has been trading for at least three years. The ethical front runner in this space is Triodos Bank. Established in 1980, it refuses to invest money in fossil fuels, mining, arctic drilling, fracking, arms and military technology. It publishes the details of investments it makes on its website to ensure transparency.

Triodos's relationship manager Simon Crichton stresses the importance of purpose-led in everything the bank considers. 'The mission and purpose of any business approaching us always comes first,' he explains, 'but if the financials don't stack up we won't lend. That said, if you went to a high-street bank it would be focused solely on financials and not concerned with purpose. As we understand the unique space we can take a slightly different view.'

In fact, Triodos concentrate their loans to the top 30% of purpose-led businesses. This will include 10% of exemplary businesses already doing good stuff well, but also businesses with a plan to transition. 'No business is perfect,' Simon adds, 'but a business may come to us wanting to significantly improve their sustainability credentials. Then, we base our decision around mitigating factors.'

Whatever the business, the bank would look for at least two years of historic accounts and two years of projected accounts before carrying out a risk assessment. The account's relationship manager would also look in depth at how any loan would be spent. Written into the lending covenant would be an agreement to use the money for the purpose intended.

'We put together an impact prism of whatever activity a business wants to pursue which maps to the UN sustainability goals,' says Simon. 'We then review this every year. If we lent a business money for a fleet of electric vehicles and it ended up buying diesel, then this would contravene the agreement and in a worst-case scenario be a potential default.'

However, a more likely scenario is that Triodos would work alongside a business to help it achieve its goals over time. By signposting it to other organisations who can offer advice, it might then build in an improvement strategy into any agreement, such as making energy-saving changes or working towards a goal to pay employees a living wage.

With all bank loans you'll have to weigh up risk, and there are typically two types of business loans:

- *Secured loans*: Most business loans will be secured against collateral. This could be your work premises or the nuts and bolts of your business such as machinery, but it could also be your house. The advantages of secured loans are that you are more likely to be able to borrow more and repayment terms can be favourable.
- *Unsecured loans*: Unsecured business loans aren't linked to your business assets, but you may have to provide a personal guarantee. This means if your business fails to make the repayments, you will need

to repay the loan from your personal funds. These are typically more expensive than secured loans, but quicker to obtain.

Before you consider a loan, be confident about your ability to repay the amount and try to build in contingency to cover any unforeseen problems. In my view, a person worrying about whether they are going to lose their home is unable to make good business decisions, and this is more so if you are a female entrepreneur with a family.

Also, depending on whether you take a secured or unsecured loan, banks may ask you to give regular reports and accounts so don't forget to factor in this time needed to collate these on a regular basis.

Personal loans and credit

Founders of start-ups unable to meet lending criteria from a bank may be tempted to take out a personal loan to cover costs. Some lenders will not allow a personal loan to be used for business purposes, or will demand immediate repayment if this is found. If a bank does allow this, you would not need to produce business accounts or projections to qualify; rather it would be based on your ability to repay.

Personally, I would guard against this. Unlike a business loan where the business is liable should you default, you will be personally liable. While a personal loan isn't secured against any collateral, such as a house, you will incur ongoing charges if you fail to make the repayments. This could result in a county court judgement (CCJ) or, in a worst-case scenario, bankruptcy which will affect your ability to act in the future as a director of a business. It will also severely affect your credit rating. Plus, a personal loan would not give you any of the access to ongoing support or a relationship manager that a business loan might.

Furthermore, while having a business credit card is a good idea, particularly for keeping a track of expenses and managing expenses, racking up unnecessary debt on credit is to be avoided. Typically credit cards have far higher interest rates and you could fall into the same repayment quagmire if you default on minimum monthly payments.

Do you need to grow?

There may come a time when you want to grow and how fast you do this will depend on what you want to achieve. Bringing in outside investment will accelerate growth a lot faster than if you steadily grow profit and invest it back into the business.

In traditional business, growth happens to maximise shareholder return, but for the purpose-led business there are other factors to weigh up. There has been much discussion over the past few years about growth and whether it is even a good thing. At the forefront of this discourse is the analysis of Oxford economist Kate Raworth, whose book *Doughnut Economics* maps out what a sustainable, universally beneficial economy would look like. She describes how, from the 1930s, businesses have become addicted to growth. As a way of keeping tax low, governments are addicted to it too, while consumers are also hooked through mass consumerism. It is exactly this untrammelled growth that has given rise to the conscious consumer.

In business, growing sales, greater market share and soaring profit are all measures of success, yet it is exactly this model that has destabilised the planet and causes regular economic resets. Even 'green' growth cannot be decoupled from resource use. Yet, in Raworth's revised model, economics meets nature: growth occurs, but at a certain point continual growth threatens the stability of society. Maturity in nature is about sustainability, and is regenerative and distributive by design.

You might wonder what this has to do with finance, and the answer is everything. In the 2020s, the narrative prevails that growth is the only trajectory. So, should a purpose-led business automatically set its sights on growth? I would say this depends on its core purpose and the impact it wants to achieve.

Here's how I think about growth: until a business is profitable, it is always going to need to grow. How it grows will depend on which investment route it takes. Up until the point of profitability it won't be able to balance the needs of the four cohorts instrumental in it fulfilling its reason for being. Here are those four groups:

Customers: Without customers or users you don't have a business, but once you are profitable the pricing of your product or service will depend on how you allocate profit. At certain points you may decide to reduce cost to the consumer to deliver further on your purpose. Or perhaps you will want to reward new customers, loyal customers, or everyone who buys from you.

Employees: Your people are the lifeblood of your business. While they need to be paid – and how much you pay will depend on market rate, statutory rate and the type of talent you want to attract – you may also want to reward them with a bonus. How much you allocate to that bonus, and how often, will also depend on how you balance profit share between your four cohorts.

Shareholders: This group receives their return in two key forms: there can be an ongoing dividend payment, which is a small income that reflects the cost of that investment. Or there's capital gain, which happens either by selling shares or the whole company being sold. If you want to invest in the business and grow it, then investors may be happy to hang on and wait for a sale and receive their return on the increased value of the business. However, if you are not looking for a short-term exit – rather that you want to run it and grow it and deliver more impact – return on capital in the form of a dividend will pay them regularly.

Future holders: This last group is instrumental on your achieving impact long term. I call these future holders because these are your customers, people and shareholders of the next generation. These are our kids and grandchildren. These are the people for whom you want to make a difference, and so the question becomes: how much profit do you invest to achieve this? This could be as simple as shifting behaviour by offering a green travel-to-work bonus, or as complicated as building a state-of-the-art factory that revolutionises a production process.

Once you are profitable, you'll find that you are constantly juggling the needs of these four groups, and this will inform if and how you grow. In addition, to have an industry voice and challenge the status quo, you'll often need to be of a certain size. Certainly, I struggled to get a foot in the door in government in the early days of Good Energy, and in the end only managed to because the sector needed the combination of challenger brand and female representation on the board of the industry body. For other businesses, there will be different drivers, such as being a market leader or innovator. Only you will know when you have reached a tipping point where your business has achieved the intended impact. For me, when thinking about growth there are three questions to ask:

○ Do I need to grow, and why?

○ If I don't grow, can I still deliver on purpose and satisfy my stakeholders?

○ If I grow, how much bigger do I need to be, to deliver on my purpose?

If you do decide on a further growth path, then how big and how fast you grow will inform who you bring in as an investor. On the one hand, an investor may be content with injecting money into a certain project and receiving a regular return. On the other, if you engage a venture capitalist, then you will automatically be on a fast growth trajectory and pulling away from this will be far harder. Sketch out a preference journey of your ideal way to raise cash, but be aware that if none becomes available you may be forced to go down an imperfect route. Know what will be a manageable compromise for you, rather than one you may come to regret.

Venture capital

If you do want to grow quickly and perhaps attract a certain set of expertise to help you, then private equity in the form of venture capital is a route to consider. In most cases, a business won't start out seeking venture capital; rather it will engage a venture capitalist (VC) fund once it has customers and market traction. In my view, many purpose-led entrepreneurs go into these arrangements not being fully aware of what they've signed up to. Venture capitalists can bring a lot to a business, but you may also have to give up a certain amount too.

Venture capitalists are looking to invest in businesses with high growth potential in return for a large equity stake. The fund is typically raised through limited partnerships which comprises a group of investors, who may be high net-worth individuals, pension funds, insurance companies and so on. As a general rule of thumb, a fund will have an average ten-year horizon and want a return of three times the amount invested over a three- to five-year investment period. After that the fund will want to exit and return profit to its investors. While involved in your business, a VC is likely to have a seat on your board and bring others on to it, as well as perhaps management. Automatically, this gives VCs an amount of control and they will want to influence the business's direction.

For this reason, finding the right venture capitalist is paramount, but equally important is the protection of your purpose through your articles of association. Without this, you could find yourself on a rapid growth trajectory that moves you from your purpose in ways that you cannot reconcile. Certainly, some business leaders believe venture capital and purpose-led businesses are thoroughly incompatible because meaningful long-term change typically needs patient capital.

If you are interested in raising venture capital, look around for who is investing in purpose-driven companies and who is specifically investing in your sector. VCs want companies with a large potential market and a unique product or service, but they also look to industries they are familiar with. When pitching to a VC:

○ Target the right fund and find out as much as you can about them. You may want a VC to bring value-added help, but not all VCs deliver on that promise. A VC who wants to nurture your company is an asset. A VC who just funds you may be a disappointment if you wanted expertise.

◌ Prepare well for your pitch, and make sure your purpose-driven mission and vision are woven throughout. VCs, in particular, are interested in your financial projection, but aligned VCs will want a plan to achieve impact.

Similar to the SEIS scheme I mentioned earlier, there are follow-on government-backed schemes to help you attract venture capital and they are well worth registering with. Full details are available on the HMRC website. There are several caveats to each scheme, but the two applicable are:

◌ The *Enterprise Investment Scheme* (EIS) offers investors tax relief to up to 30%. Businesses can raise up to £5 million each year with a £12 million ceiling over a company lifetime.

◌ The *Venture Capital Trust* (VCT) scheme also gives up to 30% tax relief on investments by funds approved by HMRC on investments of up to £200,000.

One of the most active investor growth capital funds, which focuses specifically on supporting small- and medium-sized businesses in the UK and Ireland, is the British Growth Fund (BGF), and I will declare an interest because I sit on their advisory board on climate change.

The fund looks to help founders and management teams, has a patient outlook on investments, and only takes a minority shareholding. There are some fantastic examples of founder-led stories on their website.

Public markets

It's unlikely you will list your company on the public markets early on, but a few years down the line it's something you may want to consider.

It is worth mentioning here because, again, the earlier you can protect your business purpose the better. Before you list, there are certain contractual mechanisms you can put in place to help manage your shareholders. However, when you raise capital this way, it opens you up to a different investment pool. While you can exclude certain investors from the initial allocation – for example, market makers there to buy and sell quickly with no commitment to purpose – you cannot ultimately control who investors sell shares on to in the open market. Embedding purpose legally through certification such as B Corp will give you a solid underpinning and an ongoing focus when control lessens.

As of 2022, digital consultancy Kin + Carta is the only UK B Corp company listed on the stock exchange and this also throws up regulatory questions of how an independently assessed accreditation sits within the complex framework of ESG and CSR reporting required for listed companies. Yet, as more businesses become a force for good, this will undoubtedly evolve with more clarity. Watch this space . . .

Who your business invests in

Lastly, let's explore how companies themselves invest, as defined through a pension scheme. Although pension schemes would normally sit in a discussion around employee benefits, I want to talk about it here because, in a nutshell, pensions are investments in other businesses and, depending on which funds you attach yourself to, you can be part of a growing movement of pension positiveness.

I believe pension power is the next big shift both individuals and businesses will engage in. Launched in 2020, the Make My Money Matter campaign is now calling on industry to respond to growing consumer demand by making green pensions the default for savers. It highlights that £1.7 trillion remains in schemes that have yet to align with the Paris Climate Agreement and is asking individuals to put pressure on their employers and providers to ensure their money is not causing harm to people and planet.

Undoubtedly, pensions are complicated, and 'ethical pensions' are still in their infancy, so as an employer it's unlikely you'll find an ideal solution. Whereas more bespoke private pensions are available, company pensions still tend to be 'off the shelf' and harder to tailor. However, in the same way that you can sketch out a preference list for the types of investment you want to attract, you can do exactly the same with pensions. Be prepared for compromises, but one step forward is better than doing nothing.

To help simplify pensions, let's hear from Rowan Harding, financial planner at Path Financial, the only positive impact pension advice service operating in the UK. The business is three years old and, due to increased demand, it launched a company advisory arm this year. This in itself is encouraging and shows interest in ethical pension literacy.

'Currently there are a few providers offering limited ethical investment choices,' says Rowan, 'but when you look under the bonnet of these, they are a lighter shade of green. However, the more pressure is put on providers from employees and employers, then the more change can happen.'

Since 2012 employers have been required by law to automatically enrol employees in a pension scheme if they are above the age of 22 and earning more than £10,000. Some businesses also choose to offer the scheme to those below that age. If you are new to setting up a pension scheme, you are in the perfect position to seek out ethical options. If you already have a scheme in place, then you may want to embed switching into your plans. There's a great step-by-step guide to setting up an employer pension on The Pension Regulator's website. Typically available to you will be two types of pension:

- ○ *A defined benefit pension* guarantees an amount to the employee, such as a final salary pension scheme.
- ○ *A defined contribution pension* is more common, and while it allows flexibility and is often portable, there's no standard guarantee to the amount paid out. It's most likely you'll offer this type of scheme.

'Within the defined contribution space,' explains Rowan, 'there are lots of providers and different products, such as stakeholder pensions, group personal pensions and occupational pensions, all of which do the same job but with slightly different set-ups. You may also decide to have a separate pension scheme for directors and employees.'

A good point to note is that your choice of provider may be limited depending on your payroll system, which must be compatible with a provider's underpinning technology. So, if you want to go greener, find out what system your top preference aligns with.

But what actually is an ethical pension? The answer is complex, not least because every person's idea of 'ethical' differs. Many so-called ethical funds will strip out the obvious nasties: fossil fuels, mining, or arms and military spending, but below that it gets murky. Rowan describes it as 'fifty shades of green'. At the light-green end, a pension fund may invest in a company that scores highly on one part of the ESG matrix – for example, governance but not social and environmental. Surprisingly, tobacco companies tick this box, yet their inclusion in any ethical scheme is clear greenwashing. At the darker green of the scale, funds are choosier.

Path Financial aim to direct people to funds positively impacting the world. Yet, even within this space there are compromises, warns Rowan. 'You may be against animal testing for cosmetics, but funds might invest in pharmaceuticals using animal testing for life-saving drugs,' she says.

If you're a small enough business, you can discuss such red lines with colleagues – you can ask questions about what you must divest from and what you are comfortable investing in. When you start to grow, this engagement becomes harder. As a decision-maker or a senior team, always return to your core purpose and work from there. Moreover, take specialist pension advice from an aligned business who use aligned and thorough investment analysts to guide you in making the right choice for your company and your employees.

Finance and investment . . . in a nutshell

Financing your business is one of the hardest aspects you will tackle and it's worth taking the time to consider options carefully. Aside from your own time and effort you will need investment to grow. There are lots of options out there. Used smartly, micro-finance and crowdfunding are a good option but do understand how to use these to your advantage. Building a polished investment deck will be essential and if you engage a bank or a venture capitalist then be aware of the benefits and drawbacks. Lastly, take control of who you invest in by looking into ethical pension schemes if and when you have employees.

Quick wins

- ⊘ Open a current account so you can start trading.
- ⊘ Use sweat equity to get your business up and running.
- ⊘ Register with the SEIS scheme to attract low-risk investment.
- ⊘ Engage friends and family in an initial stage of funding.
- ⊘ Put together a compelling investment deck.
- ⊘ Boost your business with innovation funding or grants or business collaboration.

Moving up a gear

- ⊘ Open a savings account with an ethical bank.
- ⊘ Sketch out an investment preference journey.
- ⊘ Engage with investors who will finance you at an earlier stage that can include micro-finance lenders.
- ⊘ Crowdfund to help finance your next stage of growth or improvement.

Going for it

- ⊘ Register with government venture capital schemes.
- ⊘ Look to grow your business by approaching venture capitalists.
- ⊘ Apply for a business bank loan.
- ⊘ Offer your employees an ethical group pension.
- ⊘ List on the public markets.

Chapter 7
The Supply Chain

In the linear economy, 'stuff' is made when materials are extracted from the ground and goods are designed to be thrown away. Entrepreneur Mart Drake-Knight, who co-founded fashion label Rapanui with his brother Rob when they were teenagers, calls it 'a giant conveyor belt that you attach growth to'. Maximising profit depends on how quickly the conveyor belt runs. In other words, how quickly you deplete natural resources and increase waste.

I first met Mart some years ago and, whenever we speak, it's his focus on problem-solving that inspires me. It's a brave entrepreneur who takes the most commonly worn fashion item – a T-shirt – and ends up remodelling its entire system of production. Yet that's exactly what Rapanui has done, even if the duo didn't quite set out to start the revolution.

'We thought it would be stupid easy to make a T-shirt made out of organic cotton and design it so that it didn't end up in landfill,' says Mart. Given that, globally, three out of five T-shirts bought today are thrown in the bin within 12 months – that's a dumper truck going to landfill every single second – Rapanui's quest made perfect sense, but they didn't factor in the systemic obstacles that would litter their journey. 'When we tried to do the right thing, the business got hammered by cost,' explains Mart. 'We thought that if we used organic and renewable materials then good things would come from it. But it was like a punch in the face. Using a single-use plastic mailer bag was ten times cheaper than a sustainable alternative. Polluting is rewarded.'

To solve the problem, Mart and Rob went back to the drawing board. Engineers by background, they started out in a shed with a laptop and £200 and an idea that they could produce T-shirts on demand. 'Whenever we received an order, we cycled to the local printer, had the design printed and then posted it,' laughs Mart. Waste was minimal even when they expanded to batches because they wrote computer software to forecast accurately. But it was when they wanted to scale up further that they hit their biggest obstacle. Most suppliers had fashioned their factories around mass production, an inherently wasteful system because it creates surplus.

'Factories have been made a certain way to produce more and more,' says Mart, 'and we were asking them to rebuild their infrastructure to fulfil a single-item order. The model of the factory itself became the problem.' The solution became to build their own factory, reducing waste by increasing efficiency through technology and developing their own print-on-demand software, now trademarked as Teemill. Every T-shirt the company makes can also be sent back at the end of its life and remade, creating circularity and reducing waste and cost further.

Today, savings pay for recyclable organic material and a living wage to its suppliers, including those abroad. 'We didn't want to pretend to fix a problem,' says Mart, 'we actually wanted to fix it and to do that you have to come at it from a different angle. If you don't get into understanding where stuff comes from, then it's like mopping a floor with the tap still running.'

But Rapanui's story isn't just about stuff. It's about people. One decision at one end of a supply chain can have a profound impact on the other. You only need to remember the devastating collapse of the Rana Plaza building in Dhaka in 2013, which housed five garment factories, killing at least 1,132 people, to understand the human cost of mass production. Many of the businesses there were working for global chains.

When it comes to the supply chain we can either tinker around the edges or we can look to reinvent, and in this chapter we'll re-imagine the supply chain for the twenty-first century by exploring Mart's journey in fashion and through two other unique start-ups in technology and food. We touched on supply chain and the circular economy in Chapter 2 when we covered refurbishing office space and recycling waste, but here we'll focus on designing precisely for the circular economy, right down to product packaging, plus look at tackling human rights abuses such as child labour. Brands who don't change their practices will find themselves obsolete. A new wave of entrepreneurs have the perfect opportunity to disrupt, with technology and a supercharged dose of determination. As Mart rightly says: 'We're all guilty of thinking of the economy as a rigid rule set that is applied to us, as if we have no say in it. We need to look at who makes the rules and understand that the economy isn't something that happens to us. It is us.'

Purpose meets product

If you do sell or make a product then traditional manufacturing places tremendous stress on people and planet, although these stresses fall differently. For example, a disposable plastic coffee cup will eat up carbon in its materials, its manufacturing and its throwaway status. Its stress will always be weighted towards being harmful for the environment.

Yet, when it comes to coffee production itself, the stress, while partially environmental, will affect plantation workers who harvest beans for little pay and operate in poor working conditions.

Working through the UN development goals, you can see how supply chains form an ecosystem where each highlighted issue interconnects and impacts on the other. Once your eyes are open, you cannot see products in silos any more. Increased production of throwaway items to satisfy mass consumerism leads to degradation of land, water and biodiversity, and what follows also has a catastrophic effect on people's lives: increased inequality, resource conflict and ultimately a question of survival. Taking a holistic product view requires a different mindset and it can feel overwhelming, but there are actions you can take to work through it:

- Study the supply chain of your product in detail and understand where the main stresses are in your chain when mapped to the UN goals. Does your product lean towards a risk of child labour? Is it weighted towards environmental degradation? Create a hierarchy of areas to focus on.
- Know that these will not be solved overnight. Be realistic and understand that you will develop solutions over time as you hit obstacles that feel unaligned with your purpose. What you can't do today, you should aim to solve through an iterative process of review and improvement.

In the future, advanced automation will give many businesses more tools to aid these goals. Among them: innovative software; artificial intelligence; the Internet of Things, which brings the power of the internet and connectivity to the world of physical objects. Meanwhile, blockchain – a digital ledger which started life in the world of crypto-currency and records transaction data shared across multiple parties – is being developed to enhance supply-chain traceability.

Blockchain technology, in particular, allows multiple parties in the supply chain to record transactions in a verifiable and secure way that is also tamperproof. This means participants can record information such as price, date, location, quality, certification or other relevant information, thereby increasing visibility and compliance, particularly when it comes to outsourced manufacturing.

Certainly, we can already see how technology is transforming businesses to enhance positive societal and environmental impact, but in the circular economy, whereby goods are designed with reuse, repair and recycle embedded from the outset (and which I'll expand on throughout this chapter), it is also collaboration that is becoming vital. For me, innovation is all about solving the climate crisis together. It's about connectivity of thought as well as process. On this journey, disciplines such as engineering and science cross-fertilise with fashion and design; twenty-first-century technology meets revivals of historical production practices, and so on. But progress starts with a commitment to pursue authenticity.

Commit to traceability

Whatever product your business makes or sells, it is likely that you will start out by outsourcing some or all of its manufacture. In the fullness of time, you may bring some aspects, or all of a production process, in-house. Up until then you will be reliant on building partnerships with other businesses. These may be close to home, but they could easily be abroad. Moreover, the raw materials you need are likely to be sourced from several places. In smaller operations, material origin is easier to trace as supply chains are shorter, but as soon as you start to scale up then traceability becomes more complex.

When thinking about supply chain traceability it's important to look beyond first-tier suppliers towards sub-tier suppliers. As I've said, supply chains are ecosystems, and if you are committing to traceability then you must consider the broader chain, which will include your supplier's supplier and your customer's customer. According to a 2021 white paper by consultants Bain and the World Economic Forum, digital traceability such as the previously mentioned blockchain will be the new supply chain revolution to advance sustainability; yet with platforms still in their infancy, businesses making the shift from linear to circular chains will need to drill down into every aspect of the product path to understand where efficiencies and improvements can be made and suppliers can be supported to make shifts in their own processes.

One observation Mart had when reflecting on Rapanui's story struck me as so important: suppliers make bad choices about people and planet because they are constantly leaned on. 'If a linear system exerts pressure and maximises cost then the foundation is broken,' he says. 'You end up forever saying one thing to suppliers, then pulling the rug out from under their feet. Yet if people are given the opportunity to make positive change, then they generally make positive decisions.' For Rapanui it's been cost reduction coupled with increased productivity that has allowed it to work smartly with suppliers, and it has achieved this by addressing the problem of waste.

Innovate with technology

When a business isn't flush with resources it is forced to innovate. For this reason, it is Mart's opinion that sustainable start-ups work better without investment for as long as possible. When Rapanui opened its first factory in 2014, this led it to focus on waste reduction – the point at which the environment and the economy work in harmony. 'Less waste is better for the environment, for the business and for the customer. At the end of that rainbow is the circular economy,' says Mart. Reduction can come in many forms, as we've already seen: whether it's reducing emissions by using less heat, or recovering heat, using less electricity or powering your operations with renewables.

Meanwhile, in the supply chain, automation can be the main driver of reduction. While not a panacea, it has allowed entrepreneurs to re-imagine processes only possible through technological advancement. The beauty of the internet is that there are tutorials available on anything from software programming to lean manufacturing techniques allowing non-specialists to log on and learn a new skill. This open-source, peer-to-peer knowledge exchange couldn't have happened in any other age.

Moreover, it is often simple technology that can optimise any operation. Rapanui's T-shirts are made by outside suppliers, but its printing facilities are located in a warehouse on the Isle of Wight. As well as its print-on-demand platform, there are robots that pick and drop T-shirts on to conveyor belts, built with parts from eBay or scrap sites. There's a 3D printer producing spare parts. All the machines communicate via Raspberry Pis, basic computers typically used to teach children. 'We've reduced labour time per T-shirt by 30%,' Mart tells me. 'There are no keyboards or mice or printers for paper "pick lists". Workstations are also reduced to a minimum as processes have become automated, designed out or digitised.'

A good way to think about how to optimise any production cycle is to identify where waste is created and this will differ depending on each product and process. The circular economy distinguishes between technical cycles which make, recover and restore products such as white goods, and biological cycles, such as in food production, which regenerate living systems such as soil or the oceans. There are overlaps between the two, and a great place to understand these in more depth is through the resources available at the Ellen Macarthur Foundation website. We'll explore the biological cycle further in the latter half of this chapter, but for technical cycles it's important to consider:

○ *Raw materials*: The circular economy requires you to understand material choices throughout the product life cycle, not as an afterthought. This means choosing safer materials from the outset that cause less harm, or none, to the environment or to human health and can be reused without polluting. To work out a way to redesign a product, you should find out what its current materials are and their chemical composition. You can do this by engaging people in your supply chain, but you may need to enlist specialist help. There's also a great free online tool called MaterialWise that can help you identify harmful materials.

○ *The design process*: Once you have created an inventory of materials for your product you need to focus on how your product is used by the consumer and what features are essential. From there you can begin to find safer alternatives that don't diminish the design function or quality of the item. This could range from changing the materials or chemicals the product is made from, or by redesigning the product by stripping out components that are unnecessary or more complex than needed. For some businesses, creating a completely new material may be an option. For example, the fashion company Camira has teamed up with the Seaqual Initiative to create a fabric that is made from plastic debris found in the ocean. A leather substitute, so-called vegan leather, can also now be made from pineapple leaves, cork or apple peels, and there are many other inspiring examples worldwide.

○ *Product afterlife*: Because in the circular economy, waste and pollution are prevented or minimised from the outset, this overcomes the need for excess recycling which in itself won't be enough to tackle the mountain of waste we produce. Instead, reuse, repair and remanufacture should sit above in the waste hierarchy, and it is only through planning at the material and design stage where environmental impact can be reduced.

○ *The manufacturing process*: reducing waste in the making process relies on employing methods of lean manufacturing applicable to your business. This can range from addressing over-production which leads to surplus, or mapping a better workflow to eliminate unnecessary steps in the process or reducing distances between processes. You may also simplify the equipment being used as unnecessarily complex machinery can lead to overproduction to recover cost. Or you can address waste in energy usage and transportation. Much of the waste in manufacturing can be stripped out using technology, but there is also human waste to consider. Processes that cause injuries or are hazardous to health lead to increased sickness and, in some scenarios, loss of life.

Meet and collaborate with your supply chain

To help you understand how waste relates to your business, one of the best things you can do is go out and meet any potential supply chain.

According to Mart, some of the best conversations he's had have been on a roadside chatting to organic cotton growers or by visiting a factory. 'One of the dangerous sustainability mind-funks we've got ourselves into,' he says, 'is going and looking at people making things. That's not what sustainability is. It's going to factories to have conversations. Go there. Ask, learn, listen, study how the product is made and work back to the design table.'

There are good reasons for doing this. Understanding exactly how your product will be made, and the pressures on the suppliers manufacturing it, will allow you to deconstruct both the product and the process to work out a way to make it better from a natural and human resource perspective.

For example, if you need many suppliers to fulfil different design elements of your product, look at ways to simplify it. For Mart, this has meant sourcing a raw material that is most compatible with nature – organic cotton. Why? Because traditional cotton production is environmentally punishing: cotton plants are ordinarily treated with pesticides. They also need vast amounts of water to grow – 2,700 litres is needed to produce enough cotton for the average T-shirt. Then, once the cotton is transported from its country of origin, it is transformed into spinning threads or yarns. From there, the slivers of yarn are milled into coarse fabric before being treated with heat and chemicals to soften the material before it is dyed. This process in itself can release toxic waste water and harmful chemicals into the air.

And T-shirts are rarely made from 100% cotton. They are stretchy and breathable. They have labels and fixtures, and it's likely that cotton will make up only a tiny amount of this. The material will be a minestrone of other synthetic fibres such as polyester, nylon and acrylic.

The Supply Chain

The chemical dyes that are used to colour the cloth also contain plastics. If this sounds complicated, the same story applies to almost any other product we buy from clothing to cars, perhaps the only difference being the rate at which we throw clothing away.

Meeting your potential supply chain will also give you an early indication of who you want to align yourself to. In Mart's case, he visited several factories which he instinctively knew were sweat shops. The same will be true of other industries, but there are some tactics you can use to get under the skin of any potential partner:

- Ask to be shown around the areas where your product or component of your product will be manufactured. Any business proud of its working conditions and way of operating will be happy to oblige.
- Ask to talk to employees and notice whether you are allowed to do this independently or under supervision. Employees are usually honest and if they are being leaned on by an employer, you will sense this.
- Talk through the manufacturing process. In a linear model, a supplier will be under pressure to produce volume at the cheapest price. When you strip out waste in your business you can make cost savings that can allow you to collaborate on a new way of working. If you have devised an alternative model, invite willing suppliers to come with you on the journey. Incentivise them with fair payment and share knowledge and expertise.
- Map your supply chain and know exactly what is being subcontracted. This is especially true if you scale up. When you become removed from your suppliers you risk losing control of the provenance of your product, so employ reputable third-party auditors to assess your chain.

Child labour, slave labour and poor working conditions

By mapping out the inherent negative leanings in your supply chain, you will also have some ideas of the types of issues to look out for, and we should focus briefly on a problem that affects many areas of production: that of child labour, slave labour and human trafficking. Indeed, social fairness forms another important pillar of the circular economy. The International Labour Organization (ILO) estimates that the number of children in child labour stands at 168 million globally, and the problem is anticipated to get worse. It's inhuman to think that another 9 million children will become child labourers by the end of 2022, according to the UN.

Currently, most child labour occurs in mining in gold, coal, diamonds, stone and salt mines. Agriculture, especially coffee and cocoa production, is also a hotspot alongside industries like fashion that rely on low-skilled labour. But there are also industries that help our green economy, such as electric car battery production, that rely on lithium-ion where underage labour is widespread or slave labour and trafficked labour is commonplace.

As I've mentioned, as a start-up you have the advantage of a shorter, traceable chain and the opportunity to know your suppliers. But if your product relies on certain raw materials and components supplied through indirect parties, you are already removed. If you suddenly grow, you may have to diversify your supply chain if your current suppliers lack the capacity to scale up. Market shocks and supply issues, the likes of which we've seen since Brexit and the war in Ukraine, can also force you to source materials quickly and from suppliers you lack a relationship with.

In an ideal world, corporates and larger companies with budgets to pay workers a living wage and departments dedicated to investigating supply chain integrity must lead the way and raise standards, but this is not happening fast enough. Currently a company with a turnover of more than £36 million is required to report annually on what steps it has taken to ensure that child labour, slavery and human trafficking are not part of its supply chain but, in my view, businesses of all sizes must and can take action:

- If you are in a business where there is a high risk of child labour in the supply chain, assume it does exist and start with the mindset that you must do all you can to ensure full traceability.
- Most child labour occurs because of poor pay, meaning families must send children to work. Reduce cost elsewhere and prioritise fair pay. For example, Rapanui pay workers more than the minimum wage in each geographical area.
- When sourcing suppliers look for marks of verification, but don't rely on these. Some verification will mean that a company has only committed to a minimum set of standards. Be sure to align with only the most reputable standards in your industry.
- Put in place procedures for due diligence and monitoring on child labour. This could include a supplier code of conduct, and follow-ups that include regular audits carried out by reputable third parties.
- Discuss from the outset with a supplier what commitment it has to human rights, and ask for documentation. If you deal with an indirect supplier, ask for proof that the commitment links to everyone it sources from.
- Include in every supplier contract a clause that requires strict adherence to your zero-tolerance stance on child labour or other human

rights abuses. Make clear that a breach of that clause may result in a hefty penalty or termination of the agreement.

⊘ Create awareness through training for anyone in your company involved in procurement or any part of the supply chain. Refer back to your purpose and values and explain what bad practice would mean for your reputation.

⊘ Even though you may not be legally required to produce a statement on child labour, slavery or human trafficking, agree to voluntarily produce one. This will focus the business on regular monitoring, but can also be used as a statement to provide assurance to customers and investors.

First life, second life and beyond

As we've seen, in the circular world you need to have an eye on a product's entire life cycle as this will dictate the materials you use, plus the product's design and manufacture. But if I turn to the tech world where planned obsolescence – the act of introducing an artificial lifespan into a product to generate repeat sales – is commonplace, then it is easy to see how unsustainable our current model is. Indeed, the practice has sparked a global 'Right to Repair' movement with campaigners demanding that everyone has the right to fix the products they own, and this includes changing regulations on how products are made in the first place. This shows the focus shifting from responsible recycling by the consumer to responsible design by the manufacturers – parts that can be made available for repair and designs that build in afterlife use.

Take the humble battery, for example. Established recycling routes for traditional lead-acid batteries exist, whether these are domestic batteries, battery packs from laptops and mobile phones, car batteries, or batteries for off-grid solar power, but not for newer types of batteries such as lithium-ion.

Even the recycling route of a lead-acid battery is far from ideal. Battery recycling itself is CO_2 intensive. Currently, goods such as fertiliser and detergent are made from a battery's sulphuric acid which is neutralised and turned into sodium sulphate. The lead and the polypropylene plastic coating are separated and turned into new batteries or used in other industrial products. Thanks to recycling, lead is now barely mined, but therein lies another problem. The lead-acid battery recycling market is now so large that there's been a proliferation of unregulated smelters in the informal economy. In India, parts of Africa and South America, it is child workers who often pay the ultimate price. Given lead is a highly poisonous material, exposure to it can affect almost every organ in the body. Worst of all is its effect on cognitive development, and high levels have been linked to behavioural problems, learning deficits and low IQ.

When it comes to the alternative lithium-ion battery, it has seen a boom in use as the world shifts to electric vehicles, and that number is only set to rise. According to the International Energy Agency, there could be 125 million electric vehicles on the road by 2030 compared to around 3 million as of 2022. Clearly this has a knock-on effect when it comes to the safety of people mining raw materials, but it also raises serious questions about afterlife use. Thankfully, there are some pioneering businesses re-imagining environmentally harmful items with little or no wastage as the end goal. It's a problem Birmingham-based Aceleron has focused in on – a start-up reinventing the lithium-ion battery for the circular economy.

'A lot of batteries coming on to the market are not designed with the long term in mind,' Aceleron's co-founder, Dr Amrit Chandan, told me. 'Yet, if you're driving down the road and something goes wrong with your car, you don't scrap the vehicle. You get it repaired. It doesn't make sense to scrap such a high-value asset, yet we do it all the time with lithium-ion'. Terrifyingly, he likens the future mountain of lithium waste as being as destructive as fossil fuels. 'By 2040 we will be able to fill Wembley Stadium 50 times over with batteries every single year, yet there is still a lot of life left in them if they were redesigned,' he says.

With circularity as its guiding principle, Aceleron has lifted the lid on the battery. It has deconstructed it, removed the resins and bonded materials that make lithium-ion recycling time-consuming and expensive. Instead, its core is held together by compression. Each part is removable and modular, meaning batteries can be dissembled and its cells and electronics serviced or upgraded easily. And its flagship battery has four times the life cycle of a traditional lead-acid equivalent. As for end of life, the business is working on repurposing battery cells to power two- and three-wheeler vehicles servicing last-mile logistics. It is also collaborating with global giant Total to repurpose waste lithium-ion material from solar cells into repairable and upgradable battery packs. This will bring power to off-grid communities in northern and eastern Africa. And once established fresh routes for used materials are found, this cumulatively tips the balance and changes the status quo.

Of course, not everything can be redesigned and we still need to find kinder, more efficient ways to recycle the goods we have already made. But start-ups do have a unique vantage point of working from a zero sum and there are some initial tips to help you build in afterlife from day one.

○ Understand the circular flows in your product. Break it down and think about where each component will go at the end of its life.

○ If your product is technical, explore questions such as how to extend the life of the product – this could be by designing in easy refurbishment, or designing so that, when returned to the manufacturer, components can be replaced. Also look at the materials you choose and decide whether some of these can be returned to a raw natural state.

○ If your product is biological, for example a foodstuff, break down every component to see what can be extracted for other applications, or how the product can return nutrients back to the earth after use.

○ For inspiration look to nature. Nature is intrinsically more holistic and circular and you may solve a design challenge through biomimicry.

○ Make a list of all the possibles for your product and then look at the potential obstacles to it being circular. Remember collaboration can really help to deepen your understanding and move forward. It can also help you discover new end-of-life use for component parts, and be mindful that these applications may be outside of the industry you work in.

Education, collaboration and the circular economy

Establishing best practice in every part of your business will give you a solid foundation and this will become more important if you start to educate and collaborate in your space. Helping others improve their supply chain is not only becoming key to improving sustainable practices across the board, but also enhancing the everyday perception of sustainability.

Arguably, items such as clothing are an easier sell in the circular economy. A T-shirt made from a used T-shirt is relatively unobjectionable. But when it comes to other goods, in particular food and drink, education must run alongside a supply chain revolution. This education is threefold:

- ⊘ The consumer must be helped to reorient its perception of waste – after all, food circularity is not, as many people assume, reusing bin scrapings!
- ⊘ Manufacturers also need help understanding how they can better use their surplus – the waste generated in their own production processes.
- ⊘ Lastly, businesses working in the same space can address waste through collaborative learning.

One innovative business that exemplifies all three of these goals is craft beer brewer Toast Ale, a social enterprise business which has circularity baked into its product to help solve the problem of over-supply of bread. Launched in 2016, it was one of the earliest food-waste businesses, manufacturing beer made with 25% bread, 75% barley alongside water, yeast and hops. Although no mainstream brewer uses bread today, records dating back to 4000 BC show that the Sumer people in Mesopotamia used fermented bread to make the drink.

When I spoke with Toast's co-founder and chief operating officer Louisa Ziane, she explained that bread is one of the most commonly wasted foods in the UK at home and commercially – a whopping 20 million slices of it per day. 'We source our bread from bakeries who are incentivised to over-produce for many reasons, including the risk that if a bakery undersupplied a supermarket, it would be fined,' she says.

The statistics are remarkable. If all UK beer was produced using 10% surplus bread, it would halve the amount of UK bread waste, thereby contributing to achieving the UN's Sustainable Development Goal. Moreover, the malt used to make beer has a high carbon footprint because of the land needed to grow barley and the energy and water used during the malting process. Toast cut emissions by using a quarter less malt, replaced by the surplus loaves.

One of Toast's suppliers is a sandwich factory in Bognor Regis. Now, through partnership, it reduces surplus into small croutons via an air-drying process. These croutons then get transported to Toast's brewers in Broadstairs where bread is added to the mix.

'When people think about waste food,' says Louisa, 'they automatically assume it's lower quality and should be cheaper, or it's about using up unwanted leftovers. For this reason, we hardly use the word "waste" in our marketing. (Louisa adds that Toast prefers to use the word 'surplus'.) 'As much as this is about creating a more sustainable beer, it's about educating people about why food is wasted and that so much of what is wasted is actually fresh, nutritious and delicious.'

Toast undertakes annual reviews of its supply chain to pinpoint where tweaks can be made, such as nudging customers towards canned beer instead of glass bottles. While highly recyclable (though less recycled than aluminium cans in the UK), glass bottles are responsible for more CO_2 in transportation given their weight and less compact size and shape. A change of brewers in 2021 now allows canning to happen on site, eliminating a journey to a separate facility.

When it comes to educating other breweries, Toast has collaborated with several to produce a series of experimental beers, in the process introducing others to the use of surplus bread. These collaboration beers also give Toast the opportunity to try out new recipes and experiment with making its supply chain more sustainable. 'Last year, we sourced organic oats and malts for a beer to support more regenerative farming methods,' says Louisa. 'However, there was limited availability and problems with crop pests from one supplier so we had to work hard to overcome these problems.'

Moreover, Toast's primary business has now sparked demand for a secondary venture, called Companion, whereby it will supply processed surplus bread to other breweries to encourage its use. 'We can overcome the challenges of sourcing surplus bread,' explains Louisa, 'managing food safety and tracking for allergens, and processing bread for efficient use in brewing. We work with large bakeries to also simplify logistics, but want to expand operations to support more bakeries to reduce waste. Ultimately, we will get Companion to a point where it is cost-competitive with malt and has a lower carbon footprint.'

Improving the entire supply chain

It's one thing to brew beer, but Toast has also set out to change the food production system. Another collaboration has been with the charity Soil Heroes who support farmers wanting to transition to regenerative farming practices. Rather than purchasing offsets for its carbon emissions, Toast funds farmers in the UK to implement practices that will improve biodiversity and water retention, as well as carbon sequestration. These kinds of regenerative practices include using fewer chemicals, no tilling and planting cover crops to protect, and rebuilding soil health and structure. However, it takes time, and financial support to farmers is needed as yield reduces in the period when the soil starts to recover.

Then there's the spent grains, a by-product of the brewing process, which go to local farms for animal feed. 'This avoids waste of the grains, but it also reduces the demand for crops grown specifically for animal feed including soya from deforested land,' says Louisa. Some bakeries send bread direct to animal feed producers, although there is an allowance for 0.15% of plastic that Toast doesn't allow. This plastic enters animals' digestive systems and can end up in the soil, and ultimately rivers and the ocean through animal faeces. Even the once discarded hops are composted at the end of their life.

And lastly, as Toast contract brews, it collaborates with its brewer to manage its footprint. Toast is currently working to gather more data on its energy use to see what can be improved and where renewable power can be sourced. In fact, only 3% of Toast's carbon footprint is from Toast's own business, whereas the remaining 97% comes from suppliers who produce and distribute its beer.

This multifaceted approach to keeping surplus out of the waste stream takes circularity way beyond a redistributive food model. Its ripple effect is felt through every touchpoint. And through analysis, goal setting and collaboration, it is constantly driving change.

Packaging

One of the most overlooked aspects of any product cycle is its end packaging. This could be an envelope, paper wrapping, a bag, a box or a plastic food container, but it could easily be a can or a bottle. We're going to concentrate on plastics and paper here and explore paper more in the next chapter, but depending on your business do investigate what the recycling rates are for whatever material you want to use and plan accordingly. So many environmentally friendly businesses do themselves a disservice when they package in unsustainable ways.

I had my eyes opened to sustainable packaging many years ago when Good Energy began working with a graphic designer called Matt Hocking – a human encyclopaedia on the subject! He runs Leap, a graphic design agency dedicated to sustainable materials and printing methods and the first B Corp design business in the UK. Matt began his mission to understand sustainability when he worked with the Eden Project in Cornwall back in the early 2000s, and he's still teaching businesses how to improve their impact. Here, he passes on some ideas and tips.

'Use packaging that can tell a story,' he says. 'It's such an important point, because the paper, cardboard or inks you choose can all feed into your brand marketing.' Matt has worked with a marine charity using paper made from algae from fragile marine environments. 'It was more expensive, but the charity understood the value of that story and came on board,' he says, adding that once businesses become early adopters of seemingly alternative materials, others do follow.

When thinking about packaging there are several points to consider:

○ Don't view packaging as waste. See it as a part of your product that can feed the circular economy. Find out how the packaging is being made and whether the company you source it from is also thinking sustainably. For example, one company called Cyclus not only make recycled paper, but also recycle their production residue into box packaging and worm food. There is biodegradable and even edible packaging made from seaweed on the market!

○ Unlike plastic, paper can be recycled around six times, so always opt for paper over plastics in the recycling hierarchy. Also, make sure the material you are sourcing is 100% recycled, rather than just a percentage.

○ The standard of recycled paper and packaging has improved over the past decade so never think you are compromising on quality by using it. On cost, don't assume recycled materials will be more expensive. Some specialist materials will be, but generally recycled paper is competitive with virgin paper.

○ If you are sourcing plastic packaging, say for a food product, make sure it is recycled and recyclable. For example, many black plastic trays end up in landfill, not because they can't be recycled, but because the black pigment used to make them is invisible to most machines that sort recycling. For this reason, use clear plastic. Also, make sure every part of the packaging is recyclable. For example, certain bottle tops can't be.

○ Make sure the inks you are using on the packaging are sustainable. Traditional inks contain heavy metals which are petroleum-based. These are not only hazardous to the environment, but also for workers. Look for printers using vegetable-based inks such as soy or water-based inks, although even the pigments in these inks are derived from fossil fuels. The newest entrant to the market, and the most sustainable, is algae ink that uses algae cells for pigments and is recyclable and compostable.

The end consumer

Finally, a brief section on the end consumer. When you start to think through all the stages in a product's life cycle where waste is created, whether it's fashion or food or electronics, our old linear system of production starts to look even more absurd. How did we get to the point where we fly food all across the world only to discard it? Or companies design so many models of a phone just to keep us buying? While it would be easy to blame manufacturers, we must also look to ourselves to understand that a symbiotic relationship between production and desire has also fed mass consumerism. While clever marketing creates a push, we also create a pull.

I am conscious that throughout any discussion of the supply chain, we as end consumers must also address our consumption habits. Do we need so many clothes? Must we replace our mobile phones every two years? But even this analysis can be reductive. The pace of technological advancement in the last few decades has also moved underlying technologies on apace. The Internet of Things, whereby your smartphone can talk to your washing machine or central heating, wouldn't exist without it. There are faster processors, cameras and so on. Arguably without this we couldn't start to design out waste through technology.

What I consider to be the most important message that you can give to the consumer is that your product is built to last, therefore it must be cared for, repaired and then reused. For some products, the 'buy me once' message will help the consumer understand why your product may be more expensive, but it will also foster a deeper connection with it and your brand. It also puts onus on you to create a product of quality, that you are not willing to compromise on. If suitable, offer a time guarantee to show your product is long-lasting. Also, always check back with your manufacturers to ensure they continue to have the same commitment to quality that you do.

Another option is to offer your product as a service. In the circular economy, satisfaction doesn't always equate to ownership. If you are producing an item that can be shared or rented, then this will also give consumers access to products and remove the need to manufacture more.

The supply chain . . . in a nutshell

Reinventing products for the circular economy requires you to consider the whole life cycle of a product, from the materials the product uses to its manufacture and afterlife use right down to its product packaging. The economy distinguishes between technical processes and biological processes, and you will need to map according to your business to understand how you can redesign for sustainability. Reducing wastage through automation will also create cost savings to pass on to your customers or make the business more sustainable in other ways. Always remember the human cost of production and take every step to eliminate human rights abuses such as child labour.

Quick wins

- Understand your product, how it is currently made and how it could be made. Have circularity at the front of your mind.
- Visit suppliers and ask questions of their processes.

- Study where waste occurs in your business and understand how technology and lean manufacturing can impact your product journey.
- Work back to the design table and see where simplicity can be built in and waste reduced.
- Understand your manufacturing process from a CO_2 perspective and also look to where you can bring emissions down or recycle energy.
- Study your supply chain from a human perspective – what are the inherent negative leanings and how can you try to mitigate these?
- Don't forget about the packaging of your product and investigate sustainable alternatives.

Moving up a gear

- Align yourself with suppliers who share your values or are willing to work alongside you to share alternative production models.
- Look to where you can reduce cost in your business through automation.
- Put in place steps to help eradicate issues such as child labour by using any cost savings to pay a living wage in any geographical location.
- Build in commitments to human rights into your supplier contracts. If abuses are found, look to how you can work with suppliers to improve, but terminate if the problem persists.

- Employ reputable third-party auditors applicable to your industry.
- Work to educate the consumer about waste through your product.

Going for it

- Build in regular reviews of your supply chain and set constant goals for improvement.
- Investigate ways in which all the component parts of your product might be reused and think beyond your own industry to find solutions.
- Be a collaborative leader in your field and share knowledge and expertise to raise standards in your industry.

Chapter 8
Reaching Your Market

Rebels in wellies: that's how I describe the individual generators who became some of Good Energy's first customers. When I think of rebels I think of people like Margarita Neri of Mexican Zapatista fame, or Esraa Abdel Fattah, the leader of the Facebook revolution in Egypt, but our renewable warriors were – and still are – heroic. Take Matthew Oxenham: 20 years ago his ex-Navy father Ken abseiled with a friend down the gorge he owned in his hometown of Lynmouth in Devon. Their mission was to build a small-scale hydro-electric power station. The piping they used to lay along the riverbed was strapped to their backs – a hare-brained scheme back then, but one that has stood the test of time.

The two men constructed the station almost single-handedly to capture the power of the West Lyn River. Today, it generates 1.5 million kWh of clean energy every year. Glen Lyn Gorge is now run by Matthew and his family, and when I went to interview him for a series I filmed called *Meet the Generators*, it took me back to those early days when I knocked on people's doors and marvelled at their solar sites or wind turbines or hydropower stations. Since then, we've seen many more community energy projects spring up and this has unlocked not just individual stories but stories of villages and towns, schools and businesses, all with a stake in how they are powered.

Luke Bigwood, marketing and external affairs director at Good Energy, likens all the people a business touches to a 'treasure trove', and it's a perfect description. It is their stories that will feed into a great marketing strategy. It builds from the old adage that people buy people. You, your customers, your suppliers, your employees and anyone your business touches are a precious asset to be nurtured in narrative form.

But marketing isn't only about knowing what makes a powerful narrative. It's about understanding why, when and how to create it. The story actually begins with your story: from the time you set up your company and give it purpose. Your product or service launch adds another layer and, when you have customers and create campaigns, it develops further as you build brand sentience. In this omni-channel world, each piece of communication must be tailored to the medium, whether that's a thought-leadership piece highlighted on LinkedIn or a funny picture posted on Instagram.

In this chapter, we'll examine the basics of marketing and signposting ways to start building and reinforcing your purpose-led brand as you grow. If you are green at heart there are also some questions to ask about how you communicate and the impact this might have on people and planet. Do you doorstep customers to attract more business? Or plan a large-scale leaflet drop? Should you rationalise your data usage to cut your carbon footprint? And how do you avoid being tempted into 'sparkling' the green, when not everything you do glitters? Finally, we'll focus in on how to build a successful campaign with an emotional heart across all traditional and digital mediums.

Who are you?

Choosing a name for your company is the first step in marketing it, but as I discovered in the early days of Good Energy it's not that simple. In our initial phase, we were an offshoot of a German company in need of a European-wide name: enter three branding agencies with different ideas. Etopia was the first name we wrestled with, but this was nixed when we searched online. To our dismay, in the early 2000s Etopia was an adult site advertising 'Asian Babes'! Next up was Energy Republic: tempting, but it sounded too campaigning and reminiscent of 'Banana Republic'. In the end, we settled on Unit[e] – it reflected our scientific thrust. Quite literally, it spelled out one unit of electricity.

Everything was going well until I did my first radio interview. As I was making the case for renewables, I realised that Unit[e] didn't translate – all listeners would hear was 'Unity'. Afterwards, if anyone wanted to search for us online, we'd be hard to find. Then, there was the problem of the square bracket. It was clumsy on a URL and it magnified the search problem. To top it all, the government's Defence, Science and Technology Laboratory at Porton Down used square brackets in its name (it still does), and soon we were facing legal action by the Ministry of Defence for using it in a marketing document (you might think they had better things to do!).

Six months in, we went back to the drawing board, but the name Good Energy wasn't born in a branding agency. Instead, it came to me after sharing a bottle of wine with a friend, Will Sankey, who had started the Good Shopping Guide. That was my light-bulb moment. We were an energy company doing good things: it was simple, you could spell it easily, it was memorable and it stuck.

Our name said what it was on the tin, but other brand names that work can also be unrelated to the industry they are in. Think of Octopus in the energy sector, Dove in the beauty space and so on. Some people use their own name or an aspirational place. Today, there are some edgy names out there – you don't want to be bland – but a name does need an emotional pull. Whatever you choose, remember that your name is going to carry everything you stand for, plus your marketing and publicity. While there's no magic formula, there are some dos and don'ts:

- Keep it simple. A name has to roll off the tongue, so after you've come up with several ideas repeat them out loud. Any name that's long or complicated won't be remembered. If you can, test your name out with sample customers, but avoid friends and family who may not give you the best, impartial feedback.

- You may want a brand name that immediately communicates your higher purpose. Don't force it if it doesn't work. Supporting straplines and surrounding marketing material can enhance that message, so concentrate on simple and memorable first.

- Have an eye on the future. A name that's gimmicky will last a short time, but you'll want longevity. It has to be focused yet flexible enough to allow your company to evolve without having to change it. Also think about how it can be added to other businesses or products if you expand.

- Consider how your name is going to translate to a website URL. Potential customers won't spend time looking for you. For this reason, using initials and non-alphabetic characters can be a disadvantage.

- Ask how your name is going to play out across all media channels. Is it going to translate from your website to social media platforms?

Or will it translate from the verbal to being searchable online? Might it be confused with another word when said out loud? And make sure it doesn't mean something rude or offensive in English or a foreign language.

- You must adhere to Companies House rules – for example, words or expressions that could imply a connection with a government department may be problematic, as we discovered to our cost! For a full list, study the government guidance on name incorporation.

- Search for your name online. Someone else may have registered it, trademarked it, patented it or it could link to a website you hadn't expected. As soon as you've finalised your name, register it on .co.uk and .com domains. And trademark it to protect it. The last thing you want is to be contacted by another business after you've spent money on a website and marketing material and be forced to change.

Know your customer

The secret of great marketing is to know your customer inside and out. To launch your business you will have done some initial research to know that there is a market for your product or service. This may have been a deep dive into your potential customer profile with a marketing agency, or it could be through a survey, or simply by talking to people.

Before I started Good Energy I embarked on a European-wide tour which included talking to renewables operators. I wanted to understand the 'secret sauce' in countries more advanced in renewables, like Austria and Germany, and what the perceived barriers might be. In fact, the message I got back was 'just do it'. I continued talking when I set up the company. Without search engines, social media or data analytics I went to events, festivals or anywhere I could connect with customers.

These days, marketing teams can reach far larger cohorts of people digitally and through a number of channels. 'Marketing is all about understanding people's motivations and there are now some sophisticated methods, such as tapping into thousands of social media conversations,' says Luke Bigwood at Good Energy, whose input I've asked for in this chapter. Having those direct conversations has certainly become easier but I still believe in the power of face-to-face. Having that initial conversation and keeping it going is so important as your business grows, because the knowledge you amass will automatically feed into any marketing strategy.

Quantitative research

It's most likely that, pre-launch, you'll engage in market research which will continue as you grow, add new services, expand a range or look to improve. Quantitative research usually takes the form of surveys, questionnaires or a poll and there are great online tools to help, such as Survey Monkey. To use these, you'll need an existing database of recipients and be GDPR compliant.

Early start-up questions may centre around whether people would use your product or service, how they might use it, what features are desirable and what other brands people are buying in your space. This will give you a sense of what your market is and how it behaves. Initially, you might want to direct your questions to a specific demographic, or sample population. After that, you may want to collect data over a longer time frame.

Quantitative research isn't just about people, it's also about understanding metrics such as peak periods. For example, winter isn't the season to hit the market with recyclable sunglasses, but research will help you understand the right time to launch and the best place to promote your brand coming into summer. Likewise, if you are an ethical food brand serving the takeaway market, knowing peak times of day for your product range will help you understand how and when to communicate.

Qualitative research

As you develop, deeper insight into your customer base and your business will create loyal, emotional connections. It's about understanding your customers' values, their psychological profiles, their perception of your brand. You are asking why people feel a certain way. This information can be gleaned from in-depth online surveys and engaging in online forums or communities, as well as analysing social media conversations.

In time you may find that face-to-face focus groups, or in-depth phone or video conferencing interviews, become more useful as you seek feedback on a new product launch, tailored campaign or marketing strategy.

Other innovative methods for qualitative research are also developing. Flashing up photographs of your product or service and getting respondents to record their emotions is one way of understanding brand impact. Hosting an event, for example if you are a food brand, and observing and listening to how customers react is another. What you are searching for is not only honest feedback, but insight that helps you understand your customers' lives, their aspirations and their desires. If you can, engage a reputable market research company to work alongside you who aligns with your values.

Listening in

It's likely you'll have a customer service element to your business. At first, this could just be you picking up a phone. Certainly, I've listened in to many customer service calls over the years. I wanted to know the areas we fell short on, or what people liked about us. Being purpose-led, callers often discussed wider issues such as questions on climate change and whether we planned to solve a particular problem. It showed customers bought into us because we were doing more than just selling power, and it helped us create content that resonated with our audience.

Today, it's easy to include a feedback form on your website. Personally, I still think the human element is needed, so following up with a phone-call to address the complaint or attending an event to address customers' queries, or to have a wider conversation, will reinforce that you are a brand who care. You will also learn so much about your customer along the way.

Building a visual brand

Building your brand continues with your look and feel, typically through your logo, colour palette and the design features you carry through to your website and literature. Often businesses start out thinking these aren't important. Yet, when you consider that an estimated 80% of human perception and learning is visual it does matter. Try to think of your brand as a personality. What traits does it possess? Is it bold, authoritative, fun or irreverent? These decisions will filter through to the visual and conversational tone you'll adopt.

All I remember in the first six months of Good Energy is poring over designs and colours and their meaning. From the beginning, we wanted to be inclusive, but trusted – a hard balance to strike. Although the company's logo has been refreshed over the years, we've never had to change the name which is often a time-consuming and expensive process. To get it right, there will be several visual aspects you'll have to consider:

○ *Impact*: Purpose-led brands want to be around for the long haul, so choose a logo that can be subtly adapted but has impact. A good place to start is by looking at other brands in your space. What's their feel? Are they comic? Romantic? Aspirational? At the very least you'll want to stand out from them, or you may want to disrupt the category entirely but don't be overly gimmicky.

○ *Font*: Font plays a critical role in conveying the emotion of your brand. Again, pinpoint your position in the market. Are you a new entrant answering an untapped need or a challenger brand? Who are your customers? What feeling do you want to elicit? Imagine an ethical financial advice service whose logo is written in playful Comic Sans. It's unlikely to inspire trust, which is exactly what a financial advisor must do. Likewise, a funky craft beer brand using a business-like font like Futura isn't going to send people rushing to the bar. Have a look at the variations within the six font classifications: Serif; Sans-serif; Slab-serif; script; handwritten; decorative – and narrow down your options from there.

Lastly, make sure the font is legible and can be read at a distance. You may also want to pair different fonts if you have a brand name and a subheading, so try out combinations. Play around with capital letters and lowercase depending on the tone you want to convey. Also, make sure your font works across all platforms including print, web and mobile. Some fonts are open-source and free, but others will need to be licensed, so do keep cost in mind.

○ *Colour*: In the same way that font expresses personality, colour adds to your voice. When Good Energy opted for yellow, there was no other energy brand sporting that colour, and it hasn't changed. We experimented with many palettes: blue was too businesslike, delivery and tech-focused. We pondered long and hard on green and red, but in the end decided they were too campaigning. Instead, yellow was optimistic, friendly, social and inclusive; perfect for our message that everybody is part of the answer to the climate crisis. Your main brand colour may be white, signifying purity; or hot pink for youth and boldness; or black for sophistication and elegance. You may also opt for a combination of colours.

Once you've found your primary colour you'll also need a palette of supporting colours. Remember that these will feature across many touchpoints including your logo, website, emails, social media, advertising, business cards, event banners and so on. After that, consistent use inspires trust, credibility and reinforces your identity so collate a set of brand guidelines and follow them. When deciding on impact, font and colour, ask yourself four questions:

- What are our brand goals? In other words, what does our business do for customers or users? Does it inform them? Help them enjoy life? Help them to help others, or something else?

- What is our higher purpose and can we communicate this through our design features such as font and colour?

- How do we want our customers to feel? Confident or happy or another emotion?

- What are our brand personality traits? If our brand was a person, would they be authoritative? Easy-going? Thoughtful? Try to link your brand's personality with your brand goals, and your messaging should flow.

Imagery

The imagery that defines your brand will range from your illustrative logo to the design features you'll use throughout your communications, alongside photographs, moving images, short films and so on. One of the first things you'll work on is a brand logo, so let's start here and move through:

- Create a logo that is scalable, so it's easily recognisable whatever its size. Anything that is too complicated will be difficult to read when scaled down. Simple, easily recognisable logos are best. Eventually you'll want people to know who you are without reading your name: think of the Nike swoosh or the Apple apple.

- Make sure your logo is visually balanced, so your tagline is not larger than your business name, or that the logo insignia drowns out the words. Alignment, symmetry and the amount of surrounding unused space are elements that should work in harmony.

- You may want to use design elements of your logo throughout your marketing literature. This will give your communications consistency. Good Energy's trademark yellow dot runs through all our material and appears as a design feature, such as a substitute full stop.

- Again, knowing what fits comes back to knowing your customer. What's important to them? What do they value? What will they find interesting? Photographs are a powerful communication tool and it's worth spending time and money on them as stock shots can feel inauthentic and impersonal. If you are using shots of people, make sure you show faces. I've seen so many brilliant companies feature people with their backs turned! And if you say you are a company pushing on diversity, show this – remember that prospective employees will visit your website so, even if you haven't met your diversity goals, demonstrate not who you are, but who you want to be.

Understanding the marketing mix

At first, you're going to be cash-strapped, or you may not have any marketing budget at all. See this as a driver of innovation rather than an obstacle. Having an understanding of the marketing mix will help you identify areas where you can use no- or low-cost content and only pay for what is essential:

○ *Earned media* is the amount of free publicity you generate, nurtured by your relationships with the media, bloggers, investors, influencers and customers. This is coverage of your brand through organic means, which can include mentions or being quoted in an article or social media, a listing in a guide, online reviews or re-shares of your content. This is some of the most difficult media to secure because it requires having something interesting to say, being noticed and nurturing relationships. And, whether the coverage is good or bad, much of it is out of your control. That said, if you can build it, it can pay dividends.

○ *Shared media* mainly covers social media platforms and it's your content shared by third parties through retweets, shares, likes and comments. It can also extend to content shared on partner websites, or through a sponsorship agreement (both of which will typically have an initial paid-for element). Shared is all about being part of the conversation and it's where having a distinctive brand personality is essential.

◌ *Owned media* is the content that you control such as your customer stories, employee stories, webinars, videos or podcasts all produced by you. It also covers your user-generated content such as your blogs, tweets, posts and so on. Another source of owned is commissioned reports or exclusive industry insight that you publish, and this can win publicity.

◌ *Paid media* includes ads you place in publications, broadcast, online or sponsored through posts, tweets and pictures. As a rule of thumb, paid-for media should sit last on the hierarchy until you know what works, when it works and why it works, after which you can be more focused. That said, you may want to pay for an affiliation partnership early on to tap into a customer base. Don't rule out paid-for media, but it has to serve a valuable function.

Of course, none of these should be viewed in silos. They all converge at points and, as you develop, one will constantly feed the other. As we briefly run through each type of media, see each through the lens of the marketing mix.

Reaching your customer

An early debate we had at Good Energy was whether we should doorstep the public to attract new customers. It's a tried and tested method for businesses to send teams out.

If I'm honest, the practice sat uncomfortably with me. If we were an ethical company, then everybody needed to be treated with respect. I put myself in the public's shoes. How would I feel if I was elderly and opening the door to a stranger? Or a lone woman faced with a man on a winter's evening? I thought of vulnerable people leaving the warmth of a living room to be faced with a hard sell from employees, financially incentivised by the quota of customers they signed up.

While many companies do doorstep – and it is a personal choice – I would guard against it. In our new business landscape, there are far kinder ways to reach customers and by doing so you may avoid any reputation damage. If you want to sell face-to-face, why not find a way to reach out to a community, so that they can volunteer to safely meet you?

Partnerships

In fact, much of Good Energy's early marketing was helped by affiliations with brands that shared a similar customer profile and similar values. Organisations such as Friends of the Earth became our trusted partners and, through a financial arrangement, we had access to their supporters. Data protection (GDPR) legislation does require members to opt in to receive marketing material from partners, but carefully managed affiliate marketing is still a great way to reach out. For new brands it's a brilliant way to benefit from what's called 'the halo effect' – aligning your business to an established name.

Affiliations can extend to becoming listed on price comparison sites or being recommended in consumer guides. Each platform will have its own criteria for submissions and adopt different payment structures, but typically a pay-per-click model means you'll pay when there's a click through to your site. Or you'll pay once a sale is made, or an app downloaded.

Plus, the halo effect is evident through social media – for example, if you are picked up by an influencer who talks about your product. A clothing brand might also hook up with a designer, celebrity or model to help design or endorse your brand. Drinks brands are now asking artists to create limited edition bottle designs. Whatever the arrangement, partnerships allow creativity to flourish. But be sure to partner with individuals, organisations and platforms that share your values. The last thing you'll want is bad publicity if something unexpected is revealed about your partner brand, so choose well.

Leaflets and brochures

Leafleting is one way of reaching your customer, whether door to door or inserted into newspapers or magazines, yet this can throw up an environmental question around paper wastage. Don't automatically assume that using paper is a no-no – paper is one of the most recyclable products around – but there are some tips for responsible usage:

- Calculate a realistic print run so you are not left with surplus. Printers will often try to upsell. Resist the urge unless you are sure that the leaflets will be used.
- Most gloss paper and photographic paper cannot be recycled, so do check with your printer before you commit. Also, using paper that has already been recycled is best. Otherwise, use Forest Stewardship Council (FSC) certified paper, ensuring forests are maintained with the highest conservation standards.
- Check with your printer what inks they use and opt for someone using planet-friendly options. Vegetable-based inks are far kinder to the environment than petroleum-based ones.
- Just because the paper is recyclable, it doesn't mean it will be recycled. Remind the reader by including a recycling graphic in a prominent place.

Print and magazine publicity and advertising

In the digital era you may dismiss print and magazines, but in fact you can target readers who have more time to browse. If coupled with a digital strategy, print may prove highly effective, so to get the most out of it:

- ⊘ Target publications that are perfect for your demographic. Print tends to favour an older readership, but not exclusively, and remember that some magazines have also moved online.
- ⊘ Think beyond the news-stand offering. Membership organisations such as The National Trust send out monthly or quarterly magazines, so this will be less scatter-gun than advertising in a national newspaper.
- ⊘ Magazines and newspapers are fertile ground for free publicity. If you have a unique story to tell, a great founder story, or can be an expert on issues related to your industry, get out there and make yourself known. Remember to target the right people in the right section of a publication. There are financial pages, lifestyle and entertainment supplements, science and tech pages and so on, so think carefully about how you package the story you want to tell. Local community newsletters can also be hugely effective.
- ⊘ 'In any communication avoid self-referencing,' advises Good Energy's Luke Bigwood. 'You may be trying to solve a complex problem in your business, but don't assume everyone has knowledge of it. Put yourself in the shoes of your customer and try to get your message across in simple ways.' This is especially good advice when communicating through print where there's more

space. You may be tempted to take an advert out to talk about your higher purpose – our original ads in the *Guardian* were full-page editorials, and although they were educational, I'm not sure they got our brand widely known.

Of course, traditional advertising also throws up ethical questions. I know of certain brands who won't advertise in newspapers whose political views or ownership don't match their values. These are complex questions, the answers to which will be unique to you. You may be a brand who wants to reach as many people as possible with an environmental message and don't feel it's necessary to judge reading habits. On the other hand, a newspaper owner may be revealed to be investing in a harmful environmental practice connected to your mission, so you'll want to divert your advertising budget elsewhere.

There are also the environmental costs of physical magazines and newspapers which include paper and ink, plus transportation costs to deliver even though, as an advertiser or contributor, that is not directly part of your supply chain. Trade-offs will always have to be made. For example, you may decide that the impact your green message will have, when targeted at a certain demographic through print, outweighs those secondary environmental costs. You may also decide that perhaps you could achieve the same goal through an alternative digital campaign. If you do decide that print reaches your demographic better, then also understand whether the publication uses eco-friendly inks and recyclable paper. The point here is to always weigh up the costs and benefits. Have your bottom line in mind but also your green hat. Ask yourself: have I thought it through, and can I justify my decision?

Social-media platforms

Technology has revolutionised the way we market, but getting it right requires the right information to be placed on the right platform at the right time. In a moment, we'll go through each main platform, but firstly it's worth highlighting that it's not just print that throws up ethical issues – digital needs the same consideration and may require similar trade-offs.

As a purpose-led business you may grapple with your conscience about whether to have a presence on big tech platforms at all. After all, the same algorithms being used to promote positive things in society can also be a vehicle for violent extremism, hate speech and fake news. Certainly, following the scandal when political consultancy Cambridge Analytica illegally targeted would-be voters using data harvested from Facebook, we did some serious soul-searching at Good Energy. In the end, we kept our business holding page but pulled our paid-for advertising for a period, and other brands boycotted the platform in the same way.

Today it is almost impossible for any business to market without the tech giants, but protest can be effective if a platform behaves unacceptably. And if enough brands do this then it forces change. Personally, I believe that we will get to the point where tech platforms and purpose-led businesses will co-exist as standards are raised and more stringent regulation is introduced, but I also predict turbulence along the way.

Then, there is the under-discussed issue of the use of digital media itself and its carbon footprint. The energy needed to offer up and download content in real time is vast. According to ethical advertisers

Good-Loop, a typical online ad campaign uses 5.4 tonnes of CO_2 which is 43% of the average annual carbon footprint of a person in the UK. I cannot see a world where brands and consumers will not use the technology available, but there are questions about levels of output and consumption. Yet there are ways to create and use content more responsibly:

- Opt for Scalable Vector Graphics (SVGs) instead of formats like JPEG, PNG and GIF. Unlike normal image files that are pixel-based, SVGs are vector-based, meaning they are made up of lines, dots, shapes and algorithms. They are smaller in size and allow you to scale up and down without any loss in quality and reduce your digital load.

- Limit the amount of images you use on your website and in your marketing content. Ask yourself whether you really need a photo or a moving image and, if you do, rationalise how often these will appear. Likewise, if you put an ad out on social media, ask whether you can reduce your emissions by reducing its length. For every second shorter your ad is, you'll save on CO_2. That said, the content of a three-minute film may have a positive net zero impact that far outweighs the footprint of the communication. Whatever you choose, make sure you have carefully considered your decision.

- If you are setting up a photoshoot or creating a short film, weave sustainability into everything you do. Ask questions like: can people get to the location by public transport or car share? Can you provide locally sourced food and avoid one-use plastics? Are your models or actors wearing new or recycled clothing? There's a wealth of material available on the AdGreen website to help you create a checklist.

Otherwise, a good media strategy is about creating perfectly curated content for each medium. And, when it comes to social media platforms each have their own unique uses and benefits:

○ *Facebook*: Targeting a chosen demographic through Facebook is cheaper than hiring an event stand and taking employees to it, as well as being kinder to the environment given the savings on transportation. Of course, don't rule out events for certain communications. For thought leadership, TEDx talks or a Q&A session at a festival can be a great way to engage, and talks can live on online to be enjoyed and to educate well after the event. But using a platform like Facebook is faster and less scatter-gun. 'If I want to reach 5,000 people between the ages of 25 and 40,' says Luke, 'who love food, are into environmental causes, who like walking, support recycling and buy sustainable clothing brands, then I can set the parameters and target people easily.'

But before you launch any paid-for campaign, start raising awareness with a free business home page to build conversations. Unlike a personal profile page, a business page connects to followers through 'likes'. Include as much information as you can, especially if you have a physical presence with a location and opening hours. From it you can link to your website, post pictures of events, customers or the communities you serve.

If you want to boost reach with a paid Facebook campaign, the platform offers several bidding categories for any budget. For most businesses new to the platform, Facebook's default 'lowest cost' bidding strategy is sufficient. For businesses wanting to target previous customers, an alternative setting such as 'highest value' may be more applicable. Tweaks are often made to the categories, so do check what's available and seek advice – there are lots of expert online tutorials to help you understand what's right for you.

According to most recent Facebook figures, 2.7 billion people use the platform each month globally. Of people aged 18–29, 86% use Facebook, as do 77% of people aged 30–49. More Facebook users – 54% – are female, compared to 46% male.

○ *Twitter*: a great medium for short, sharp observations or news-led tweets. Currently, it has 330 million monthly users, split 50% between men and women, with its core audience (38%) aged between 18 and 29. Perhaps there's an announcement on a topic related to you, or you want to start a conversation about something you're passionate about. Your aim is to build a community of like-minded followers, but be measured about what and how often you post. Users don't want their feeds clogged with unnecessary brand content, so it has to be engaging. And don't overuse Twitter hashtags. Instead use one or two relevant to your tweet. Similar to Facebook, you can pay for promoted tweets or Twitter ads.

○ *Instagram and TikTok*: Users flock to both sites to be entertained in bite-sized bursts, so don't ever feature a long-winded interview talking about the benefits of wave power here. Given that Instagram users' ages range from 25 to 34, it's a far more spontaneous and creative space which is great for building visual stories as well as posting short- or long-form videos. In total, Instagram has 500 million worldwide daily users with its core demographic roughly split between male and female. Some 67% of people aged between 18 and 29 use the platform. TikTok, on the other hand, favours silly and catchy videos, which is perfect for fun and more irreverent content. It appeals to a much younger audience with 43% of its global watchers aged between 18 and 24, of which 57% are female and 43% are male. Again, think carefully about what you feature. Engaging, from-the-heart and unique content works far better. Everybody wants their posts to go viral, but don't spend time chasing this. Instead, concentrate on authenticity.

○ *YouTube*: YouTube works for a variety of short, catchy videos, but it's also good for long-form content and value-added content, for example, talks or more in-depth interviews. Worldwide, it has 2 billion monthly users with the same equal male/female split. Some 81% of people aged 15–25 use YouTube, but it also enjoys an older audience with 66% of people aged between 46 and 55 also using the platform. If you want to target on-trend influencers then create shorter, sharper content. Try to post regularly and at the same time to build consistency and interact with others to build your community. Remember that the tags you use should reflect keywords associated with your business and should chime with what your audience is searching for online. Each video also needs a thumbnail. This could be a still from the video but creating a bold, eye-catching custom thumbnail can draw viewers in.

Building people-centric narratives

Whatever media or platform you use, building human narratives around your brand connects people. These narratives can start with telling a founder story to reflect the passion behind the business. For me, being a lone woman in the energy sector meant I stood out and it gave me opportunities to speak across platforms. While it also presented challenges, I understood it to be a superpower and I used it to my advantage. Other superpowers might be your charisma or storytelling ability, and there are enough successful founder-led examples to learn from. Despite always feeling underprepared in the early days, I always said yes to radio and broadcast interviews as it was a no-cost way of getting my message across. My advice is to invest in some media training to improve your confidence.

Your superpower is also every person your business touches. I started this chapter with one of our generators, Matthew Oxenham. Likewise, if you have a supply chain then get to know the people in it. What's their story? Highlight the unique relationship your brand has built with this person. This is all part of the 'treasure trove' Luke described: a wealth of experiences you can dip into and keep your audience updated. If your higher purpose is to benefit communities in the developing world, then tell these stories to show how your brand makes a difference. And always look for what is unusual in a person's story – that way you build authenticity and interest.

Lastly, look to the people within your business, in other words your employees. If you want to build a positive culture around your brand, dig into their experiences and feature it in your communications. See your brand as a network of people all working to make the world a better place.

Communicate your journey

You will not be perfect on day one, year one or year five, so it's equally important to communicate your journey. You are striving to be better, and there will be times when you can say this. Perhaps you want to source a more sustainable material for your product but you haven't got there yet, or you have a goal to power your business with 100% renewables, but this is in the pipeline. Positively updating your audience will demonstrate you're a progressive, forward-thinking organisation, not happy to rest on its laurels and eager to reach another milestone.

Along this journey, please resist the temptation to greenwash and sprinkle some extra glitter on your operations. Be worth everything you say you are, and that includes being honest. I cannot stress enough that greenwashing is corrosive, unethical and it is not solving the climate crisis. And, if you are exposed, bad press and reputation damage comes at a huge cost, and it will take time and valuable resources to get back on track.

Moreover, if you make a mistake, put your hands up. 'It is far harder for brands to hide from mistakes these days,' says Luke, 'so be transparent and communicate what you are doing about the problem.' And, if you say you are solving the problem, do what you say and update your audience. For example, if you are an ethical chocolate brand who's found child labour in your supply chain, communicate what steps you have taken to eradicate the problem or source elsewhere. Obstacles will always be there and curveballs will come your way, but it's how you navigate them with integrity that counts.

Building a successful campaign

Finally, we approached Joss Ford, founder of Enviral, an ethical brand marketing agency, for advice on how to build traction by formulating great campaigns. For Joss, the magic ingredient to building any successful purpose-led brand is to achieve word-of-mouth status through authenticity, consistency and targeted action. In other words, any campaign should bring together all the elements described in this chapter.

'All businesses are different so there is no single way to build a campaign, but there are some overarching guidelines to set you apart,' Joss says, adding that everything should flow from having a single-minded proposition and knowing your customer.

Have a strategy and nail your brief

Any communication or campaign must have a solid strategy behind it. Whether you are working in-house or with a marketing agency, understanding what you want to achieve and who to target is key. Perhaps you want to build brand awareness, get people to sign up to a newsletter, or increase the sales of a product. Always start with a clear brief. 'The best briefs boil down to one paragraph,' is Joss's advice. 'Know what it is you want to do, in what time frame, what medium you want to use and what end result you want. Spend time honing your briefs.' Not only must it be clear to you, but to everyone working on it. This could be an outside agency, a photographer, or a film crew. 'If, along the way, you've picked up analytics that alter the brief,' adds Joss, 'make sure it is changed and well communicated to everyone.'

Understand your budget and what it can do

You're likely to be working on a limited budget, so don't assume that you need to spend a lot to achieve your goal. 'You could spend £10,000 on an advertising campaign,' says Joss, 'but you could also respond to a tweet with an authentic message that gets far more traction. Sometimes one powerful post on the right medium is better than five.' Getting the tone spot-on, according to where the communication will land, will also help you work within your budget. 'Don't attack everything in one go,' he says. 'There's no use running campaigns on LinkedIn, Facebook,

Twitter, YouTube plus TV and radio. Know who you are speaking to and why. This comes back to having a clear strategy and brief.'

Joss advises any start-up to concentrate on building an organic following first, either through well-placed publicity, building your network through social media pages, or repurposing content such as news or comment pieces. Always credit the source if you do this, and add your opinion or reaction. 'Be careful not to repurpose worthless information for the sake of it,' warns Joss. 'The digital world is overcrowded.'

Also, don't assume the only way to build a following is by attracting celebrities or known people who may be expensive to hire. 'Asking your local running club to try out your lifetime water bottle can create an equally powerful network of supporters,' says Joss.

As you progress and understand what works, you will spend your budget more wisely when it comes to every campaign. In addition, learn how to create an overarching campaign narrative that can be reworked, shortened or spun differently across mediums such as print, broadcast and digital. This will save time, money and embed consistency in your message.

Product first, sustainability second

Environmental or sustainability stories are difficult to tell, not least because you may be communicating a catastrophe before it has happened. The added danger is that your audience remembers the catastrophe but not your brand. With this in mind, tell customers about your product or service first and follow on with its impact on the world. It's only when you are easily recognisable that you can launch in with an impact story. 'Sustainability has always had a brand marketing problem,' says Joss. 'In the past, it hasn't connected the masses, so you have to put it through the lens of your product or service.' If you are selling a bamboo toothbrush, your user will want it to be a fantastic product before they understand it's made with less harmful materials or their purchase will finance the treatment of preventable gum disease in the community where the bamboo is sourced. 'Have your core elements in place,' says Joss, 'such as look, feel, quality and usability. Without these, no one will buy your brand and the sustainability aspect will be lost.'

Be authentic

Once you've locked in your brand guidelines, such as your colour palette, logo and tone of voice, then any communication needs to authentically flow. You'll get an idea of what works and what doesn't by trying and testing communications when you build an organic following. 'Your voice needs to be easily recognisable and feel human,' says Joss. 'No one goes on social media platforms to be talked to by a corporate. They want to be entertained and engaged, so talk to people as people. Don't always talk about how great your product is, talk about the story behind your product and why it's interesting. Later on, you can build narratives featuring people in your supply chain.'

One golden rule, says Joss, is never to put the onus on the individual to do the right thing. 'Blaming people for their behaviour when it comes to the climate emergency is a turn-off,' he continues. 'Instead, tell them about you, your impact and show your values with people-oriented stories.' As you tell these stories, don't heavily script these or use stock imagery. Audiences can spot inauthentic content. While developing an inspirational, conversational tone is an art form, once you find your voice, replicate it across all touchpoints.

Test and learn, measure and analyse

Believe it or not, the measure of success is not just about click-through rates on a website, email sign-ups or even sales. The ultimate metric is to get people talking about your brand. 'You do need patience,' says Joss. 'In the first three years your brand is probably not going to reach 300,000 followers on Twitter, but you'll get better through measuring and analysing.'

Testing and learning is key to improving, but one mistake many businesses make is to simply see peaks and troughs superficially. You may have had a surge in interest, but this could coincide with a government decision that concerns your space, or an influencer recommending your brand. Understanding the 'why' is more important than analysing the 'what happened'. 'There are so many reasons for spikes and troughs,' says Joss. 'Dissect each one. Ask what worked and what didn't work. Was it the look of the communication? A complicated hashtag? Did you use a personal story rather than a funny tweet? If you sent your product out to 100 influencers and no one picked it up, ask them why and get feedback. Never react to an analytic until you are sure of the "why".'

Lastly, keep testing and learning. This also applies to analysing data from your quantitative and qualitative studies. After that you can start to create a six-month strategy followed by longer-term strategies. 'Don't think too big too quickly as you will adapt as you learn and may end up having to redo the work,' says Joss. And if you do work with an outside agency, make sure they understand how to tell purpose-led stories. You can't afford for consistent mis-messaging to kill your communications.

Internal marketing strategy

Finally, in this section, I wanted to talk about an internal marketing strategy. Employee-focused communication is as important as your external marketing strategy. While the latter polishes your brand on the outside, the former keeps the day-to-day cogs whirring, and ideally the two should work in harmony.

In the first instance, you will be selling your business to prospective employees. Here, a strong, consistent external brand image will create an impression of an exciting, fresh place to work. But as you build your reputation, the task becomes less about selling your proposition and more about attracting people through the business's established culture.

There are different ways of telling people about your internal culture, either through your website or on business sites like LinkedIn. Enhancing this via testimonials is a great way to showcase what people recommend about your business. For example, we put together a montage of employees highlighting different aspects of the company they liked. Some focused on the purpose-led aspect while others said they valued the work-life balance we encouraged. In the same way your customers and supply chain are your best advocates, your employees are a superpower too.

If you're putting out a call for prospective employees on social media platforms, choose the right one. A cutting-edge company might put out a tweet, but work-focused sites such as LinkedIn are probably more tailored to job seekers and business news. There, you have the opportunity to build a more detailed view of your company: this could be through blogs; linking to a profile or Q&A with your CEO; or linking to a thought-leadership piece. Remember that prospective employees will also look at who your company connects with, and these associations will help build your online profile.

Internal communications

A comprehensive internal communications strategy is essential when you start to grow, and you perhaps won't all sit in the same room. An increase in flexible working may also accelerate that need when it's more difficult to talk informally. Or, you might work with people across different time zones.

A good strategy will ensure the business runs smoothly and has a positive knock-on effect on the service you provide to the customer. Yet internal communications are not a one-way street. Crystal-clear, top-down messaging is crucial, but so is feedback fed from employees. If you say one thing to the outside world but don't live your purpose internally, then your authenticity will come under scrutiny. As Luke says: 'Purpose falls down if you treat your staff badly. Today, there are enough recommendation sites where employees can post. Once consumers find out it can be very damaging, so you have to have your own house in order.'

How you create your internal communications mechanisms will change as you scale. At first, you might send a weekly email with news or links to external communications. Over time, this could grow to a monthly newsletter detailing sales figures; digital page impressions or unique users; the number of new customers; a purpose-led goal that's been achieved such as recycling targets. Keeping everyone up to speed on upcoming campaigns will also be vital to certain departments who will handle a surge in interest. You may also want to include outcomes of board meetings, future plans or goals. And don't forget about the softer element, too, such as announcing work accolades or birthdays.

Later on, you might find it easier to invest in an internal digital portal. Intranets can range in sophistication from sites that keep staff up to date with news or advertise positions internally, to an all-bells-and-whistles system that also manages employees' pay, holidays, personal development and benefits, and so on. Always gain employee feedback as you develop your intranet site, and don't see it as a dry communication platform for functional communications. Just as you build your brand externally through compelling storytelling, employ the same techniques internally.

Reaching your market . . . in a nutshell

A great marketing strategy starts with knowing who you are and knowing your target audience inside out. Once you've developed your look, tone and created a set of brand guidelines, look to reinforce these by consistent use. When it comes to using print or digital platforms, understand where your target audience communicates and use each platform in a targeted way. Build compelling people narratives around your brand, and don't forget your internal marketing is just as important as your external. Building a positive work culture through a well-crafted strategy will keep things running smoothly.

Quick wins

- ⊘ Find a name that has impact and emotional resonance.
- ⊘ Build your look and feel through your logo, font, colour and design features.
- ⊘ Create a tone for your brand by understanding your brand personality.
- ⊘ Do some initial market research and testing to get better insight into your customer.
- ⊘ Decide how you are going to reach customers and make sure you are comfortable with each method.
- ⊘ If you decide on a leafleting campaign, make sure it's sustainable.
- ⊘ Initiate partnerships with other aligned brands to create a 'halo effect'.

Moving up a gear

- ⊘ Start developing campaigns, depending on what it is you want to achieve at any given time.
- ⊘ Research mediums, such as print and digital platforms, and understand how each can be optimised for your target audience.
- ⊘ Understand hashtags and tagging and how to reach audiences through using these effectively.
- ⊘ Test and learn constantly to get your voice, timing and content right.

- ⊘ Concentrate on developing compelling, timed content rather than lots of it.
- ⊘ Understand how to tell purpose-led stories and build authenticity.
- ⊘ Continue to build word-of-mouth by targeting influencers and networks that you know are talking about subjects in your space.
- ⊘ As you grow, develop an internal communications strategy.
- ⊘ Know that all content has a carbon footprint and work to minimise this.

Going for it

- ⊘ Develop compelling narratives by looking into your supply chain or organisation to tell unique, people-oriented stories.
- ⊘ Develop an omni-channel campaign across several touch-points, tailoring each to the platform.
- ⊘ Keep analysing the metrics and ask why an action worked or didn't work, rather than just looking at the numbers.
- ⊘ Create an internal intranet and make the content engaging.
- ⊘ Hold focus groups in the run-up to a campaign so you can be sure how to resonate with your target demographic.

Chapter 9
Transport

Back when Good Energy didn't yet exist, I remember hopping on a plane what seemed like every week. Our German parent company had offices in Frankfurt and, as a consultant, I was required to be there in person on a regular basis. Funny to think that the Channel Tunnel wasn't open, Zoom hadn't been conceived of, and the budget flight industry was just taking off.

As a business operating on a shoestring, it also meant my waking up at an unholy hour to shuttle on to a plane at Heathrow to cut the cost of travelling at peak times. Often, I'd travel at weekends because Saturday flights were cheaper. This did have some upsides. It turned out that the music industry also travelled off-peak. Not being the best of fliers, I'll never forget taking off from Frankfurt airport with zigzagging lightning all around and being talked down by the only other passengers on the near-empty Lufthansa flight – the 1960s band Manfred Mann! Another flight to Portugal was shared almost exclusively with the iconic Britpop band Blur.

Despite these momentary glimpses into a jet-set lifestyle, the glamour of air travel soon wore off. And when I thought about it, the experience itself wasn't satisfactory. By the time I was airborne, I could squeeze in a half-hour of work before the cabin crew prepared us for landing. It's something that always stuck in my mind when I came to formulate our own transport strategy at Good Energy. Travel is not just about the 'why' and the 'by what means', it's about the 'how we feel' when we do. At front of mind were my concerns around the environmental impact of flying, but also, looking at transport experientially informed whether we should encourage trains, cycling and walking and other forms of kinder travel.

Of course, if you are a business that ferries goods around then transport takes on a much wider meaning. Investing in a fleet of vehicles to reach your net zero goals can present challenges. And then there's the last-mile delivery businesses springing up – you might be one, or use one. The past few years has seen an explosion in delivered goods – in particular during the Covid-19 pandemic. According to the Office for National Statistics, internet sales are now around 32% of all retail sales, all of which will be delivered to a home or a click-and-collect destination.

In this chapter, we're going to be talking planes, trains, automobiles – electric obviously! – and a whole lot more. We'll explore how employees travel to and for work and asking questions such as: how do you implement an inclusive green travel-to-work scheme? Should you spend your life video conferencing instead of meeting face-to-face? I'll cover fleet management. Along the route we'll hear advice from those who've worked through reducing their emissions. There's also some great innovation happening around transport infrastructure, particularly electric vehicle charging. So, strap in for the ride . . .

Work-related travel

While a nation of office workers persevered with being glued to a screen for the duration of the pandemic, many of us mourned the loss of human contact. Without doubt, Covid-19 has changed how we work forever, with more flexible approaches being adopted in many organisations. As we found in Chapter 2, shared office space is on the rise, as is the use of video conferencing, hot-desking and the home office.

That said, nothing beats face-to-face for certain tasks. After all, we are social animals and projects, particularly in the creative sphere, thrive on people coming together and bouncing ideas around. But how do we square the environmental factors when it comes to work-related travel?

As a former CEO who has had to think hard about this for my own business, I do believe that it is not simply a top-down approach that leads to better decision-making, although employees can be incentivised by clear policies that shift behaviour. Employees must be empowered to make the right choices in a range of situations. This can only happen through education so that greener, healthier ways to travel become natural options. When thinking about travel priorities:

- Create a hierarchy of sustainable travel related to CO_2 emissions but do so with the needs of your business in mind (see below). For example, if you are a law firm prone to meetings abroad, cutting flying completely may be unrealistic, but know that there will be ways to limit impact.

- Don't limit thinking about travel as simply a method of getting from A to B. As well as convenience, speed and workability, consider the *experience* of travel. Walking or cycling can feed into a work-life balance policy or encourage an active, healthier lifestyle among your workforce.

- Communicate your travel sustainability targets with your employees. Highlight that if the business reduces flights, or chooses conference venues closer to home, then this equates to a certain percentage reduction in carbon emissions. Update your employees regularly with progress, so every choice they make feeds into achieving the business goal.

So, what should we prioritise? Now we'll examine a travel hierarchy based on carbon emissions that includes both the employee commute to work and employee travel for work.

Online

The wide range of digital communication, whether it's Zoom, Teams or an in-house Slack platform, has revolutionised communications. Certainly, online comes out best on emissions, but it is not a panacea. Unless the data centre you connect to is powered by renewables, then you will be clocking up carbon with every meeting you hold, so choose carefully.

What you will probably end up with is a mixture of online and face-to-face meetings, but you'll need to judge what is right for the kinds of meetings you hold and who you connect to, whether in the UK or abroad.

- Face-to-face is preferable if you're meeting someone for the first time. Pitching and project proposals also work better in person, as do complex sessions that require abstract thinking or brainstorming. Employee appraisals or team-building sessions are also hard to hold remotely.
- Update meetings, ongoing project meetings, regular round-ups and check-ins are all low-complexity meetings that can work via video conferencing and will save on CO_2 if not everybody can attend in person.

When deciding between online and face-to-face meetings, also factor in how online may affect certain members of your business – a point which comes back to employee inclusion.

- Certain neurodiverse people may find it difficult to read body language and pick up on visual cues, all of which are impeded online, and a 2019 research paper for Microsoft highlighted the challenges and stressors of video calling specifically for autistic people.
- Screen fatigue is also a reality, so do consider the impact online has on your employees' mental health.
- Remember also that informal interactions and opportunities all happen when people are present and visible. Certain cohorts, most likely women, can miss out on these as they opt for flexible working to juggle caring or childcare duties. Balancing presenteeism with online can reduce the unintended consequences of gender, and other, inequalities.

Second and third on the transport hierarchy are walking and cycling and we've asked green travel expert Aidan Chisholm from the walking, wheeling and cycling charity Sustrans to help unpick each. 'Promoting active travel for businesses means analysing the opportunities and challenges that your workplace presents,' he says, 'but it all starts with fostering a workplace culture whereby active travel is open to everyone.'

While the impetus to foster an active travel culture may come from employees, employers are also being asked to meet environmental and wellbeing goals so it's important to analyse what you can offer top down.

'The first place to start is to survey your employees to understand how they travel to work, how they might like to travel and what barriers are in place,' says Aidan. The next step is to understand safety concerns around each method and Aidan advises working alongside your local authority so that there is constant communication around issues or hotspots. 'Planting a seed of travelling with a walking or cycling work buddy can also be a game-changer,' he says.

If you want to work more formally to embed an active travel plan, then there are also accreditation schemes such as Modeshift STARS who can help you achieve your workplace goals.

Walking

Walking to work has so many plus points, only a fraction of which are environmental. These include improved physical and mental health. Certainly, I know that getting out in all winds and weather and walking my two dogs clears the cobwebs and I come back to my desk feeling refreshed and ready to start the day. But as well as boosting morale, walking also promotes employee cohesion, is known to prevent absenteeism and encourages employee retention, so there's a pretty good business case to promote it.

Of course, encouraging your employees to walk will depend on where you are based. If you are in a more rural location this may present accessibility challenges, whereas in urban areas, safety may be more of a concern. However, there are simple actions to help mitigate this:

- Help with route planning. Once you know of employees who would like to walk to work, do a site survey to understand what challenges they may face and create safe routes. There are several third-party charities, like Sustrans, that can help with this.

◌ If there are employees who live near each other, set up a walking buddy scheme or a scheme where more experienced walkers initiate others by showing people the best routes to take.

◌ Set up a walking WhatsApp group so if someone is walking alone, especially on a winter's night, then they can report arriving home safe or share any issues that others should be aware of.

◌ Offer employees walking confidence and safety training. Again, a local charity or your local authority may provide this. Also, consider issuing alarms for lone walkers or hi-vis vests or bands for dark nights.

◌ If you can, provide lockers for employees to allow people to change their clothes, in particular on wet days. A place for footwear is also a good idea so shoes don't stink out colleagues. This can really put people off!

◌ Encourage employees to walk to out-of-office meetings, too, but be aware that the need to wear a suit or smart clothing may be a barrier.

Cycling

Likewise, cycling has a range of physical and mental health benefits that transcend emissions reduction. And, thankfully, its poor image is changing. The angry 'middle-aged men in Lycra' group are not so visible these days and it's great to see cycling being embraced by people of all ages. I began cycling whenever I had to come to London because I couldn't bear being stuck in queues of traffic or underground on a stuffy Tube. Not only can being a road warrior take time off your journey, but experientially it can be fun!

There are great ways that workplaces can promote cycling and support cyclists, and some come at a very low cost:

- 'Starting with something as basic as mapping out public bike stands and directing employees to them with messaging and pictures can really make a difference,' says Aidan. If there aren't public stands or lock-ups available nearby, talk to your local council about installing some.

- If you have an area at work to lock up bikes, make sure these are visible rather than tucked at the back of a building where safety may be an issue.

- Buddy systems and travel champions also apply to cycling. These can be a little time-consuming to set up, but do create their own momentum.

- The government Cycle to Work scheme comes in two parts: firstly, employees can hire a bike from the employer as part of salary sacrifice or you can offer an interest-free loan to employees to buy a bike and/or safety equipment such as lights, clothing and helmets, which they pay back from their salary. These can be an agreement between employer and employee, or a third party if you use a scheme provider. Various providers support the scheme, do all the paperwork for you and provide the bikes. An alternative is to buy a small fleet of bicycles and offer a pool scheme, which can be great for off-site meetings.

- Provide employees with safe route maps, but also offer bike proficiency, safety and maintenance courses.

- Create a wider cycling culture by promoting being part of a group. National events like Bike Week and Cycle to Work Day are a fun way to encourage cycling, or you could create your own organisation-wide challenge.

- Lastly, a workplace with a shower or facilities to change in are always a massive plus if you promote cycling. No one wants to breathe in bad body odour all day, not even your own!

Disability

In any walking or cycle-to-work scheme, understanding the challenges that disabled employees have will create an equitable travel policy. Wheeling rather than walking should be encouraged, but be mindful that there may be barriers along any route, such as parked cars blocking pavements.

With this in mind, specific route planning that takes in the needs of more vulnerable employees is needed, and you may also want to work with a local authority to highlight where routes can be improved.

For some people with disabilities, cycling is easier than walking. Depending on the person, the cycle can be an Electrically Assisted Pedal Cycle (EAPC), or an adapted cycle, or a unique cycle such as a tricycle, hand cycle or cargo cycle. Most are catered for in cycle-to-work schemes.

'It's really important to let employees know that active travel is open to everyone, and that the support is there,' says Aidan.

Public transport

Public transport sits one rung down on the hierarchy and it should be something you've already thought about when choosing the location for your business. The greenest option is to base yourself near to a transport hub, whether that's a local rail or bus station or a location that's well serviced by bus or tram. In more rural locations frequency of services will also be a factor. However, in a post-Covid world, some vulnerable employees may not feel able to travel on public transport, and as an employer you must be sensitive to this. But there are ways to encourage others:

○   As a start-up, it's unlikely you can offer a free season ticket to employees, but do investigate a tax-free loan so employees can buy season tickets and pay the cost back monthly as a salary sacrifice.

Otherwise, public transport is most often used when employees have to travel for meetings, conferences or other work-related business and you can control what choices they make by having a clear expenses policy.

At Good Energy we prioritised train travel, but ultimately we wanted teams to take responsibility for making decisions about their carbon footprint. This required a shift in mindset for managers often more used to minimising cost rather than carbon. Here's how we structured our policy:

○   We allowed car or plane travel if the journey time increased by 100% by taking a train. For example, to get to our wind farm in Delabole it took eight hours by train, but three hours by car, so in that scenario we permitted driving.

○   Where travel took less time by train than by car, train became the obvious choice, unless there was more than one person travelling. We also highlighted the experiential benefits of the train. Not only can a person move around, but they can also work for the duration.

○   When it came to air travel, we took account of time spent travelling to the airport, plus check-in time, flight time and time getting to a destination. For some meetings plane is quicker and often cheaper, but we guided on time and carbon emissions.

In situations where employees can't access public transport, for example if they work late or early morning shifts, there is no legal requirement for you to provide it. However, the idea of placing people in potentially unsafe situations would not sit comfortably with me. Instead:

- ⊘ If employees work shifts and public transport can't deliver them on time, look at flexible working for those times. This can work well in call-centre operations in a way it doesn't for more manual work.
- ⊘ Investigate a taxi service, and if you are providing this for a group, make sure the taxi drops people off via the most economical route. Try to work with a taxi firm who has a green fleet. This has now become a unique selling point for some firms, especially in urban areas.

Cars

Next up is driving which, thankfully, has become greener due to the explosion on to the market of electric vehicles. But, as I've highlighted, this comes with its own cost to planet and people. Until there are established and widespread recycling routes for EV batteries, then raw minerals will be intensively mined, so think holistically about the car life cycle, even with electric cars.

That said, all employees who do drive to work should switch to pure EV if they can. The technology is moving so fast that even plug-in hybrids that switch between fuel and EV look like they will become obsolete over time. To encourage pure EV:

- ⊘ Again, offer a salary sacrifice scheme. It's one of the most cost-effective ways to nudge behaviour. This is essentially a company car that an employer rents from a supplier to rent to the employee. Road tax, insurance, servicing and maintenance, breakdown cover and accident management are typically included in any scheme. While there is already a benefit to an employee, given that the payment is given up before PAYE and National Insurance contributions, tax on an EV is also low at 2% until 2025, meaning there are good savings. As an employer you will also benefit as NIC and VAT savings can also be substantial.

○ If you use pool cars, then also opt for EV. As well as this being kinder to the planet, it's also a great way to get employees to test out an EV car as people often have initial reservations.

Of course, encouraging EV use needs to be backed up by the right charging infrastructure. To understand more about how this landscape is evolving I spoke to Melanie Shufflebotham, founder and COO of Zap-Map, a business that maps public charge points allowing EV drivers to search for chargers, plan journeys and pay for charging via an app.

The business itself grew out of an online buyers' guide to lower car emissions. 'In around 2014 we started creating a map of charge points on the site,' says Melanie, 'and this became a really important element, so we set up a separate platform to respond to growing demand.'

Currently there are around 30,000 public charge points across the UK. Whenever one is set up, Zap-Map is informed and it adds it to its network. Users can then find out where the best place to charge is, and its live availability status, while there is also a route planner to tell drivers the optimum locations to charge at based on the mileage they are covering.

For Melanie, EV for business is now a far more viable option and public charge points are mostly used by businesses for on-the-go top-up charging. 'In around 2017, there were around ten different cars, but the sheer number of EVs available has since exploded to around 90 pure electric models so there's real choice,' she says.

Likewise, charging range has increased from around 120 miles to between 200 and 300 miles on a standard car. Charging points are also increasing at roughly 30% each year, with an estimated 300,000 public points expected by 2030 – 250,000 of these are likely to be standard-speed chargers and 50,000 rapid speed which give around 150 miles charge in 30 minutes.

While we'll talk specifically about fleets in the last part of this chapter, it's worth noting that, while Zap-Map currently cater for cars, vans is an area it is starting to track so it can offer a tailored service.

'Fleets have specific needs,' says Melanie, 'and so we've teamed up with a fuel card payment service so fleet managers can see consolidated information on petrol, diesel and electric costs each month. In the fullness of time, we'll be able to give them lowest cost and lowest carbon information too.' Another feature the business is working on is mapping bays of different sizes so vans know the best locations to charge.

You may also be in a position to install charging points if you have a parking area. Certainly it was something we looked at very early on at Good Energy, simply because many visitors to our office asked for it. When thinking about this option remember that:

○ The price of a charger depends on the model and communications required, but typically it comes in at under £3,000. On top of this will be installation costs, and these can vary depending on where you want your charge point and how far it is from an electricity source. Do also check on annual running costs.

○ Government help is available through the Workplace Charging Scheme which is a voucher-based scheme that provides support towards the up-front costs of the purchase and installation. Check with the Office for Zero Emission Vehicles whether your business is eligible.

In addition, you may want to look at car-sharing schemes to make more environmental savings. This can also be a great solution if your office lacks parking space, not to mention the financial savings for employees in travel costs – being part of a share scheme can save people on average around £1,000 every year. But there are social and health benefits too. Just like walking and cycling together it can enhance networking and office cohesion. Moreover, sitting in traffic alone can be stressful and even having someone to chat to at the end of a long day can relieve anxiety. You can set up a car-sharing scheme in one of two ways:

○ If your business is relatively small, then it's just a question of who lives near who and an informal arrangement and payment mechanism. Once you grow, then you might want to set up a function on your intranet or an app that allows employees to share a rota, timetables, payments and other information.

○ If you want to join a wider car-sharing scheme then there are many available, and this would mean employees would find suitable share partners from the local area. Platforms such as Liftshare are free, but also offer a paid-for bespoke business service – although check with your local authority to see if it runs a scheme.

○ There are also car clubs to hire vehicles by the hour, which may also be an option for one-off journeys. Some of these are also prioritising sustainability, such as Co Wheels whose fleet is 33% electric and the remainder mainly plug-in hybrid. Again, this can be a great way for employees to try out electric – in my view, once tried, you won't go back!

Mostly, car sharing schemes are about people taking the first step, and there's often anxiety about days when people are not free to join. Make sure employees know car-sharing doesn't have to be an all-or-nothing arrangement. Even car sharing twice a week will make valuable savings. Do also incorporate a review of arrangements if a car share is not working out. After all, it is supposed to be an enjoyable experience!

Air travel

In terms of carbon emissions, air travel is without doubt last on the list, but sometimes it will be unavoidable, or even crucial depending on your industry. While many businesses opt for carbon offsets to balance out flying, this doesn't actually change behaviour and, in my view, is a version of greenwashing. Reduce first, but if you do have to fly, always try to limit the impact by:

- Grouping meetings together rather than taking the same journey over and over. For example, if you visit a client in the States, see what other meetings you can fit in around this while you are there. When you are there, avoid travelling by air while in the country and look to the bus or train.
- It's unlikely you'll be sipping champagne in first class when you start out, but flying economy emits four times less carbon than if you did. If you travel with a budget airline, where the plane is usually fuller,

you'll also cut your carbon footprint. That said, budget may be fine for very short-haul flights, but do think of the experiential aspect for long-haul.

- Fly direct if you can. Taking lots of connecting flights equals more take-offs and landings which make up a quarter of a flight's overall emissions.

- Choose an airline with a newer fleet. Contemporary built planes typically use less fuel. The charity Atmosfair publishes an annual index of CO_2 emissions for the airline industry, and is a great resource for cutting through greenwashing claims. Greenwashing also happens when air carriers claim to be sustainable by using reusable packaging for its food or cutting down on disposables by asking passengers to bring their own headphones. Clearly, when it comes to flying this is sustainability light!

- Reduce the weight you take with you. If there's less weight on the plane, it needs less fuel, and every little helps.

Incentivise your staff

As I've said, embedding a green travel mindset in the workplace is as much about knowing your employees and their travel habits and opening their eyes through education. At first you may want to bring in an outside party to help, but if you assign this within the organisation, make sure it is someone genuinely enthusiastic who can motivate others around the benefits.

In addition, promote greener ways to travel through marketing. It could be via an email, on the company website, via a newsletter or on public noticeboards. Telling employees about the benefits of walking with communication helps to educate people alongside people who can fly the flag.

I always saw green travel as a way we could achieve long-term impact. It was an element to invest in for our future holders – our custodians of the planet long after we are gone. This became a reason why Good Energy made it a key performance indicator, and to help us with that goal we offer employees a green travel-to-work bonus.

Climate perks for employees can be set to different goals, for example a bonus is given if a person travels to work in a green way two days of the week. To help you further, there's a great campaign called Climate Perks which can focus your mind on formulating a green travel plan. Do have a look on their website which also includes a handy policy document example.

Delivery management

Depending on what business you are, you may run a fleet of vehicles outside of pool cars or pool bicycles. Or you may begin by employing a third party to collect from your suppliers or collect from you to fulfil your customer delivery arm. How your product gets from A to B is as important as how your people travel.

Thankfully, fleet management is something I've never had to grapple with, so I've called on Zac Goodall, head of sustainability at organic veg box company Riverford Organics. The business began in 1986 when its founder Guy Singh-Watson began delivering produce from his family's organic farm in Devon. It now delivers close to 50,000 produce boxes across England and Wales every week. It's a brilliant example of a small business that's grown from humble beginnings and has had to evolve and adapt to meet its environmental goals.

Currently the business run a fleet of 15 44-tonne articulated lorries that are used to transport goods from its network of fruit and veg suppliers to its two pack-houses. The same-sized heavy goods vehicles then transport packed boxes to around 30 distribution hubs. From there, a fleet of medium-sized high-top vans make final deliveries to customers.

'When Riverford first started opening up to the UK,' says Zac, 'we used a third party and then a franchisee network. This has now gradually been brought in-house as we've grown. Although franchisees were aligned with the brand, there's an environmental efficiency in our system around routing, fuel and the types of vehicles we use.'

Broadly, there are three types of vehicles that a business might use, with lots of variations within those categories. However, there are some overarching things to be mindful of when building a sustainable fleet.

Lorries and trucks

Currently there is no mainstream electrification around heavy goods vehicles, although it is a space where we are seeing more and more innovation and change, with innovation grants being prioritised in this area.

Until these become mainstream, most HGVs traditionally run on diesel, and now increasingly biofuel, although a limited number now run on hydrogen. When it comes to hydrogen, I see it as a component of the low-carbon transition but not a solution. Hydrogen can be produced from a variety of resources, such as natural gas, nuclear, biogas and renewable, but currently most hydrogen produced is 'blue hydrogen', meaning it comes from non-renewable sources. According to the International Energy Agency, 96% of hydrogen produced worldwide is made using fossil fuels – coal, oil and natural gas – in a process known as reforming which involves combining fossil fuels with steam and heating them to around 800°C.

Transport

Riverford changes its fleet every three years, as is standard for a business of its size, and so it has used hydrotreated vegetable oil (HVO), a type of biofuel but one that uses waste cooking oils and crop oil waste. The fuel can be used as a replacement for diesel with no modification needed to the vehicle, and half a tank can even be topped up with diesel should HVO be in short supply. However, this may not be the case for some older vehicles, so do check if you are buying second hand as you may run into an engine problem or invalidate the warranty.

For Zac, it's not a long-term solution: 'It is something of a stepping stone because it is still a biofuel, albeit made from waste and not putting additional pressure on land use. However, because of the amount the UK and Europe are using, there's a danger that in the next few years we take so much out of the Asian market that this indirectly drives a change in land use to grow crops to make biodiesel. It's one to watch and basically we need to get cracking on what's next.'

Because of the types of fresh produce Riverford delivers, it doesn't need multi-temperature vans – rather, fruit and veg can sit comfortably at an ambient temperature. For its small selection of refrigerated items, it moves these in reusable ice packs and reusable insulated cardboard boxes.

If your business does need to use temperature-controlled trucks then there is a higher environmental cost, although some all-electric refrigeration systems are being piloted by forward-thinking companies. Again, this is an area where I would expect to see much more innovation in the future.

Vans

As a result of bringing its transport operations in-house, Riverford has gradually replaced its van fleet with electric. Current CO_2 savings stand at 2,500 tonnes of carbon per year as a direct result of this.

'When looking at vans, think about how much space you actually need,' says Zac. What you want to avoid is under-filling space as this is inefficient, and Zac prioritises size over vehicle make.

With an increased fleet of electric, the business also knows that it will need charging facilities outside of any public network. At the time of writing, it is assessing its hubs to see what is possible in terms of space.

Transforming its fleet will also have a knock-on effect on cost as it works towards its goal of having a fully electric van fleet by 2025. 'Electricity cost is going to double for us, so we're looking at a range of options such as trying to get as much renewable energy into the business as possible,' says Zac, adding that some energy will be self-generated. Where hubs are on short-term leases, it is looking to use power purchase agreements (PPAs) whereby it will purchase energy directly from a renewable energy generator.

If you do want to invest in new electric vehicles, do also remember that these also qualify for super-deduction tax relief, announced by the government in 2021 which runs until 2023. Full details and eligibility are available on its HMRC website.

Last-mile delivery

Last-mile deliveries can be done via a number of ways, and there have been a proliferation of micro-businesses fulfilling this need. Riverford use vans for all deliveries, but have in the past trialled a third party e-cargo bike company – bikes that are pedal cycles with a bit of electric ooomph!

'E-cargo is great for urban areas and on particular routes,' explains Zac. 'We trialled them in Oxford and we could get around 45 veg boxes on one bike, so they can take a significant load.'

One drawback the company found was that while e-cargo worked on ultra-urban rounds, there were certain rounds that worked better with a van. Moving between the two caused problems with staffing as it reduced a van driver's hours per day. 'It was too much upheaval with employees' hours,' says Zac, 'and we realised some rounds were made for e-cargo and some were not. If you haven't yet got established routes then e-cargo is great, but not so good on tightly packed rounds.'

In other urban areas, traditional bike delivery may be an option, too. If you are considering using any last-mile delivery service, whether it's e-cargo or traditional pedal cycle, there are a few points to bear in mind:

- Several have been criticised for their underpayment of employees and use of zero hours contracts. Do your homework and find a business that aligns with your purpose.
- Third parties may not uphold your vision of what the customer journey should look like. While you can mitigate some of this by choosing a business that aligns, it may never be as perfect as bringing transport in-house. You could be the best, most sustainable brand in the world, but if a customer opens the door to an unhelpful driver or delivery person, then it can damage all the hard work you've put in.
- If you do find a company you want to work with, remember that using a third party for the last mile will increase costs that you may have to balance out elsewhere.

Routing and backhaul

How you manage fuel comes down to effective routing, and in the world of logistics this is crucial to your sustainability goals. Many businesses now operate underpinning platforms enabled by telematics, that automatically figure out where your lorries, vans and other delivery vehicles go, when they go and via what route.

For Riverford, who have regular orders but also experience customers joining, dropping off or placing an order more infrequently, then this needs constant calibration. It also took the decision that it wasn't going to compete with the supermarkets and offer precisely timed delivery slots.

'We don't give customers the insane choice of slotted delivery,' says Zac. 'Rather, they know the day we are coming. We have opted for a joyful acceptance of our customers understanding this.' It's an important point because in our push for ultra-convenience, slotted delivery eats carbon. This is because the route is calculated by time rather than location and fuel efficiency. In other words, a route may zig-zag, using up tonnes of carbon on the way. And while the big boys can benefit from economies of scale, you won't have that luxury. If customers don't understand why you can't deliver 'on the dot', make sure you effectively communicate the sustainability message to them.

If you are employing a third party, it's also good to understand how it uses routing to minimise carbon emissions. Zac found one franchisee who was delivering to two streets only yards apart on different days. An efficient operation would have consolidated both deliveries into the same day.

And pay attention to backhaul as this is also a consideration for some businesses when it comes to route planning. For example, Riverford arranges to pick up from suppliers in areas where it has delivered to a distribution centre that morning or afternoon. 'We've worked with many suppliers for years and so we contact them and arrange pick-up. This way our lorries aren't driving back empty,' says Zac.

You will get a feel for how you can best manage backhaul as you grow, and you may even find yourself collaborating with other businesses to pick up for them at a price on certain routes where you know you will come back empty. There are lots of complex arrangements out there, some more informal than others. Five key points to remember when looking at fleets are:

- Always look to consume less fuel, which is all about driving fewer miles. Advanced routing software will save time and effort as well as reducing delays and unnecessary idling time.
- Minimise empty miles. Vehicles running with nothing in them adds to pointless vehicle wear and tear, and burns carbon for no purpose.
- Constantly review the data to see where you can be more efficient. This way you can identify habitual problems, delays and diversions from plans, giving you the opportunity to tweak and improve.
- Encourage your delivery employees to build up relationships with customers they deliver to regularly. Personal service counts for a lot when you can't compete with supermarket delivery services, and your delivery staff can spread the sustainability message.

Managing your deliveries

If you are delivered to by your supplier or a third party, then you also need to consider how you can best manage your deliveries with people and planet in mind. The best lesson here is to plan ahead. If you do this then you won't need fast, last-minute deliveries that eat up carbon. Also, if you have space, create an area where your delivery can sit if you can't be there, and let the driver know. This way fuel isn't wasted on a re-delivery.

However, when it comes to any delivery – whether it's delivery of goods to you or goods to your customer – it throws up the thorny issue of which selling platform to use and therefore which third-party delivery company to partner with. Amazon is clearly the big beast, and many smaller companies will use it to reach their market. However, you may choose to boycott Amazon on account of its poor record on carbon emissions, not to mention being dogged by complaints over its working conditions and labour practices. And then there's its shady tax arrangements! Also, it's worth remembering that Amazon owns many of the other platforms you may use in other parts of your business – such as the messaging platform Slack. Always remember to do your homework so you are not inadvertently supporting a company that doesn't sit comfortably with your mission.

That said, although I would advise the use of Amazon as a last resort, it can be difficult to compete with, and you may find that you choose it as an initial step before you can get to a size where you are in a position to boycott it. One of the main reasons customers use Amazon is that there is one login and you don't need to input your payment details every time. So, if you want complete control over your selling platform and your third-party delivery company, then my advice is to invest in a decent website that has great content and a simple payment process (you might want to use a payment service like PayPal). If you are using eco-friendly last-mile deliveries, this may also be something you want to shout about on your website. Make the fact that you don't use Amazon a selling point!

When you are considering who to use, it's also worth looking around to see who is operating in your specific space. For example, Wob is a B Corp online bookseller. There are also sites like Traidcraft, who may not reach a wide audience but who are always highly rated across our green touchpoints. Ethical Superstore is a bigger operation and may also fit the bill. Ethical Consumer reviews selling platforms and highlights some of the greener alternatives, so it's a great place to start your research.

Transport . . . in a nutshell

Transport is likely to be the most carbon-heavy aspect of your business. Whether it's the way your employees commute to work, or the travel they do for work, there are ways to incentivise green travel to build a cleaner, greener, healthier culture for your business. And don't just think of travel as getting from A to B. Also factor in the experiential aspect. If you manage a fleet, then constantly challenge the business to be better. This may include replacing a fleet with electric, using routing platforms and not offering the customer the ultimate in convenience.

Quick wins

- Carry out an employee survey of how people travel, how they want to travel and find out what would incentivise them to travel greener.
- Create a travel plan for your business looking at its specific needs. Understand compromises will have to be made, but always look to minimise the impact within these categories and state these clearly.

- ⃝ Create a policy for meetings – what can people do online and ideally what should be done face-to-face?
- ⃝ Pay special attention to vulnerable or disabled employee needs.
- ⃝ Advertise in a public area where your nearest public bike stands are.
- ⃝ Encourage walking and cycling to work by bringing in a third party to help with route mapping or kick-starting a walking or cycling group.
- ⃝ Appoint an enthusiastic walking or cycling champion who can answer employee questions and induct others.
- ⃝ Through marketing, highlight the health and wellbeing aspects of active travel.
- ⃝ Create a wider active culture by getting involved in events like National Bike Week.
- ⃝ Negotiate a discount with a local store for walking shoes, bikes or safety equipment.
- ⃝ Set up or join a car-sharing scheme.
- ⃝ Introduce employees to platforms such as Zap-Map who can help with public space EV charging.
- ⃝ Employ a green third party to start out delivering your product/service.
- ⃝ Encourage flexible working or align with a green taxi firm if public transport doesn't fit with shift times.

Moving up a gear

- Educate your staff to make choices about how they travel for work – this is most easily done through a clear expenses policy.
- Put in place salary sacrifice schemes for bikes, electric cars and public transport season tickets.
- Install a bike stand or lock-up shed.
- Buy pool bicycles or electric cars for employee trips.
- Provide lockers for employees who walk or cycle to work.
- Install a shower.

Going for it

- Install EV chargers if you have car-parking space.
- Make green travel a key performance indicator.
- Incentivise staff with a green travel bonus or climate perk.
- Bring your delivery fleet in-house choosing the greenest options.
- Investigate the most climate-efficient fuels and use the best you can.
- Invest in a telematic routing platform to optimise your routes.
- Pay attention to backhaul so your drivers don't travel with empty vehicles.

Chapter 10
Achieving Impact

When Mahnoor Kamran heard on the news the story of a nine-year-old girl who had died of an asthma attack, she began to join the dots. Ella Adoo-Kissi-Debrah was the first person in the UK to have air pollution listed as a contributing factor to her death following an inquest. The coroner ruled levels of nitrogen dioxide near Ella's home on a busy London road exceeded World Health Organization and European Union guidelines. 'Suddenly I realised that polluting and climate change was going to affect everybody, not just in the global south but in the global north too,' says 17-year-old Mahnoor.

Mahnoor has a unique perspective. Having grown up in the bustling city of Karachi in Pakistan, before moving to the UAE and Oman, and then settling in the UK, she witnessed at first hand the devastating effects of climate change. 'Karachi is a coastal city,' she says. 'It's got hotter and the monsoons are getting much worse. But the Middle East is also a global emitter of CO_2 through oil and gas. When I saw the report about Ella, I realised for the first time that all these issues are interconnected.'

Mahnoor is one of the six teenagers aged between 13 and 18 who sit on the Good Energy Future Board, set up by Good Energy with my support in 2021 through the educational charity Eco-Schools. The board meets in person and the group also juggle their schoolwork with continual online debate about policy issues affecting Good Energy's everyday decision-making. 'We've looked at the energy price cap with the policy team,' says Mahnoor, 'and debated inclusion and diversity with the people and culture team. We discuss everything, from what politicians are talking about to what corporate businesses are doing.'

In particular, she's passionate about people and how decisions made about our sustainability affect vulnerable communities. 'All the elements that go into wind turbines and electric cars are mined in places like the Democratic Republic of the Congo, which is the reason why global inequality and human rights abuses exist. I have an intense hatred and disgust for companies perpetuating these inequalities but channelling it in a positive way through activism can create meaningful change.'

It's encouraging to hear Mahnoor say that, because I saw the creation of a future board as one way that a purpose-led company can achieve impact way into the future. After all, it is today's children who will be at the brunt of the climate crisis long after my generation is gone. And the board don't have the high stakes of being a shareholder or an employee. They can speak freely and honestly without fear or favour. Through them, we can understand their concerns, and also hear their solutions.

In my view, impact is all about speaking truth to power. It's about being a critical voice where the status quo prevails, and giving teenagers like Mahnoor the education and tools to make their voices heard. It takes a lot of guts to speak out, but when you see how activists like Greta Thunberg or Jamaican-British activist Mikaela Loach have inspired a generation, then it gives hope to those of us who started on this journey so many years ago.

Yet, when it comes to achieving impact in business, you have to start small and grow – making gains where you can before reaching out further. So, in this last chapter we're going to look at the various ways in which a purpose-led company can change their sector and influence wider societal change. When I started Good Energy, I wanted to shift the energy market from the ground up. More than 20 years on and it still hasn't sufficiently changed, but the progress is tangible. Twenty years ago, renewable energy made up 2% of the UK's energy mix. Now it is more than 40%. We became part of that journey by simply existing. Impact takes determination and patience. So how do you begin?

When to consider impact

You may start in your business with higher goals about how to change the world, but unless you get your business right you will never shift the dial.

That's the view of Guy Singh-Watson, founder of Riverford Organics, a company I featured in the previous chapter. 'However great your ideas are and your values, you have to be competent,' says Guy. 'Otherwise you only end up letting people down: you'll let your employees down, your customers down, your suppliers and your investors. You can't contribute wider until you understand whatever challenges your sector throws up. Know your industry and under-stand its weaknesses.'

Guy hits the nail on the head there, and it goes back to why I wanted to write this book. Purpose-led businesses face specific challenges, but to bring an established order to the tipping point of change, the first rule is to stay in business. According to government figures, fewer than half of all start-ups make it beyond five years. It's a sobering statistic and a salutary reminder that unless your company has a great proposition, is well run, manages risk sensibly and walks the walk of being purpose-led, then your chances of success are slim.

Having made the full transition to organic farming in 1987, Guy didn't aim for impact from the outset. Instead, this has developed over time. 'I was increasingly surrounded by stories,' he says. 'Unless you think that we were put on this planet to serve our own needs, how could you not want to become an environmentalist or address social issues?'

As well as organic farming being a guiding principle, Riverford has become employee-owned, again rejecting business norms by rejecting outside investment. It is also piloting an agroforestry project, introducing beehives to boost pollination, as well as launching the Riverford Planet Fund that invests in biodiversity, renewables and sustainable farming in partnership with charities, farmers, food producers and local communities.

Yet, simply by existing, Riverford's alternative method of food production has been an influencer. I would say, too, that simply by existing, Good Energy has achieved its fundamental goal to decentralise the energy market. However, the reality was that we could not push for wider change until we found our feet, became profitable, and could channel resources into doing more good stuff.

That said, I do believe that having an eye on impact from the outset, along with a collaborative mindset, will alter the way you think and lead you to positive incremental change both within and outside your sector. As we've seen through businesses like Toast, it is working steadily to influence the bakeries it sources bread from, other brewers, its farmers and ultimately the consumer. Once there are enough businesses in its space successfully tackling food waste in innovative ways, then the balance will start to tip.

Map impact to UN goals

A good way to start considering impact is by mapping your business to the UN's Sustainable Development Goals, which you'll now be familiar with.

All businesses large or small, and regardless of which industry they operate in, can contribute to the goals through sustainability strategies, policies and processes. In fact, I would say small businesses are uniquely placed to do so, simply because they are agile with shorter decision-making chains. By way of example, Good Energy has two primary goals:

- Our first maps to the UN goal 13: climate action. Our whole reason for being is to disrupt the energy market and help save the planet.
- Our second maps to goal 7: affordable and clean energy. Naturally, our focus on trading exclusively in renewables ticks this box.

If you are a food waste business your primary goals will more likely map to goal 2 of zero hunger, or goal 3 of good health and wellbeing. Likewise, a marine conservation business will map to goal 14 of protection of life below water, and so on.

Aside from our primary goals we also have secondary goals, which reflect the interconnectedness of thought and action across the sustainability landscape. Our core business is energy, but I wanted to shift the dial on:

- *Goal 5: Gender equality:* We worked at this by introducing family-friendly policies such as flexible working plus maternity and paternity care.

271

○ *Goal 8: Decent work and economic growth:* Becoming a living wage employer was crucial for me. Not only did I want to attract talent to the sector, but I felt it was vital that people were paid a fair wage for the work they did. I wanted to retain a healthy churn of employees and empower people through our self-development programme.

○ *Goal 9: Industry, innovation and infrastructure:* When we engaged small-scale generators in energy production we fundamentally changed the energy industry, but since taking over our first wind farm in Delabole we began on a journey to develop renewable infrastructure. In doing this, we fed back into goal 8 of economic growth and goal 11 of sustainable cities and communities.

○ *Goal 11: Sustainable cities and communities:* Our solar and wind farms power communities and change communities. This is because each project has a community fund attached to it to ensure local people benefit from hosting renewables. Support ranges from investing in digital equipment for schools, providing horse-riding facilities for disabled children and funding nature-friendly initiatives such as communal green space.

Remember that these initiatives and programmes have been developed over time. So, while you can map from the outset, be prepared to spend the first few years of your business honing your product or service, getting its delivery right, building up your loyal customer base and meeting your in-house sustainability targets.

Impact within your business

As we've shown throughout this book, the first place to achieve impact is within your business, whether it's tackling your emissions through heat loss, inefficient energy usage or transport, to name a few. These are known in business as scope one and scope two impacts. Mostly, these are within your control, although certain elements may not be, for example if you don't manage or own your own building. In both, measurement and monitoring is key.

When it comes to environmental goal-setting there are two ways to go: by adopting science-based targets or net zero targets. There is some debate as to whether science-based targets, established to reduce emissions in line with climate science, is the best guidance for everyone. Put simply, these targets translate the action needed globally down to a business level. Certainly corporates use them, but one size does not fit all. The alternative net zero target does allow for measures such as a limited amount of carbon offsetting and don't operate in as strict a time frame. It's worth familiarising yourself fully with both, and deciding what's best for you.

There are some caveats when it comes to measuring. Instead of becoming fixated on certain aspects of the business, you should consider your operations holistically. For Guy at Riverford, this point hit home when the food sector began measuring food miles and cutting imported produce. 'The industry got obsessed with food miles,' he says, 'and as a result people were happy to grow food in heated greenhouses, which is insanity. They weren't measuring the carbon impact of what they were doing locally.'

Of course, it's unlikely that at first you'll have the time or resources to measure everything all of the time, but knowing which of your activities release significant emissions will give you a hierarchy to work with. And, if you have secondary targets that impact the culture of your organisation, such as employee diversity, then you can add these to the mix and use the same measuring and monitoring techniques.

Remember also that the quality of the data you collect is important as you'll want measurements to be accurate. A good way to do this is to:

- Create a spreadsheet. This way it can be easily understood by everyone and updated over time.

- Typically, collect data over a 12-month period and monitor performance throughout the year. To focus minds, report internally on a regular basis and break down consumption, targets and progress into different functions of the business. Not only will this give you a detailed overview but, if you have employees, it will give them ownership of certain goals.

- Where you can, collect data from primary sources. Calculate from electricity bills the total kilowatt hours used, rather than estimates. It's the same for gas and water usage. Fuel and employee travel can be recorded from invoices and receipts. Waste to landfill is another highly measurable statistic that your waste provider can give you. Staff churn is also a good indicator of the internal health of the business.

- Commit to publishing your data, even if you are not legally required to do so. This will focus your efforts but also let your customers, investors and any other stakeholders see that impact is a priority for you. This information is also increasingly being asked of companies.

- Know that impact does not happen overnight. Instead, work steadily. Changes that can't be made today can be made tomorrow, and there will be a range of factors to juggle such as budget, time, industry volatility and so on. Impact is a journey, not a sprint.

Impact across your touchpoints

Impact in your wider chain is known as scope three impact, and these relate to the activities of the people you work with across your value chain. Naturally, these are more difficult to measure because they can concern elements outside of your control. But, demonstrated by all the businesses in this book, impact can be achieved in the following ways:

- Engage with suppliers or third parties and help them reduce their emissions. Work collaboratively and develop a two-way communication that can be developed with regular monitoring and incentives for action.
- Look to where you can fundamentally change the business model, as fashion company Rapanui has done. Designing for the circular economy can shift established manufacturing processes as well as lowering the life-cycle emissions of your product.
- Analyse your supply chain and look to where you can source materials, components, products or services from suppliers with a lower carbon footprint and from businesses that adhere to human rights protocols. Always work with people who align or are willing to change practices with you to create a virtuous circle with everyone working towards the same goal.
- Keep an eye on advancing technologies. Data analytics, smart sensors and developing platforms such as blockchain will enhance traceability across the value chain, help to reduce emissions and create efficiencies to improve your business's bottom line. Many of these are still in their infancy, but in the future they will revolutionise the way we do business.

◌ Educate your customer either through marketing or direct education. Help them to make better choices about what they buy, how often they buy, how items are delivered to them and how to care for and value their purchases. Pass on the reduce, reuse and repair message.

◌ Always think about where your investment is coming from, and who you are investing in, such as through your pension scheme. This will shift investment away from environmentally harmful businesses such as the fossil fuel industry, again creating another virtuous circle.

Impacting your sector

Once you are competent you can start to raise your head above the parapet and be a voice in your sector. Thought leadership and sharing expertise is a great way to start, and again there are some effective techniques to do this:

◌ Contributing to industry publications, public speaking or blogging can be a brilliant, low-cost way of becoming a sector influencer. Here, don't be limited to your business. Understanding wider issues and highlighting them will open you up to being part of a broader movement for change.

For example, you may be an innovation business who wants to attract more women. By thinking outside of the box, you could align yourself to a schools' programme to encourage more girls into Science, Technology, Engineering and Maths subjects, known as STEM, like the amazing Stemettes with whom we did several workshops in local schools. You may be an ethical beauty company who takes a stand on cosmetic surgery. Or a financial services company who campaigns for better financial inclusion for marginalised groups. Finding satellite partners, perhaps a charity or community group, will help you stretch out your tentacles.

Although it makes sense to align to causes that reinforce your brand and purpose, it doesn't stop you from being interested in issues that relate indirectly to your business. Take LGBTQ+, for example. You may have a policy encouraging employees to bring their whole selves to work. Posting a blog to celebrate Gay Pride and what it means to your business could feature on your website. When Good Energy ran its campaign against greenwashing we used our blog to discuss greenwashing in fashion and food and other industries. Our message was: 'We're concerned about our own industry, but we're campaigning on behalf of everyone.'

Joining an industry body can amplify your voice, as these act as lobby groups to government. And, as representatives of your industry, trade associations understand sector-specific issues and are a wealth of knowledge on best practice, in particular on sustainability. You'll not only have access to information but perhaps the chance to contribute to round-table events or conferences. Panellists and speakers are always needed. Put your name forward or say yes if you are asked! Being an assured voice doesn't always come easily. I once taught maths to a class during my postgraduate years, meaning that most audiences that came after seemed like puppy dogs by comparison! But there are other ways to boost your confidence. Public-speaking lessons or media training is an investment. Over time, being an opinion former will become second nature.

⊘ Networking groups will also give you access to others in your industry and beyond. These could be local sector-specific groups or national groups with local arms. Many host events and seminars, give you access to training or peer-to-peer socialising. And there are networks with cross-industry affiliations such as the British Association of Women Entrepreneurs, a membership organisation set up to give women in business a support network and platform. The organisation Meaningful Business exists to support, connect and inspire progressive leaders. Through a series of events run with various partners, it helps businesses and business leaders consider some wider impacts they can have through their business, from accountability to leading on mental wellbeing.

Impacting policy and regulation

Being aware of the legislative and regulatory changes across your industry will happen naturally if you are part of a trade body, and reacting to these can also be a powerful mechanism for change.

You're unlikely to have a policy department, even after a few years, unless you are in an industry that's heavily regulated, but it is important to keep abreast of government debates and bills going through Parliament that will have an impact on you and your wider industry.

Of course, not every business is affected equally. Being in the energy sector we were inextricably linked to policy and regulation. I understood how energy is, and in most ways continues to be, skewed towards fossil fuel and large, centralised generators. We made sure from the outset that we interacted with policy-makers every step of the way, always pushing for a rebalance back to renewables.

Achieving Impact

In many ways, being a pioneering business meant we had a unique vantage point, and you may find the same. Being on the front line of running a business means you intricately know what regulation has an impact and what needs to change to make your area of work successful.

⊘ *Local, regional and national boards and partnerships:* whether it's campaigning for access to funds or shaping policy, there are lots of reasons for becoming an influencer. City or county councils are directly involved in issues related to business and they often need volunteers for boards, committees or community events. You may even find yourself running for elected office!

Regionally, throughout England there are 38 Local Enterprise Partnerships that make decisions on issues including transport, local labour markets and set investment priorities. The network also lead on how business is regulated locally and help deliver national programmes such as digital infrastructure or renewable energy projects. LEPs do not exist in Wales, Scotland or Northern Ireland, but there are similar partnerships between local government and the private sector. While boards are made up of different representatives, volunteer board members are often asked for from entrepreneurial or SME backgrounds.

When it comes to national boards, these can also be sector-specific. Regulatory boards will set standards for your industry and act as an advisory to government. But getting a foot in the door is not always easy, so you will need to persevere. Typically, big business has the ear of central government, and as I've mentioned I was lucky to be a challenger company in a science-led space and a woman to boot, all of which gave me an 'in'. When it comes to contributing to departmental round tables, it's most likely you will have to be of a certain size to be invited in. However, if you are known for your expertise this may well be surmountable.

○ *Calls for input:* Both government departments and independent regulatory bodies make regular requests for evidence from people with specialist knowledge before it consults on specific proposals for reform. The call will set out the objectives and the scope of the review and will typically ask which reforms should be taken forward and how they should be prioritised.

○ *Consultations:* Green papers are proposals put out to public consultation by government. This gives people – both inside and outside of Parliament – the chance to feed back on its policy or legislative proposals. If you are a member of a trade body it will typically represent the views of its members and submit a statement, but as a business or individual you are also free to contribute independently. Depending on your business you may find yourself responding to many consultations – certainly Good Energy have answered hundreds. Likewise, regulatory bodies like Ofgem or Ofcom also ask for feedback on regulatory proposals and decisions. The best way to keep informed of relevant upcoming government and regulatory consultations is to sign up for notification online. But do bear in mind that responding can take up time and resources which you may not have initially. If you feel this is important – either directly or indirectly – to your business, finding an appropriate trade body can provide you with a voice, although you will still need to provide information to them to ensure your point of view is put across.

○ *Reports:* As well as work carried out within government, there are a variety of charities, think tanks, unions and government-funded public bodies, all of whom produce regular research reports and need information from specific sectors. Or you may initiate a report yourself and approach a partner to help you. For example, Good Energy worked with innovation agency Energy Systems Catapult to research if the UK could reach its net zero target only using renewable resources. The Renewable Nation Report, which contained exclusive findings, then fed into our public relations and marketing strategy. The benefit of commissioning your own report is that its findings will be exclusive to you – this way you can position yourself as a driver of opinion and change.

○ *Academic studies:* Teaming up with a university or further education college can foster innovative partnerships to address the wider social issues you may be trying to tackle through your business. In 2020, the food waste app Olio teamed up with the University of Nottingham to create a food poverty map to help local authorities target food support through machine learning. Likewise, Riverford Organics have an ongoing relationship with the University of Exeter to examine the company's carbon footprint and improve it.

These types of Knowledge Transfer Partnerships (KTP) can provide vital insights for your business and fill an expertise gap. Not only will you feel an immediate impact as fresh ideas and skills are injected into your proposition, but you can also achieve long-lasting impact by furthering its success.

○ *Landmark campaigns:* Aligning yourself to campaigns that will make, break or amend law is another collective contribution to get involved in. In 2022 Mary Portas launched a campaign to change the law that governs business. Through the Better Business Act she has brought together a coalition of more than 1,000 businesses to amend section 172 of the Companies Act. If passed, it would mean that any business will be legally responsible for benefiting workers, customers, communities and the environment as well as delivering on profit – many of the touchpoints I've covered in this book.

Likewise, the Make My Money Matter campaign sets out to make ethical pensions the default for savers. Where this campaign has legislative impact is that it wants all pension funds to be required to notify savers on how their money is invested. It also demands that funds be clear about how they are positively impacting people and planet, and that their portfolios are consistent with the Paris Agreement, achieving net zero emissions by 2050.

These campaigns, and others like them, may not be your core activity but in the interconnected world, being part of them can create a ripple effect that will have a direct impact on your business over the long term.

Awareness raising

In Chapter 8, I discussed how awareness-raising through marketing and publicity forms a vital part of achieving impact. However, as a start-up you will be operating on a shoestring budget, if you have any marketing budget at all. Yet I've explored lots of innovative ways you can get your message out. That said, if you are innovation-led, you may have a bigger hill to climb. Your potential customer base will have to make a conceptual leap to understand your product, and there may be a price differential that is harder to communicate. When you think about it, the electric vehicle has been around for decades – it's how milk floats are traditionally powered – yet it's taken the climate crisis plus improved design and technology, plus a proliferation of choice, for the mainstream to make the shift.

So, if you are pioneering technology, you need to pay extra attention to communicating your proposition clearly and in fresh and exciting ways. My advice is to start by making the wider public aware of the issues you are trying to solve. Presenting these as real, people-centric stories will automatically foster a human connection. For example, we told stories about climate change that included how it affected people in the world's growing regions, impacting on agriculture and viniculture, and human stories about how climate change is fuelling migration.

Where the issue you are trying to solve feels remote or your product is untested in the market, it takes a constant drip-drip of exposure for the message to hit home.

  ○ *Broader campaigns and social movements:* Aligning to other campaigns or movements is another way of positioning yourself as an influencer. However, picking causes just because you think they will chime with your customers or hit a zeitgeist is never a good strategy. Your support has to be authentic. There's no value in supporting a campaign on race equality if you are discriminating in your own organisation. And never speak out against greenwashing if you are doing it yourself. Riding on a bandwagon runs the risk of being exposed. Besides, it's just plain dishonest.

Furthermore, if you authentically put your name to a campaign and this attracts criticism, stick to your guns. Whether it's Black Lives Matter, #MeToo, support for Extinction Rebellion or whatever movement you connect with, your purpose and values will guide you to know it's the right cause for you.

⊘ *Your campaigns:* Closely intertwined with achieving impact through external campaigns are the campaigns you initiate. At first this might be a campaign launched on your website with accompanying PR which could take the form of a petition for customers to sign, or a call to action.

But, as you grow, you may decide to go a step further and set up your own charitable arm. An inspiring example of this is the fashion brand Finisterre who set up its foundation with a focus on helping marginalised people have equal access to the ocean. It supports charities through grants which range from giving inner-city kids the chance to surf, to encouraging women into the water through innovative sea-suit design, or championing access by adapting wetsuits for people with mobility issues.

Again, my advice is to support causes that truly align with your purpose-led heart, that you are genuinely passionate about and where you believe you can make a real difference.

Feed a wider ecosystem

It may not be an obvious or tangible way of understanding impact, but over time you will see how the partnerships you foster and the procurement choices you make feed a wider sustainability ecosystem.

A brilliant example of this was when, in the early days of Good Energy, we employed Matt Hocking, who we featured in Chapter 7. Matt's design agency Leap was an outlier, ploughing a pioneering but lonely path of sustainable inks and paper. Through working with him we were able to formulate our own sustainable strategy for stationery, paper and printing which we would never have done had we not found Leap.

Then, through working for us, Leap could showcase the work it did with us and give confidence to other clients, including the National Trust – a larger, more influential organisation who Matt persuaded to use alternative materials and inks for its in-house publications and marketing material. So the chain reaction continued. It's why, if I find a groundbreaking company or individual to work with, I always share the love and pass their name on to a business who I know wants to explore sustainable options.

View success differently

It now goes without saying that for purpose-led businesses, success is not all about the bottom line. Of course, you have to stay in business and, in my view, make a profit, but it's how you use that profit that will set you apart from traditional businesses. I always saw profit as a way of 'doing more good stuff' and investing in the future, but notions of success will differ from business to business.

Success is usually defined by what you can measure – but it can come in other forms that aren't so easily tangible, such as the indirect impact of employing another sustainable business for an aspect of your work. Yet, contributing to the sustainable ecosystem is a vital part of climate action.

To understand what success looks like for you, you will need to think carefully about the outcomes of your work, and you can do this by returning to your purpose, vision and values:

⊘ Start by looking at your direct impact, in other words the scope one and two impacts of your business. Your actual product may reduce impact to people and planet – Toast's mission is to reduce bread waste, Rapanui's is to make fashion circular, Good Energy's is to reduce CO_2 – so remember that continuing to exist is the first benchmark of success.

⊘ Next are the direct impacts you can measure, in other words your outputs. How successful you are will depend on setting meaningful targets, achieving them, and understanding whether you have improved the business as a holistic whole rather than simply in certain choice areas.

⊘ Indirect success broadens to your value chain and this requires collaboration. How has your message spread and changed others' working practices? Indirect success also extends to how well and by how much you can influence people in your local, regional and national network, as well as influencing policy-makers at every level.

⊘ While your success will centre on your primary goals, don't forget about your secondary goals, for example, if you've successfully attracted more women to your sector, or been able to pay a supplier a living wage.

⊘ If you are a front runner, success may also be a proliferation of other businesses following your lead and popping up in your space. Increased competition means that new and exciting ideas and ways of doing business are germinating and impacting the status quo.

Recommendations on reporting

Once you are achieving impact, shout about it! As a start-up or a small business, the legal requirements for formal reporting are less. However, getting into the habit of collating an impact report will focus your internal operations but also show you have a commitment to transparency.

Achieving Impact

If you are a B Corp then it will already be a legal requirement to create an impact report which is a continual process for certification. But even if you are working towards a B Corp then it's worth doing.

Already many companies will produce an annual report, which you are legally required to do if you are a listed company, but it's a personal choice whether you incorporate impact reporting into annual financial reporting or whether you produce two separate reports. Personally, I believe combining the two fosters a different mindset which is why Good Energy integrate both. Hopefully in the long run, these will become one and the same!

Whatever you decide, make your report clear, engaging and use compelling stories throughout. Don't think of it as a dry document but another piece of great marketing. My advice is to:

- Take professional advice on getting your report right. Companies like Leap also now advise on impact reporting.
- Decide what you want to include according to your business and your achievements for that year. This could include: your carbon emission reductions; other sustainable businesses you've worked with or influenced; what you've given charitably and to whom; if you've given time through mentoring or training; whether you've encouraged greener travel; or what your future commitments are. Your benchmarks will be clear to you. And remember to:
  - Use engaging photographs and visuals to illustrate your report.
  - Cut through heavy or technical information by using tables, diagrams or infographics.
  - Invest in having it well designed.

Impacting future generations

I started this chapter with Mahnoor, but in fact I started my business and this book with young people like her in mind. For me, the future board she sits on is the embodiment of how the company I started wants to invest in our sustainable future, but it does not stand in isolation.

Meaningful and long-lasting change comes through continual exposure, education and equipping young people with the knowledge and tools to change how we do business in the future. It took me many years to establish the board, and it's encouraging to see other businesses doing the same. The sustainable period company DAME has created its own board of six girls aged between 17 and 18 who want to change the conversation around periods. The ecosystem of change really does work.

If you're not at a stage where you can put in place a formal mechanism like a board, start small. There are so many ways you can inspire and inform our business leaders or change-makers of the future. Here's a few ideas:

- Talk at a school or a youth group.
- Sponsor or provide equipment to a youth project that aligns with your message.
- Get involved in 'industry days'. These are days schools and colleges hold where outside speakers are invited in to talk about their industry.
- Give your time through regular mentoring or teaching – for example, if you are innovation-led, this is a great way to inspire children in STEM subjects.

- Team up with educational charities such as Eco-Schools who engage young people in environmental education and action and understand how you can contribute.
- Be a beacon in the communities you serve by sponsoring or getting involved in family events.

Most of all keep going, keep striving for success, keep learning from those around you, keep collaborating, keep innovating and keep inspiring generations to come. And make sure you have fun along the way! Changing the status quo isn't easy, but when our planet and our future depends on it, action is everything.

Achieving impact . . . in a nutshell

Achieving impact sums up everything a purpose-led business works towards. Internal impact is green goals your business is striving for, but external impact is also a crucial factor in challenging the status quo. Becoming an influencer, whether it's by shifting government policy or changing your industry, requires you to put yourself out there and play a leadership role. Investment in future generations will also ensure you make a difference for many years to come.

Quick wins

- Work at being good at what you do.
- Map impact to the UN goals and understand your primary and secondary goals.

○ Look within your business at impact – measure and monitor it.

○ Involve your employees in goal-setting and give them ownership of goals.

○ Join an industry body or trade association who will lobby on your behalf.

○ Join a networking group.

○ Get involved in local decision-making through your council.

○ Launch your own impactful campaign and support others.

○ Feed a wider ecosystem of change through procurement of goods or services and recommend people who are doing good work.

○ Talk at a school or youth group or get involved in industry days.

○ Sponsor community events.

Moving up a gear

○ Focus on impact across your value chain and influence new processes.

○ Adopt advancing technologies to help you achieve your goals.

○ Respond to calls for evidence or consultations by government or regulatory bodies.

○ Sit on a regional decision-making board.

○ Contribute to or commission your own reports and create exclusive coverage from these.

- ○ Team up with an academic institution to foster knowledge transfer partnerships.
- ○ Commit to producing an annual impact report.

Going for it

- ○ Sit on a national board or government round table.
- ○ Start your own charitable foundation.
- ○ Initiate your own landmark cross-industry campaign.
- ○ Team up with an educational charity for specific projects.
- ○ Create your own future board and inspire the next generation.

Acknowledgements

One of the many things I am not is a natural writer. This book would not have happened if it hadn't been for my partnership with Helena Drakakis, who is not only an amazing writer but also an amazing interpreter of ideas. What she has done in taking my ramblings, ideas and thoughts, and bringing them together in what I hope is a coherent and, above all, readable book, is not just commendable but brilliant. Thank you, Helena, it's been a joy working with you.

To my friends and family who have been supportive and, at some points, challenging But always loving throughout my life. Thank you for being there.

Thanks to Luke and Ian from Good Energy. Without their encouragement this book would never have been conceived.

And thanks to Maggie, my agent, for introducing me to a completely different world and guiding me through it.

Useful Resources

Advertising and marketing

Ad Green: www.weareadgreen.org

Ad Net Zero: adassoc.org.uk/ad-net-zero/

BAFTA sustainable production: www.wearealbert.org

Planet Pledge: www.wfanet.org

Brand names and trademarks

Companies House: www.gov.uk/government/organisations/companies-
house

Intellectual Property: www.gov.uk/government/organisations/intellectual-
property-office

Buildings and workspace

BREEAM: www.bregroup.com

Green Building Council: www.ukgbc.org

Historic England: www.historicengland.org.uk

Historic Scotland: www.historicenvironment.scot

Julie's Bicycle: www.juliesbicycle.com

The National Trust: www.nationaltrust.org.uk

Passivhaus: https://passivhaustrust.org.uk

Royal Institution of Chartered Surveyors: www.rics.org

The Sustainable Development Foundation: https://sdfoundation.org.uk

Well Building Standard: www.wellcertified.com

Campaigns

The Better Business Act: www.betterbusinessact.org

Carbon offsetting schemes

Carbon Footprint: www.carbonfootprint.com

Certified Emission Reductions: www.unfccc.int

Climate Impact Partners: www.climateimpact.com

Forest Carbon: www.forestcarbon.co.uk

Gold Standard Verified Emission Reductions: www.goldstandard.org

My Carbon Plan: www.mycarbonplan.org

Quality Assurance Scheme for Carbon Offsetting: www.direct.gov.uk/
    offsetting

UN Offsetting: www.unfccc.int/climate-action/climate-neutral-now

Verified Carbon Standard: www.verra.org

Certification and accreditation schemes and tools

B Corp: www.bcorporation.net/en-us

Cruelty-Free International: https://crueltyfreeinternational.org

Fairtrade: www.fairtrade.net

Farm Assured Welsh Livestock: www.fawl.co.uk

Forest Stewardship Council: www.fsc.org/en

Global Organic Textile Standard: www.global-standard.org

Northern Ireland Farm Quality Assurance Scheme: www.lmcni.com

Quality Meat Scotland: www.qmscotland.co.uk

Rainforest Alliance: www.rainforest-alliance.org

Red Tractor: https://redtractor.org.uk

SDG Action Manager: www.unglobalcompact.org

The Soil Association: www.soilassociation.org

Vegan Certification: www.vegansociety.com

Circularity

Circular Design Guide: www.circulardesignguide.com

Circular Product Design Framework: www.circle-economy.com

Ellen Macarthur Foundation: https://ellenmacarthurfoundation.org

Material Wise: https://www.materialwise.org

Crowdfunding

Crowdcube: www.crowdcube.com

Crowdfunder: www.crowdfunder.co.uk

Ethex: www.ethex.org.uk

Seedrs: www.seedrs.com

Triodos Crowdfunding: www.triodoscrowdfunding.co.uk

UK Crowdfunding Association: www.ukcfa.org.uk

Employment

ACAS: www.acas.org.uk

Disability Confident: www.disabilityconfident.campaign.gov.uk

Equality Act: https://www.legislation.gov.uk/ukpga/2010/15/contents

Gender Decoder: www.gender-decoder.katmatfield.com

National Living Wage: www.livingwage.org.uk

Status of Workers: www.gov.uk/employment-status/worker

Stonewall: www.stonewall.org.uk

Energy

Biomass Information: www.forestresearch.gov.uk

The Carbon Trust: www.carbontrust.com

The Centre for Sustainable Energy: www.cse.org.uk

The Energy Saving Trust: www.energysavingtrust.org.uk

The Environment Agency: www.gov.uk/government/organisations/
environment-agency

Finance, banking and investment

British Business Bank: www.startuploans.co.uk

Finding Finance (CDFIs): www.findingfinance.org.uk

Funding Circle: www.fundingcircle.com

Government Capital Venture: www.gov.uk/guidance/venture-capital-
schemes-apply-to-use-the-seed-enterprise-investment-scheme

The Prince's Trust: www.princes-trust.org.uk

Responsible Finance: https://responsiblefinance.org.uk

Food waste

Feedback: www.feedbackglobal.org

Food Recycling: www.thefirstmile.co.uk

Love Food, Hate Waste: www.lovefoodhatewaste.com

Soil Heroes: www.soilheroes.com

Stop Food Waste: www.stopfoodwaste.org

GDPR

Information Commissioner's Office: https://ico.org.uk

Green roofs, living walls

Green Roof, Living Wall Centre: https://greenroofslivingwalls.org

Renewable Energy Hub: www.renewableenergyhub.co.uk/main/green-roof-information/green-walls-living-walls/

Health and wellbeing at work

Menopause: www.wellbeingofwomen.org.uk

Menopause at Work: www.womens-health-concern.org

Men's Health: www.menshealthforum.org.uk

Mental Health First Aid: www.mhfaengland.org

Mental Health Foundation: wwwmentalhealth.org.uk

Mind: www.mind.org.uk

Workplace Wellbeing Charter: www.wellbeingcharter.org.uk

Innovation grants

British Growth Fund: www.bgf.co.uk

Horizon Contact Points: www.h2020uk.org/national-contact-points

Horizon European Fund: www.ec.europa.eu

UK Innovate KTN: www.ktn-uk.org

Insulation

The British Board of Agreement: www.bbacerts.co.uk

The Cavity Insulation Guarantee Agency: www.ciga.co.uk

National Insulation Association: www.nia-uk.org

IT and cloud data

The Chartered Institute for IT: www.bcs.org

Green Web Directory: www.thegreenwebfoundation.org

Networking

The Better Business Network: https://thebetterbusiness.network

Business in the Community: www.bitc.org.uk

LEP Network: www.lepnetwork.net

Meaningful Business: https://meaningful.business

Women in Business: https://wibn.co.uk

Paper and packaging

Confederation of Paper Industries: www.paper.org.uk

Forest Stewardship Council: www.fsc.org

Love Paper: www.lovepaper.org

Pensions

Make My Money Matter: www.makemymoneymatter.co.uk

The Pensions Regulator: www.thepensionsregulator.gov.uk

Planning

Planning Portal: www.planningportal.co.uk

Recycling

Electronic Recycling: www.iwaste.co.uk

Plastic Recycling: www.plasticexpert.co.uk

Relieve Furniture: www.relievefurniture.com

Useful Resources

Rubbish Please: www.rubbishplease.co.uk

UVPC Recycling https://www.upvc-recycling.co.uk/

Window and Door Recycling: https://veka-recycling.co.uk/

Schools

Eco-Schools: www.eco-schools.org.uk

Stemettes: www.stemettes.org

Supply chain

Business and Human Rights: www.business-humanrights.org

Ethical Consumer: www.ethicalconsumer.org

Fashion Transparency Index: www.fashionrevolution.org

The Good Shopping Guide: www.thegoodshoppingguide.com

Guidance on Global Supply Chain: www.oecd.org

United Nations Global Compact: www.unglobalcompact.org

Support services

Accounting for Sustainability: http://www.accountingforsustainability.
org

The LSA: www.legalsustainabilityalliance.com

Transport

Atmosfair: www.atmosfair.de

Climate Perks: www.climateperks.com

Cycle to Work Scheme: www.cyclescheme.co.uk

Footways London: www.footways.london

Foundation for Integrated Transport: www.integratedtransport.co.uk

Government Cycle to Work Scheme: https://www.gov.uk/government/
publications/cycle-to-work-scheme-implementation-guidance

International Council on Green Travel: www.theicct.org

Living Streets: www.livingstreets.org.uk

Modeshift: www.modeshift.org.uk

Paths for All: www.pathsforall.org.uk

Sustrans: www.sustrans.org.uk

Transport for All: www.transportforall.org.uk

Wheels for Wellbeing: https://wheelsforwellbeing.org.uk

Visually impaired

Guide Dogs for the Blind: www.guidedogs.org.uk

Royal National Institute for the Blind: www.rnib.org.uk

Waste

Waste Resources Action Programme: https://wrap.org.uk

Windows

The British Fenestration Rating Council: https://www.bfrc.org

The Glass and Glazing Federation: www.ggf.org.uk

And thanks to all the businesses and organisations who gave generously of their time:

Abundance: www.abundanceinvestment.com

Aceleron Energy: www.aceleronenergy.com

Bates Wells: www.bateswells.co.uk

Caplor Energy: www.caplor.co.uk

Carbon3IT: https://carbon3it.com

Useful Resources

Enviral: www.enviral.co.uk

Finisterre: https://finisterre.com

Good Business: https://good.business

Good Energy: www.goodenergy.co.uk

Huckletree: www.huckletree.com

Julie's Bicycle: https://juliesbicycle.com

Leap: www.leap.eco

The LSA: https://legalsustainabilityalliance.com

Path Financial: www.thepath.co.uk

Peppy Health: https://peppy.health

Portas: https://weareportas.com

Rapanui: https://rapanuiclothing.com

Riverford Organic: www.riverford.co.uk

Small World Consulting: www.sw-consulting.co.uk

Theatre People: www.theatrepeople.uk

Toast Ale: www.toastale.com

Triodos: www.triodos.co.uk

Wyke Farms: https://wykefarms.com

Zap-Map: www.zap-map.com

Endnotes

Chapter 1

p.12 According to one 2018 survey, 58% of Gen Z want to own their own business and 14% are already owners of entrepreneurial start-ups.
Ready or Not, Here Comes Z, Global Study, XYZ University, 2018

p.14 And these consumers are a growing tribe: a 2021 survey by Deloitte found that one third of UK consumers now look for brands with strong sustainable and ethical practices.
Sustainable Consumer study, Deloitte, 2021

p.16 Over the last 60 years, markets have emerged for corporate control and the idea of maximising profit as the sole purpose of business has prevailed.
Principles for a Purposeful Business, The British Academy Future of the Corporation, 2019

p.18 However, the extent to which both businesses were built on the exploitation of labour in the colonised countries they sourced raw materials from is a subject currently being researched by Rowntree's own philanthropic society in the wake of the Black Lives Matter protests.
Statement from the Board of Trustees, The Rowntree Society, April 2021

p.20 The average family throws away £700 worth of food each year, which adds up to £12.5 billion of food going straight to landfill.
Enabling Food Innovation Project, Mohamed A. Gedi, University of Nottingham, 2017

p.21 According to one 2019 report, which brought together the work of climate experts, the 20 largest investor-owned and state-owned fossil fuel companies, including household names such as Shell, ExxonMobil, BP and Total, produced carbon fuels that emitted 35% of the global total between 1965 and 2018.
Carbon Majors: Update of Top Twenty companies 1965–2017, Climate Accountability Institute, 2019

p.22 Research in 2018 shows that 72% of companies now mention the UN's Sustainable Development Goals in their annual corporate or sustainability report, with 61% identifying climate action as a priority.
From Promise to Reality: Does business really care about the SDGs? PWC Report, 2018

p.26 According to a 2015 global study by Harvard University, this competitive advantage is already visible. It found that a firm's level of commitment to purpose influenced its growth and broader success. Businesses where purpose was clearly articulated and understood were more likely to achieve more than a 10% growth between 2012 and 2015 than businesses where purpose was not well understood or communicated.
The Business Case for Purpose, Harvard Business Review and EY Beacon Institute, 2015

p.26 It is estimated that employees who believe a company has a higher purpose than just profits are 27% more likely to stay working for it.
Employee Retention Report, Tiny Pulse, 2018

Chapter 2

p.28 Offices, retail space, industrial buildings, health and hospitality contribute to 71% of total non-domestic energy consumption.
Net Zero Whole Life Carbon Roadmap, UK Green Building Council, November 2021

p.28 Staggering when you think that, by comparison, UK air travel accounts for 7% of the UK's total greenhouse gas emissions overall.
6th Carbon Budget, Aviation, Climate Change Committee, 2018

p.33 This included creating more holistic and efficient building designs but also adopting measures such as reusing building materials and using non-fossil fuel powered machinery.
Decarbonising Construction, Building a Net Zero Industry, Royal Academy of Engineering, 2021

Chapter 3

p.60 Nuclear, on the other hand, takes around 60 years to decommission and the site can be off-limits for up to 10,000 years.
How to Build a Nuclear Warning for 10,000 Years' Time, BBC Future, 2021

p.60 Nuclear accounts for 17.4%, while renewables, which includes solar, wind, hydro and bioenergy, accounted for 36.9%.
UK Energy in Brief, UK government, Department for Business, Energy and Industrial Strategy, 2021

p.71 To put this falsehood into context, a 2022 report by Imperial College in London shows that respectively Norway, Finland and Sweden have the highest number of heat pumps installed across

Europe – not exactly the warmest countries on the planet! Norway boasts 517 heat pumps per 1,000 households compared to the UK's mere seven.

The Future of Home Heating, This Energy Futures Lab Briefing Paper, Imperial College, 2022

p.77 Cement, ceramics, iron and steel, glassmaking, chemicals, paper and pulp, and food and drink account for two-thirds of all industrial emissions in the UK.

Barrier and Enablers to Recovering Surplus Heat in Industry, UK government Department for Business, Energy and Industrial Strategy, 2016

p.79 Moreover, all three are aiding the fossil fuel industry with lucrative contracts with oil and gas companies offering AI and data analytics to maximise both production and profit for the fossil fuel sector.

Oil in the Cloud, Greenpeace Report, 2020

Chapter 5

p.115 A 2019 report by global management consultancy McKinsey found that corporates with more than 30% women on the executive team were 25% more likely to enjoy above-average profitability compared with those with the lowest.

Diversity Wins, How Inclusion Matters, McKinsey & Company, 2020

p.116 Yet, a 2017 study found a connection between gender diversity in business and increased carbon disclosure and enhanced performance on carbon emission reduction.

Women in the Boardroom and their Impact on Climate Change Related Disclosure, Social Responsibility Journal, Vol. 13 No. 4

p.116 Yet businesses need to include female colleagues, customers, and investors if they are serious about meeting net-zero carbon emissions by 2050. The report is well worth a read.
The Climate Action Gender Gap report, Oliver Wyman Forum, October 2021

p.117 'Different societal actors have a key role to play with public engagement with net zero . . . these all have an important and different role to play in overcoming key barriers to action on climate change and in empowering different groups of citizens,' the report read.
Net Zero Public Engagement and Participation: A Research Note, Dr Christina Demski, UK government Department for Business, Energy and Industrial Strategy, 2021

Chapter 6

p.161 In a 2021 report by Reclaim Finance, campaigners highlighted the bank's investments in coal giant Glencore and European company RWE, who currently has no real plan to shut down its coal assets by 2030, the date NatWest has said it will stop financing coal. Although, at the time of writing, full details of NatWest's policy are also to be clarified. Elsewhere on the high street, Barclays and HSBC are also leading providers of fossil fuel finance.
City of Coal: The Climate Crimes of UK Finance, Reclaim Finance report, 2021

Chapter 7

p.182 According to a 2021 white paper by consultants Bain and the World Economic Forum, digital traceability such as the previously mentioned blockchain will be the new supply chain revolution to advance sustainability; yet with platforms still in their infancy, busi-

nesses making the shift from linear to circular chains will need to drill down into every aspect of the product path to understand where efficiencies and improvements can be made and suppliers can be supported to make shifts in their own processes.

Digital Traceability: A Framework for More Sustainable and Resilient Value Chains, White Paper, Bain and the World Economic Forum, 2021

p.188 The International Labour Organization (ILO) estimates that the number of children in child labour stands at 168 million globally, and the problem is anticipated to get worse. It's inhuman to think that another 9 million children will become child labourers by the end of 2022, according to the UN.

Child Labour: Global estimates 2020, trends and the road forward, International Labour Organization (ILO) and UNICEF, 2021

Chapter 9

p.243 Certain neurodiverse people may find it difficult to read body language and pick up on visual cues, all of which are impeded online, and a 2019 research paper for Microsoft highlighted the challenges and stressors of video calling specifically for autistic people.

Managing Stress: The Needs of Autistic Adults in Video Calling, Microsoft, 2019